Johnny Holliday:
From Rock To Jock

By
Johnny Holliday
with Stephen Moore

Sports Publishing LLC
www.sportspublishingllc.com

Project Manager: Jim Henehan
Director of production: Susan M. Moyer
Dust jacket design: Kenneth J. Higgerson
ISBN 1-58261-461-X

Printed in the United States of America

Sports Publishing LLC
www.sportspublishingllc.com

To Mary Clare, my daughters, my sons-in-law, those six dynamite grandsons, and my Mom and Dad, whom I hope are smiling down from above, saying, "Way to go, son. You did it. You made it."

———————————————

Johnny Holliday

To my family, Margaret, Charles, and Suzanna, with love.

———————————————

Stephen Moore

Contents

Acknowledgments

My heartfelt appreciation goes to my wife, Mary Clare, daughters Kellie, Tracie, and Moira, my sister Charlene, and brother Bobby for their contributions and advice. My deepest gratitude goes to Joel Chaseman, Neil McIntyre, Arnie Schorr, and Shelby Whitfield for helping me create and sustain my career.

I had the pleasure and advantage of uplifting my own story with personal memories and conversations by the talented folks who have shared my adventures. To chronicle events with benefit of encouragement of family and a host of prime players in sports and radio is gratifying. There'd be no Holliday story without their support.

I am indebted to my present and past University of Maryland friends, Gary Williams, Dr. Debbie Yow, Ralph Friedgen, Dr. Dan Mote, Joe Krivack, Jack Scarbath, Jack Zane, Greg Manning, Chris Knoche, Jonathan Claiborne, Tim Strachan, and Mark Duffner for their time and thoughts.

I extend special thanks to my friends Rick Barry, Sal Bando, Charley Casserly, Morgan Wooten, Tony Roberts, Carl Maduri, John Feinstein, Don Lewis, Sal Licata, Cokie Roberts, Robert Novak, Ed Walker, Willard Scott, Ed Hider, Scott Burton, Fred Manfra, Mike Rizzo, Doug Limmerick, Doug Hill, Buddy Piccolino, Len Deibert, Jack Kyrieleison, Chris Core, Joe Beaumont, Paul Hornung, Denny McLain, the Scotti Brothers, Bruce Morton, Rick Kell, Ira Mellman, Mike Kinnahan, Nick Howey and Toby Orenstein for their stories and observations.

Stephen Moore and I enormously enjoyed writing this book together. I've known Steve for 17 years, and I sincerely appreciate the time he invested in helping me pull this together. He's family now, and I only wish he'd return the lamp he borrowed from the living room. (Steve. Please return it. No questions asked.)

Steve and I especially thank Tony Kornheiser and Dick Vitale for generously contributing the Foreword and Afterword and Mike Pearson, Jim Henehan and Susan Moyer at Sports Publishing for their editorial assistance.

Many other friends and professional colleagues helped us with this undertaking. At the risk of omitting names, and with appreciation and apologies to anyone overlooked, we publicly acknowledge those who encouraged and willingly assisted us by sharing memories and editorial guidance, tracking down clippings and photos, and combing through old records and radio air checks to complete this project: Ben Fong-Torres, "Buzz" McClain, Patricia Cooper, Peter Altshuler, Paul Lee, Jimmy Lee, Art Thompson, Grace Slick, Larry Kirby, Mike Dawson, Jerry St. James, Steve Lawrence, Jay Hunt, Ted Parker, Donn B. Murphy, Bill Gilbert, Bruce Kaplan, Linda Powell, John Toomey, Jim Cypher, Bob Moke, Greg Lance, Peter Murphy, Terry Morgan, Michael Terrance, Dave McKenna, Bill Gilbert and Dave "DCRTV" Hughes.

Our thanks also to David Diehl, executive director of The M Club, and Andrew Plenn, president of The Terrapin Club.

Articles and citations reprinted by permission:
"You Never Forget Your First Jock," Ben Fong-Torres, *The Hits Just Keep on Coming*, Backbeat Books, www.backbeatbooks.com
Billboard
Voice Lessons John Feinstein
"Johnny Holliday: Superfan" Buzz McClain, *SportsFan Magazine*
"Cheap Seats" Dave McKenna, *Washington City Paper*

An Opening Word

The year was 1957. I was sitting in the stands in Perry, Georgia, describing high school basketball play-by-play into an unwieldy tape recorder. Not-yet-Senator Sam Nunn was the star player for the Perry Panthers. The next day I played my tape on WBBN-AM 980, a 500-watt daytime-only station. That's how I began my radio career.

A journalist once pegged me as an "institution," referring mainly to my 23 years as play-by-play radio voice for the University of Maryland Terrapins basketball and football teams. That word makes me uncomfortable. Did he mean "institution," or *"institutionalized?"*

Some of my pals may indeed consider me one hinge short of a nuthouse door to be in broadcasting for 45 years and still take obvious, glowing pleasure from every game and radio gig I tackle, as if someone were doing *me* a favor for the chance to participate.

But think about it. Who wouldn't get excited to hop a plane, travel to Anaheim, *and get paid* to cover Maryland playing the NCAA tournament against the number-one seed in the West, and the second-ranked team in the nation, the Stanford Cardinal? It was a game the Terps would win, earning them their first trip to the Final Four in the school's history. And then in the following year, to reach the Final Four again—win the national championship—and see the Terps ranked number one in the basketball polls for the first time ever. What a thrill!

How about pocketing a paycheck to help introduce the Beatles to a hysterical Candlestick Park, or chat with Janis Joplin, the Jefferson Airplane, and other rock stars as I did when I worked as a Top 40 disc jockey in New York, Cleveland, and San Francisco? Consider my opportunities to broadcast 20 years of Olympic highlights for ABC Sports, *pitch* at Yankee stadium, sing Sondheim at an intimate dinner theatre, sportscast over a thousand airwave frequencies throughout America, and *repeatedly* travel to every major town in the USA to cover games.

I'm not crazy, man. I'm lucky! I enjoy what I do today more than ever and can't imagine stopping. I know it's the people—not the events and not quite the money—that keep my attention focused and enthusiasm high.

With my wife, Mary Clare, three daughters, and six grandsons, my life has been one of constantly changing adventures with many of the most interesting people in America.

I won't be modest in this account because, frankly, I'm not *that* great. If I get a little carried away with details, I hope readers and critics will forgive me. You'll soon see that I am sold on the idea that if I don't say it here and spell it out, it may get lost in the shuffle—especially accounts of the unsung heroes I've known during my persistence in the business. They deserve more than a footnote in media history.

I also hope this book can be an encouragement to young people considering a career in broadcasting. My life proves that you don't need tons of talent, a deep voice, or a sultry, syrupy delivery to make it in radio. You *do* need a certain style and a strong desire, and if you know that you want something bad enough, then you can go out and get the job done. You've got to think you're the best. If you have any reservations, then don't let them show.

Another loftier goal is to sway readers into believing that their lives can be directed by enjoyment without sacrificing values and integrity. Enjoyment in "the doing" has always guided my career choices. Hopefully, my story can show others how they can approach their own callings with dedication, optimism, and community spirit—essential ingredients for my 45 winning seasons in radio broadcasting—and, in my view, the basic recipe for a full life.

Add a good sense of humor to the mix and you are probably ready for anything that comes your way. Rock on! Play ball! And thanks for reading.

Johnny Holliday

Foreword

By Tony Kornheiser

You're in the car. You're driving down a lonely highway. The moon is up, and when you lean your head out the window you can see stars twinkling. You drive along for a while, passing telephone poles and advertising signs, and there's a certain peace to the hum of the engine and the silence of the ride.

But suddenly you feel alone, absolutely and startlingly alone. Occasionally, you see some headlights coming toward you on the other side of the road, and you realize other people are out driving. But you feel disconnected from them. You want something or somebody to reassure you that you're not alone.

So you turn on the car radio.

And you hear that voice, the familiar voice of the deejay or talk show host. You hear that welcome voice you've heard so often.

And you've got a friend in the car with you.

That's the business Johnny Holliday got into over 40 years ago. That's the business Johnny Holliday is in today.

All the great radio voices have this one thing in common: They are your friend.

In New York, where I grew up, there was Dan Ingram, Murray The K and Cousin Bruce Morrow. In Los Angeles, there was Robert W. Morgan, Casey Kasem and Rick Dees. Every city had a few special voices that cut through the lonely night and made everything all right.

Johnny Holliday was one of them. In Miami, in Cleveland, in New York, in San Francisco, in Washington, D.C. Over the years, hundreds of thousands of kids in city apartments and suburban tract houses and rural barns tuned into Johnny Holliday, eager for his voice, knowing he was speaking just to them. This is the special connection of the radio. Brian Wilson of the Beach Boys identified it so many years ago when he sang, "I hit the radio dial and turned it up all the way." Knowing the voice was just for him.

I didn't know Johnny when he was a rock 'n' roll disc jockey. In the 20 years I've known him, Johnny's been a sportscaster and the voice of the University of Maryland basketball and football teams. But one day we were driving to play golf, and Johnny played a tape somebody had sent him. A tape of Johnny on the air in Cleveland.

"Listen to this," he said with a big laugh.

And about 30 seconds in I heard him introduce himself to the teenagers of Cleveland in the early '60s as "Every teen queen's dream."

It broke Johnny up. I laughed too. But when he went to pop the cassette out of the tape deck I asked him to leave it in for a while, let it keep playing. Because I was 15 once too, and I listened to the radio late at night, when I should have been asleep, and I wanted to be every teen queen's dream, too.

And I'd heard that voice before. Maybe not Johnny Holliday's. But I'd heard somebody's voice just like his, somebody still young enough to remember the pain of bad skin and the crushing finality of the pony-tailed girl in your biology class telling you, "I wouldn't go out with you if you were the last boy on earth." Every day of his life a teenage boy faces the end of the world. If he's like me, he turned to the radio for comfort and hope. And a voice just like Johnny Holliday's had always given me some.

The power of radio is amazing. I've written in newspapers my whole working life. Nothing I've ever done professionally is more thrilling to me than having a byline. No matter what else I do, I'll always be a newspaper writer. But these last 10 years I've also done a radio show, and I'm stunned by the difference. I've found that even though lots of folks have been quite complimentary about my writing and like my writing and have told me my words are "exactly" what they felt, the connection between a newspaper writer and a newspaper reader is still rather distant. They know I'm not writing just for them. And the fact they can put the paper down for a while and then come back to it removes the intimacy.

But radio listeners have no such critical distance. You're in their car with them. You're in their house with them. Just you and them, across time and space, dancing to the same beat. You're in their ear! What could possibly be more personal?

Sometimes when I go on the radio I tell people I'm hungry and I wish I had some food. It never fails within a half hour somebody brings me a pizza or a hamburger or some pastry. They drive to the station and deliver the food themselves. To me it's an unbelievable gesture of generosity and humanity.

When I ask them about it, they always say it's because they listen to me every day and they feel close to me; they feel we're friends, and it's the least they can do for all those hours of enjoyment. Let me just say I've written a newspaper column for 20 years, and nobody ever sent me a pizza. Radio is where the true connection lives.

Johnny Holliday has spent his whole life in radio making friends across time and space. He was there at my start in radio; for three years Johnny and I did a pregame show together on Sunday mornings outside RFK Stadium before Washington Redskins games. The first time I was as wobbly as a puppy on linoleum tile. But Johnny was kind and calming. He smiled at me and told me there was nothing to worry about. We were just two guys talking, like we'd talked before. "The only real trick to it is that there's no trick to it," he told me. "Just be yourself, and you'll do fine." And I did.

Over the years Johnny and I have played golf together and gone to dinner together. He is unfailingly upbeat. I'm sure he's had down days, but I can't imagine them. Being around him is like passing Go and collecting $200. And if I go some time without seeing Johnny, I know I can always turn on the radio and hear his voice, his wonderful, singular voice aimed at just me (and you, and you, and you). That voice everyone turns on the radio to hear. That special, familiar voice of a friend.

I'd know that voice anywhere.

Chapter One

Warm Up in Miami

Have you ever taken a personality test? I took one to prepare for this summary of my life. I answered a battery of questions to see what a psychological analysis might reveal. Maybe an unbiased profile of my nature might help readers get a sense of how I'm wired.

According to the test results, my personality type is best characterized as "the journey is more important than the destination." I'm an "outgoing, practical thinker, free from the biasing influence of theory, tradition, or emotion." Action is my middle name. I thrive on it and create it when life gets too boring. My type applies "a flexible, common-sense reasoning approach to any problem we tackle. Just don't try to sell us on fantasies and abstract ideas. Spontaneous, competitive, and generous, my personality type turns work into play, whenever possible, and applies the model of an athletic team to all relationships. Teamwork matters."

I generally agree with these results, as does my wife, the lovely Mary Clare. By the way, I always refer to my wife as "Mary Clare" when I am talking about her, and always "Clare" when I am talking to her. Never, ever just "Mary."

And she always calls me "John," or occasionally, "First Class Dummy," but never, ever "Johnny." I also refer to her as "My Trophy Wife" and occasionally as "Original Parts," since she has never been reconditioned or artificially enhanced. She's as impressive today as the first time we met.

I was born John Holliday Bobbitt on October 15, 1937 in Miami's Jackson Memorial Hospital. What mattered most when I arrived in Miami was the continued construction of resort hotels. Miami was the unquestioned Mecca for East Coast tourists—glitzy, stylish, and the weather was there. "It's Always June in Miami" was a slogan back then.

The tourist waves continued until World War II, when the military took over the growing resort area. My father, John Charles, better known as "JC," joined the army as a private. My mom, Dorothy, with my little sister, Charlene and me, moved in with my grandmother during the war years.

One remarkable childhood memory was the "Freedom Train" visit to Miami in '47. The Freedom Train carried an exhibit of historical documents to Florida and to the rest of the (then) 48 states. It was Uncle Sam's attempt to show us the importance of our heritage. People stood in line for several hours to see such rarities as a letter by Christopher Columbus on the discovery of America, the 13th century manuscript of the Magna Carta, and Abraham Lincoln's 1863 Gettysburg Address.

What impressed me most was the shining red, white, and blue locomotive that brought that rolling history show to my town.

Probably what *excited* me the most as a young boy was my first serious crush on Mrs. Hill, my fourth grade teacher at Shadowlawn Elementary School,

In the fifth grade I sang "Adeste Fidelis" for a school program. I probably knew then that pleasing an audience was something I liked. I sang on key, or so they told me.

The *Miami News* selected my family as the "Average American Family" around the Freedom Train event. Our pictures were in the paper, and reporter Grace Wing wrote the following article. It's almost twilight zone strange that she led her piece with a radio reference.

"Four Freedoms Enrich Even Humble Home"

As the radio announcers say, let's look in for a moment on the family fireside of the John Charles Bobbitts, in a small duplex at 51 NE 43rd St.

It is early evening and as the Bobbitts cluster together in the light— youthful John and Dorothy with their two youngsters, Johnny and Charlene— they look like just what they are, an average American family.

And yet, close knit as the little group appears, there are four others present, invisible except in the happy serenity of the Bobbitt's faces. They are the Four Freedoms: freedom of religion, freedom from want, freedom from fear, and freedom of speech. It is the people like the Bobbitts who make America...

Ten-year-old John Holliday Bobbitt scratches a knee reflectively as he leans against his father's chair to get a hitch with his homework. Curly-haired Charlene, three and a half, dozes in her mother's lap, lulled by the purring diction of a high-priced news commentator on the radio.

"Aw, cut him off, Mom...I'd rather listen to Henry Aldrich," puts in Johnny before his attention is jerked back to the lesson in a hurry by his father.

A sudden knock on the door would bring no fear among them. They'd know it was only the traffic officer trying to find an address for a Western Union boy. Uniforms hold no threat for Johnny because he's got one, too. He's a Cub Scout.

The head of this average American family is a 31-year-old tobacco salesman, who married his high school sweetheart in 1934 the same week they got their diplomas. An infantry veteran, he was halfway across the Pacific when the war ended and sustained nothing more than an attack of jaundice. Winding up his sick leave at home, he broke his ankle playing football with his son.

Like thousands of other service wives, Dorothy stayed with her husband's family during his two-year absence. Now they are renters with ambitions of owning their own home...

And between themselves and God, there is a private understanding on which no one intrudes.

A fine article except for a few omissions. For starters, we didn't have any money. Things were tough. I was born just after the Depression, and then came the war. When we moved back in with my grandmother, I slept on a couch. So much for freedom from want.

Furthermore, our family was less than the average in many ways. My dad had been the big star athlete in Ada M. Fisher High School on Miami Beach. He was also an amateur lightweight boxing champion and a champion bowler. He was great in all sports. And he was a very handsome guy.

Because of the nature of his various jobs—he first worked for Phillip Morris, then for Budweiser, and was frequently on the road—he'd often end up at parties with a constant cigarette in one hand and a succession of cocktails in the other. When he'd come home after those parties, he'd scare the hell out of us. He was a Jekyll and Hyde. I'd sometimes lock myself in the bedroom, hoping he wouldn't break the door down.

So much for freedom from fear.

I'd try to talk to him on the mornings after these episodes. "C'mon, Dad, what are you doing?" He'd sincerely apologize, but the alcoholic pattern continued. The loud, drunken arguments with Mom. Over and over.

My mom didn't share Dad's acute alcohol problem, but she went along and joined him in the drinking and smoking. I suppose it was her way to cope.

Outgoing, beautiful, and an outstanding dancer, my mother really kept the family together. She was my biggest supporter and encouraged me to do chorus and theatrics in school. Following Dad's most serious binges, my sister and I would think, "OK. That's it. She's gone. She's not going to stick around for this." But she stayed.

It was job to job with JC, and when he left Budweiser, he found work with a laundry service. I'd travel with him down through the Florida Keys every Thursday to help him deliver laundry supplies. I missed one day of school every week and tried to make excuses as best I could.

Sometimes he'd take me on longer weekend trips for his job, but when we'd hit the hotel, he'd hit the bar. It was really disappointing to be a young boy sitting alone in those rooms. I remember this as if it were yesterday.

I probably had it best in the family. I was there before my dad went completely downhill. He'd play sports with me. We had a relationship. It was harder for my sister, Charlene, who is six years younger than me. She internalized the family "problems" in ways that I didn't. Charlene's take on it was: "What's wrong with me? What am I doing that causes Mom and Dad to drink and fight so much?"

Today Charlene is a legal secretary in Hollywood, Florida. We both cried when I showed her the draft of how I was planning to portray our parents in this book. Then she let me know I was painting too rosy a picture.

"It was much worse than John remembers it," Charlene says. "Dad was a good person until he started drinking. When he was drunk, he was abusive and mean. We lived in constant fear. I only remember being struck by him once, but he would physically abuse my mom, and she'd retaliate. Once, when John and I were hiding in my bedroom, Dad broke the door down, and Johnny climbed out the window to get help from our neighbors.

"Mom was gorgeous. There wasn't an evil thought in her mind, and I see much of her personality in Johnny today. But, unlike Johnny, she was weak in some ways. She loved us, but we just didn't have a good childhood.

"Still, she had to have done something right, because we all have turned out well. We value our homes, our families. We didn't grow up with this. There was a lot of pain when she was alive. But I miss her now every day and every night.

"I was only 12 when Johnny went off to work in radio. I looked up to him and really thought he had it together. I take real pride in all that he has done with his life. Mom was also thrilled with his accomplishments and would always file away everything Johnny would send back home concerning his career.

"The one thing about my older brother: He never bragged about his successes. Sometimes, he'd never mention them at all. For example, when he was named Washingtonian of the Year, we didn't know about it until we read the magazine. Johnny's ego is buried so deep you'll never find it."

My baby brother, Bobby Lee Bobbitt, was born in 1954. Today, he's an evangelist in suburban Atlanta with the Church of Christ. Although I see him when the Terps play Georgia, Charlene mainly keeps tabs on Bobby.

"Bobby is a wonderful person who adores his family. He has a wonderful wife and two great kids. Bobby was a DJ for a time. I believe he was trying to be like Johnny," says Charlene.

It was the hardest for Bobby Lee, because he remained with Mom and Dad when the family situation was at its worst. Because he is sixteen years younger than me, we aren't as close as we could be. That doesn't mean I don't love my baby brother, because he knows I do.

Bobby Bobbitt: "Charlene is right when she says I grew up wanting to be just like John. He was the successful one in the family. John had to care for all of us at some point. My parents waited for the $100 check he'd send every week. Then they'd drink it away. John would also send me his hand-me-down clothes.

"Our relationship has matured over the years. The bottom line now is that I want us to be closer. He put his arm around me and gave me a kiss the last time we got together. My 18-year-old son, Brandon, liked seeing us together like that."

Both of our parents eventually died of cancer. Dad was 57, and Mom was 69. They'd be 86 years old today and should be enjoying their grandchildren and great grandchildren. It makes me so angry that they passed away so young.

By age 14, I was captivated by Miami radio, especially by Jerry Wichner of WINZ 940. His show was VERY BIG in Miami, and beyond, as the station signal went east to the Bahamas. Jerry was a low-key DJ, in his late 20s, and our suspicion that he wore a "rug" was confirmed when some kid pulled off his toupee at a Bayfront Park auditorium dance. This made the local papers.

From the WINZ studio on Biscayne Blvd, Wichner played the pre-rock and roll tunes of Joni James, Ralph Marteri, and the like. Because I thought it would be fun I called Jerry at the station and asked whether he needed an assistant. "Sure, come on down," he said, so I ended up working for him, helping to file his records away and running his errands after school. Since he was a quiet, older man, I never got to know him well.

He never paid me anything for assisting him, but it was a kick to see how real radio worked. Wichner went on to nighttime radio on WNWS-AM 790 and spent the remaining years of his career in talk radio on WFTL 1400 before his retirement in 1994. When I tried to track him down for this book, I learned that he died in his sleep at his Hollywood, Florida home a few months before this project began. Jerry gave me my very first experience in radio.

As the population of North Miami grew, the town needed a high school. Edward L. Constance High opened in 1953, with grades 7 through 10. The name changed to North Miami High the next year, and the upper grades were added as we moved through the years. Principal John C. Maguire had coached my dad in football.

We were nicknamed the "Pioneers" because it was a new school. I pitched the first "no-hitter" against Coral Shores High, but, again, everything we did was a "first." My teachers could confirm that playing sports with my buddies was always my top priority.

Making friends has never been a problem for me, because I genuinely like people. With no axes to grind and never prone to "dish the dirt," my approach to people has always been easygoing and collaborative. Mary Clare says I've made so many pals in the broadcasting business because I'm not an SOB.

Bob Geissinger, Joe Gomez, Butch Grubbs, Jack Jung, Don Lewis, Sal Licata, Vennie Pent, Bob Petrie, Joe Ryan, Tom Sgro, Joe Sheaks, Edgar Smith, Bill "The Duck" Terry, and Paul Gleason were some of my best Florida buddies. We played football, baseball, basketball, and hung out together in what were, for all of us, our Florida glory days.

On the female side, there was Deanna Keith, Georgeanne Hartman, Sandra Howard, Shirley Parzow, Suzanne Mayer, Beverly Edwards, Jo Moore, Diane Rowland, Madeline Fusco, Carol King, Sue Lowell, and Sharon Hazelrigg.

Paul Gleason went on to become an actor ("with an attitude," the columnist Leonard Maltin once said). Paul's credits include the teacher in *The Breakfast Club* (1985) and the police chief in *Die Hard* (1988). He's known for playing authoritative "sleazebags," and we actually nicknamed him "Bags" when we played sports together. That handle came about because we all thought he wore the same athletic supporter for four years.

Paul was being interviewed on Ed Walker's AM Washington D.C. TV show in the seventies when I anonymously called in to ask how he got the nickname "Bags." It was fun to see his pained expression.

My closest buddies were Don Lewis and Sal Licata. In our senior class yearbook, Don was voted the "Most Popular," Sal was "the Friendliest," and I got nothing. This should give some hope to kids today that aren't singled out in high school. (Sal recalls that he voted me "Most Likely to Succeed," but, obviously, nobody else agreed.)

Don Lewis and I formed a comedy team—"Lewis and Bobbitt"—at North Miami and did what we thought were funny routines and impressions.

"Johnny, you've got a bump on your head."
"Yeah, I was putting toilet water on my head and the lid fell down."
Or, doing my best Jimmy Stewart impression:
"My new movie is called 'Don't close the blinds on me. It makes me shudder.'" Badaboom!

One of our teachers, Mrs. McClure, cheered us on to keep the act going, and "Lewis and Bobbitt" even appeared on Jack Cobb's local TV variety show on station WTVJ. The guest that day was humorist Sam Levinson. After the show, Levinson told me that he thought we were really funny. (Sam has long passed on so he can't dispute my memory on this.) One of his many quotes fits "Lewis and Bobbitt" to a tee: *"The virtue of being very young is that you don't let facts get in the way of your imagination."*

The fact is we weren't very good.

The station even flew "Lewis and Bobbitt" to Patrick Air Force base to amuse the troops, which shows how desperate our Florida servicemen were for entertainment. When I told our first joke, we heard only one person applaud. Then we realized he wasn't applauding. He was trying to get ketchup out of a bottle.

Today, Don Lewis is an Atlanta financial planner. He's done quite well in the money business. Don reflects on our early days:

> **Don Lewis:** 'I was always Johnny's best audience going back to when we met in the eighth grade. Whatever he said broke me up, and I think it was the same for him. We clowned around, and everybody seemed to enjoy it. Mr. Dutton, our chorus teacher, encouraged us, gave us pointers.
>
> "However, I remember—and Johnny doesn't—the time he invited us down to WINZ when he worked for Jerry Wichner. There was a studio they weren't using, and Johnny brought us in and started playing records and working the controls. He was pretending to be on the radio, and we were all amazed by that."

Around this time, Miami station WGBS announced an amateur disc jockey contest with the winner to be decided by mail-in votes. Unknown to me, Don Lewis entered my name as a gag. When the contest instructions arrived in my mailbox, my first thought was "Don Lewis did this." I got into it immediately and convinced all my relatives and friends to flood the station with "Johnny" votes.

My big moment came. WGBS gave me the contest script, which consisted of record introductions and news. My half-hour "on the air" flew by. When the votes were tallied, I lost to a University of Miami student from the farm town of Jennings, Florida. His name was Andrew Prine. My guess was that I didn't have enough relatives to out-vote Prine's university pals.

Just a few years later Andrew Prine took the lead in Broadway's *Look Homeward Angel* and by the time I got to Cleveland in 1959, he was in movies like *The Miracle Worker* and showing up on TV westerns like *Wagon Train*.

One thing about many of Prine's later western movies: He says he mostly played the "peacemaker" and he usually got shot to Swiss cheese…which served him right for beating me in the DJ contest.

Sal Licata, my other closest friend, was an all-star guard in basketball and one of the best athletes at North Miami. I was his backup but hardly ever played. Why? Because Sal was an *all-star guard* in basketball. Sal, also an all-star first baseman, was the key to the success of our baseball and basketball teams. A Brooklyn boy who arrived in Miami with his parents in '51, we all thought Sal would really make it in the major leagues. He was that good. But he totally blew out his hamstring in the Phillies' training camp, and that took care of his sports career.

Sal and I have come a long way from where we started. His first job in Florida was in ladies' handbags at Burdine's while I worked in the stock room at Dick Richmond's store. At $40 a week, Sal cleared $34.06. When I finally became established as a WHK broadcaster in Cleveland (covered in *excruciating* detail in chapter three) I got in touch with Licata. Here's how Sal remembers it today:

> **Sal Licata:** "In 1961, Johnny tracked me down in New Jersey where I was working a summer job in a hotel. Johnny told me to take a bus to Cleveland. Johnny had talked with Eddie Rosenblatt on my behalf about a record promotion job in the Ohio area, and he got me the job. Eddie went on to be president of Geffen Records (but put his name in small print since he didn't pay me much in Cleveland). I stayed in Cleveland for a year and got an offer from Big Top records to come to New York.
>
> "From there I went in regional sales with Tower Records and Johnny came to work at WINS so we were in New York together. I joined Blue Thumb Records as a sales manager and worked my way up to president of the label over a period of four and a half years. I broke the Pointer Sisters on Blue Thumb, releasing their debut and follow-up albums, both of which exceeded a million dollars in sales. Next I was the president of Chrysalis Records for seven years, and we broke artists like Jethro Tull, Robin Trower, Blondie, and Pat Benatar. Clive Davis, of Arista, brought me in as senior vice president, and I retired in July 2000 as president of EMI Records.

"But I can tell you that if Johnny hadn't invited me to take a Greyhound bus to visit him in Cleveland, I might have finished my career driving the bus. And of all the things I've done I consider those days at North Miami High as the best part of my life. "

I think Sal made it big because he was real and not just your typical "finger snapping, hey baby" record guy. He didn't just play the game; rather, he did things the way he thought they should be done. Sal's a bottom-line guy. When he took over EMI he recognized that the label was top-heavy with too many artists not bringing in revenue. Boom. They were gone.

Licata has it right about the fun times at North Miami. Once, my pals and I went down to the Bayfront Plaza Hotel and commandeered an elevator. In those days the elevators required a human operator, so when we found an empty one we took off with it. We next heard the security yell, "Please come out, we are calling the police." We raised the elevator to another floor and heard, "It's time to give up the elevator. *We've got you surrounded.*" Somehow I eluded the security by jumping off and hiding behind an overstuffed couch in the lobby. Unfortunately, the "heat" grabbed one of my pals, Tom Sgro, and held him. We were all in our early teens, just goofing around.

Another prank was to plant one of our friends outside the neighborhood movie theatre while a group of us drove by in our car. We'd screech the brakes and yell out, "What did you call us?" and then pile out and pretend to beat up our friend. Then we'd jump back in the car and speed off. The bystanders would be flustered, but they rarely intervened. I think this stunt was Don Lewis's idea, which, in retrospect, shows leadership qualities. (One note about Don, Sal, and yours truly: None of us graduated from college. You probably guessed that by now.)

In 1956, my parents moved from Miami to Unadilla, Georgia, where my dad and grandfather were born. Unadilla was an unrenowned community until recently, when a tragedy made national headlines. A U.S. military plane transporting soldiers from Florida back to a naval base in Virginia crashed in bad weather, killing all 21 people on board. I was personally saddened when this news hit the wires.

After high school graduation, I went back to visit Unadilla for the summer to play some amateur baseball, leaving a series of Miami jobs that included delivering parts for Tropical Chevrolet. I even hauled windows around town for a glass company. That job was a "pane in the glass" as my inexperience was transparent. They could see right through me. The jobs proved that I still had no idea what I really wanted to do with my life and no inkling whatsoever that I would choose a career in broadcasting.

In Unadilla, hanging out in my grandfather's drug store, Bobbitt's Pharmacy, was the next best thing for enjoyment off the ball field. One day a fellow named Al Evans walked in.

Evans, along with partner Joe Beaumont, owned radio station WBBN in Perry, 18 miles north of Unadilla. He was there trying to sell my grandfather advertising time. Unexpectedly, my grandfather introduced me to Mr. Evans with the words "Meet my grandson, the disc jockey."

Of course, Granddad only said that because I had been a contestant in that DJ contest. I wasn't telling anyone that I wanted to be a disc jockey. Again, I had no clue what I wanted to be.

Even more surprising to me, Evans said, "Hey, I'm looking for someone," and invited me to his radio station to read some news, to audition for a real radio job. So I went.

Since my voice was really high then, I recall being more than a little apprehensive during my audition. I was scared I'd flunk.

Incredibly, he hired me at $32 per week.

"So you are Johnny Bobbitt? You'll need a better radio name. Do you have a middle name?"

"Yes sir, it's Holliday," I answered.

Mr. Evans brightened. I officially became Johnny Holliday the day I joined the WBBN radio staff. Holliday was my mother's maiden name.

Recently, I met Art Linkletter in Maui for the first time and introduced myself as a "fan, along with millions of other Americans." The first thing he said was "Johnny Holliday? Sounds like a show business name to me." He was very gracious. He told me that he began as a sportscaster. The "Holliday" name continues to serve me well professionally, although my legal name remains John Holliday Bobbitt.

In case anyone is wondering how I felt when the "cutting edge" news broke of Lorena and John's marital misadventures, I can honestly say that it didn't bother me at all. And I have no desire to learn whether we are genealogically related. No thanks. The only similarity between John Bobbitt and Johnny Holliday Bobbitt I can think of is that my 1960s New York radio career was also unexpectedly cut short.

WBBN was one small, square building set off by itself on Highway 40. My recollection is one control room, one studio with a piano, and Al Evans always wearing a bow tie. "You name it" pretty much describes the programming.

Mornings opened with real country music by George Jones, Web Pierce, Skeeter Davis and the like. Joe Beaumont, the station co-owner and our "Mr. Smooth," hosted "Dream Awhile" in the afternoons, playing (as he describes it) "very selective, moody, romantic ballads."

Joe Beaumont, now 76, recalls: "Al and I built the station in '48. Now I have four grandkids, one in the Coast Guard, two in college, and one in high school. I don't know where the hell the time went.

"I opened up WBBN many mornings. This is because our morning man, Jack Rupert, was so undependable. Jack looked a lot like Drew Carey. I'd wake up and turn the radio on to hear nothing and have to run down to the station to start it up when Rupert failed to show.

"WBBN had a good number of listeners, including Warren Robbins Air Force Base. Radio was fun, and I really enjoyed it until the wailing, screaming guitar crap came in and drove me out of the business. I couldn't stand that garbage. But we all had a good time at WBBN."

The local Dodge dealership sponsored my Lawrence Welk show. I had only seven records, so I was flipping them over quite a bit.

At noon we'd present the "Stumpus Family," sponsored by the Perry Feed and Grain Supply Company. This bit was Evans as "Uncle Joe Stumpus," his wife as "Aunt Sally" and me as "Little Johnny Stumpus." Aunt Sally played the piano while we all stood around the microphone.

> *"Today the Stumpus family is gathered around the breakfast table.*
> *"Can I have some more eggs, Dad?" I'd ask.*
> *"No, Little Johnny. First, you must finish the eggs still on your plate,"*
> *Dad replied.*
> *"Aw, c'mon Dad."*
> *"Give the boy some eggs," snapped Aunt Sally, "because today we have*
> *a special hymn to sing dedicated to the Ladies' Sewing Club at the Perry*
> *Baptist Church."*

We'd do 30 minutes of this stuff. We just made it up. Sometimes Evans had an outline, but we'd usually just be doing it off the cuff. Once in awhile it went somewhere. Mainly it went nowhere. That's how bad it was.

Everybody seemed to love it. Go figure.

One of my fellow jocks was Jimmy Lee, who's now with the Georgia Farm Bureau in Macon. He remembers it this way:

Jimmy Lee: "Johnny and I got our first jobs in broadcasting at WBBN. I thought I would succeed quicker because he came from further out in the sticks than I did. It didn't really matter because he just had a naturally rich talent for radio. Plus, he had a real radio name, "Johnny Holliday." Man, there are jocks who would fight for that kind of name. He called his first basketball game and the station's first game on a tape recorder from the stands and it was played back on the station the next morning. He has been setting precedents ever since. I am proud our paths crossed in the early years and that we continue to have fond memories of our broadcasting roots together. I have been in farm broadcasting for almost 43 years now and Johnny's journey led to sports broadcasting. So I guess I moved out in the sticks and Johnny came to town."

My first radio job at WBBN lasted from July '56 through May '57. When I started, Mary Clare and I had already decided to marry. I mailed my debut WBBN publicity photo to Mary Clare, inscribed "To my darling Clare, the most wonderful girl on this whole earth. To you, honey, with all my heart. Nothing will ever separate us. I promise what a terrific wife you are going to make. All my love, Johnny."

Looking back, it's funny that *I was promising her* "what a terrific wife" she would make.

Mary Clare and I met on a blind date in Miami. One of my pals, Bill Stirrett, was dating her best friend, Jane Shea. The four of us went bowling. Clare was a high school junior, three years younger, and somewhat on the thin side as I recall. I got her on the rebound just as she had broken off a relationship.

One drawback to marriage was my religion, which was Southern Baptist in name only. Clare was devoutly Catholic. I readily agreed to convert. The priest presiding over my instructions, Fr. James McGowan, turned out to be quite inspirational. As I studied Catholicism, and got more and more absorbed in this new religion, I unexpectedly found myself confessing to the priest that I should *also* consider the priesthood.

"HOLD ON," said Fr. McGowan. "This will wear off. You're getting married!"

I was baptized in the Catholic faith on Good Friday, 1957. My parents were happy with this positive step in my life and were most supportive.

At WBBN, I approached Mr. Evans and asked him if I could broadcast a Perry Panthers high school basketball game. He said, "If you can sell it, you can broadcast it."

Bobbitt's Pharmacy was the first sponsor I lined up. The second was Harry Hamrick's Furniture Store.

Many kids who are absorbed in sports have probably pretended to announce a game at one time or another. I'm sure I did that. So when this opportunity came, I jumped at it. The station had a huge tape recorder that I lugged to the gym. It certainly wasn't a portable, and I had to worry about kids kicking the plug out while I concentrated on the action. We were a daytime station, so the game was a day old when it aired.

Just like John Miller, who got his job broadcasting for the Oakland A's by going in the stands, taping the game, and sending it to A's owner, Charlie Finley, I did almost the exact same thing in Perry, Georgia. I sure wish I had saved that Perry tape. This was my first play-by-play. I had no idea what I was doing. It just felt right. The kids were thrilled to hear their school on the radio. This was a big deal.

The star Perry player was high school senior, Sam Nunn, a pretty good athlete as I recall. Twenty-six years later, after I settled in Washington, D.C.,

I read that *Senator* Sam Nunn was "raised in the small town of Perry, Georgia." Retired from the Senate, it's Professor Nunn these days at Georgia Tech.

After I "knocked 'em dead" in Perry, I felt that I was more than ready for the big time. I headed back to hometown Miami—with audition tape in hand—and made the rounds of the stations looking for my next job. Since I had been *so good* on the air in Perry, I figured that the Miami market would be dazzled by my abilities and some smart program director would rapidly hire me.

WRONG!

Chapter 2

Practice in Rochester

"Johnny looked to be about 14 years old. The record hop kids didn't believe he was our DJ until he actually got behind the microphone and started to speak. Most of them couldn't believe it."
Arnie Schorr, *Program Director, WVRM, Rochester, NY*

Have you ever heard the expression "couldn't get arrested?" That was Holliday returning to Miami. The parable of the Prodigal Son had nothing to do with my return. No one would give me the time of day. I visited almost every radio studio in the Miami market and came up sucking air. I realized that the only two stations that I didn't try—or that *hadn't* rejected me—were rhythm and blues, or R&B, formats.

Remember that this was nearly a half-century ago. Miami was fiercely segregated. The pre-Elvis era R&B music was still regarded as "race music" and hadn't yet crossed over to find acceptance by a white audience. Nat King Cole was enormous then and could easily sell out his engagements at the Fontainbleau Hotel. However, when his show ended, he had to travel back to the Lord Calvert Hotel in the black community's Liberty City to get a room for the night.

So a white boy on a black station? In 1956? And, in Miami, Florida of all places? You gotta be kidding.

But what the heck, I thought. I felt that this was my final option. With no job offers from the white stations, I had nothing to lose by trying R&B. And so I did. Luckily—and I really mean *luckily*—I met Arnie Schorr.

Arnie, along with his father, Herb, mother Lillian, and his father's best friend and business partner, Harry Trenner, owned station WFEC. Honestly,

I believe that if I had never met Arnie Schorr, I would not have had the radio career you are reading about now.

My first impression of Arnie was that of a very dapper guy. He was kind of early Preppie, with horn-rimmed glasses, and he was someone who really knew his stuff. He and I sat together and had an honest talk about my experiences at WBBN and what I wanted to do with my "career." He was more than open to my pitch for a chance to prove myself. I could immediately tell that skin color wouldn't be an issue.

Today Arnie is a retired broadcasting executive living in Orlando, Fl. His career has been a long string of fabulous radio successes that included owning or managing stations like KGFJ and KHJ in Los Angeles.

> **Arnie Schorr:** *"Johnny was a gangly, funny-looking kid who had no apparent reason or right to be in radio. It was his enthusiasm that sold everyone on Johnny. His desire to be a disc jockey was so intense. I took him to meet my father and the first thing he told us was that he loved rhythm and blues. We were in that transitional phase between old-time radio, with the soap operas, and this brand- new format, Top 40. At that point we had been negotiating to buy a Rochester station and launch the first Top 40 station there. Basically, we needed to build a staff, and Johnny convinced us that he was the right guy at the right time."*

Although I would have much preferred working at WQAM or one of the other big-time Miami outlets, I was still blown away with the job offer. I eagerly accepted Arnie's invitation to join the team.

It turned out that my timing was great. The Schorrs and Trenners had just purchased WRNY, a small station in Rochester NY, and were waiting for FCC approval. They needed energetic broadcasters and were willing to bring me along. "Join us and be a part of this new, exciting adventure in Rochester radio," was the spirit of the discussion.

Herb Schorr previously served as sales manager of New York City station, WOR. Harry Trenner, his best friend since childhood, had just left the William H. Weintraub ad agency. They purchased WFEC together. While they awaited the final FCC approval papers for the New York WRNY sale to be processed, I was offered the job at their Miami station.

WFEC was located alongside the railroad tracks of the Florida East Coast Railway. This location gave the station a hometown "River City, Iowa" feeling the instant we heard the whistle of the 4:33 whiz past. A single non-directional tower beamed the broadcast from a single studio. The transmitter was actually *in the studio*—unheard of then as well as now. WFEC had one engineer who worked in the closet. That's right. *He sat in a closet.* This was a tiny operation barely making any money. The $3.00 per commercial fee—

compared to $20 for our competition—kept WFEC afloat. There were no tape cartridges back then, so commercials were live.

Arnie assigned me the midmorning shift. The dynamite WFEC lineup included "Rocky G" Groce from Brooklyn who reminded me of a wrestler or linebacker, or better yet, a baseball player—which he was. He had traveled to Miami in the minor leagues. Herb and Harry brought him on board when the team dumped him.

With his thick New York accent, Rocky G. spun Basie and Ellington records that he brought from home. Indeed, most of the jocks played their own stuff since there was no set playlist and not much of a music library. It was strictly ad-lib.

Rocky also had a beautiful Buick, and we'd often see him washing and waxing his pride and joy in the parking lot, minutes before he'd go on air.

I also played baseball in a summer league with Rocky, and man could he play! Rocky G would eventually go to NYC station WWRL, one of the premiere black Top 40 stations, where he eventually became the program director.

We also participated in a media baseball game—the radio team versus the newspaper print guys—and I was the pitcher. (This sparked an idea that I would later exploit in Cleveland.)

And then there was King Coleman. King *was* the King at WFEC. To this day I still carry the vivid image of the King walking into the studio wearing silk Bermudas, knee high socks, a beautiful and very expensive shirt, jewelry that matched his clothes, and dark shades. With a set of pipes that would make Lou Rawls sound like a tenor, King also had a band, the King Coleman Revue, that played Miami nightspots.

I was instructed to call him every day at home about 20 minutes before his radio show, just to be certain he was awake and able to make his one o'clock shift. King's late-night music life included frequent after-hour encores with many lady friends. Thus the need for the wake-up call 20 minutes before show time, if you know what I mean.

Most of the King's on-air activities were actually one-sided conversations with even more of his female "fans." He dedicated all the real bluesy tunes to his ladies.

Terry Johnston, who went by "T.J. the DJ," was the only other white deejay at WFEC, but he didn't sound quite as Caucasian as I did. Terry's very soft and light voice was more suited for a jazz audience. His was not an announcer's voice. Terry was also openly gay. While we all accepted this without prejudice, we never discussed it.

In addition to working with these terrific people, I also had the good fortune of having my own hometown friends listen to me. That is *if* they could find me on the dial, since most of them were not R&B fans. On the air, I was often laughing when I got calls from young black listeners asking me "Are you white?" Funny how they knew that.

WFEC also did some remote broadcasts from the rooftop gardens of the Lord Calvert Hotel with performers like Lena Horne and Louis Armstrong. The music was terrific. We were having a ball.

All in all, the WFEC listeners were very supportive and accepting of me. It was a great experience. The six months I spent at WFEC prepared me for my next step up the ladder.

In August of '57, I flew up to Rochester. Arnie paints this picture of me stepping off the plane: *"Johnny got off wearing what was then known as a Mal Malkin suit, a long zoot suit with pointy collars. He was becoming a fashion plate."*

The Schorrs and the Trenners set up shop at the new station, changing the call letters from WRNY to WVRM. We stole our slogan—and our theme music—from a company who made hi-fi record players at the time. Their "Voice of Music" trademark became our "Rochester's Voice of Music" slogan. We even pirated a piece of their commercial music for our radio jingle.

And that's not all we stole. I got someone to tape Miami's WQAM every week and ship us the tapes. We'd dissect those tapes every week like football coaches reviewing game highlights. We'd plagiarize everything we could.

Rochester was something of a shock to my system since I had never been any further north than Atlanta, Georgia. I was excited to see snow first-hand, and boy, did I ever see it in Rochester. My first home was on Alexander Street, across from the hospital. David Abramson, fresh out of Brown University, became my roommate. David was a member of the WVRM sales staff, along with Budd Schmidt, Bill Weintraub, and the Trenners' son, Doug. The on-air personalities were Rocky G, Bill Edwards, Bob Bohrer, and yours truly. Our newsman was David Miller. The staff was small but energetic, and Arnie was our program director.

Arnie was like a brother to me. I even went so far as to buy my clothes from the same store as he did. Clothes I really could not afford. But I wanted to dress just like him, be like him. We were one big happy family.

> **Arnie Schorr:** "It wouldn't have worked if we hadn't had the chemistry. Nobody expected anything from us in Rochester, so when it all blossomed it was like a birthday present. The DJs were so alive, and Johnny, especially, had phenomenal timing. He really became absorbed in studying the WQAM tapes each week, and he was learning all the new tricks of Top 40.
>
> "You have to realize that Top 40 was a completely new thing emerging. In old-time radio you waited for the record to end before you spoke—primarily because you had engineers who were playing the records. Top 40 did away with that as the jocks began to run their own production. Eventually, the engineers just sat there sometimes doing nothing.

"The Top 40 recipe was simply to create excitement and play the most popular records over and over. The music was the whole ball game. The only reason we had news is because the FCC demanded it. Rochester was a very dead city when we arrived, and it became very alive when we caught on. Everything we touched was successful, and it almost scared us. We really didn't understand how it happened."

The WVRM studios broadcast sunrise to sunset in the Lowes Theatre building. We had one control room where the music shows originated and a second studio where newscasts and production were done. We had two turntables, a console in the middle, and three portable tape recorders in the studio. Everything recorded was on two-inch reels of tape. When one tape was almost finished, I'd have to be ready to hit the second machine. When I got to the third, I had to start rewinding the first one. Around and around I went with those tape recorders.

In August of '57 we hit with the new format and it took off like crazy. Our competition at the time was WBBF, which had some big names like Nick Nickson, Jerry Fogel, Joe Deane, and Leon Marguerite. It took us about six months to knock 'em off.

I opened my 6-9 a.m. broadcast with a character I had "borrowed" from the morning man at WQAM, Chuck Daugherty—or "Chuckie from Kentucky" as he referred to himself. The character was "Little Red, the Bloodshot Thermometer." Using an oscillator filter on the mike, "Little Red" announced the weather and made wisecrack comments throughout the morning. In hindsight it was a '50s version of Billy Biceps, a character I later inflicted on my audience when I went to WWDC in Washington, D.C.

At the time, Arbitron did two ratings books a year, although we couldn't afford to subscribe to the ratings service. WVRM went from nothing to number one in the first book.

One of our promotion stunts was to hide a $100 bill in a plastic box somewhere in the city—always on public property, mind you—and then give the listeners clues to its whereabouts. The police once complained that we were tying up traffic when the clues started to zero in on the Rochester city park. Again, I think we stole this idea from WQAM.

Radio historians agree that this era was a heavy-duty transitional time for radio. There are many theories on how Top 40 evolved. It seemed like many of the old-school radio professionals were moving to television. Young guys like Arnie (who was only about four years older than me) and I were experimenting and trying to create a station personality or special sound that could move us ahead of the competition. This was true both in both Rochester and at my next assignment in Cleveland.

The true "inventors" of Top 40 were probably the Bartell Family, three young Wisconsin brothers and their sister, Rosa. In 1947 they put together a programming grab bag of popular music, weather reports, a local "polka king" segment, a "Here Comes the Bride," showcase, and later an airborne traffic report on station WEXT. The Bartels found success with this segmented, lighthearted approach to radio and began building stations around the country. Slowly the popular music segments were expanded, by disc jockeys with names like "Lucky Logan" and "Mad Man" Michaels. Top 40 began to spread to the major cities.

One way to look at it is that there weren't enough guys like me to fill the growing demand for the new format. I think that's what Arnie means when he said I was the right guy at the right time.

We didn't even have enough announcers at WVRM to cover seven days a week, so every Sunday morning Arnie hosted "Sinatra and Strings." He taped soundtracks of Sinatra speaking and played his music around these intros. Although it was completely prerecorded, it got ratings as high as our other music programs. At noon we went Top 40.

I started doing record hops at the Rochester roller rink to supplement my $75.00 per week salary. Bob Bohrer and I did some record hops together in nearby Lyons, NY. I was skating on thin ice because I hadn't yet perfected the "Holliday Record Hop" routine that would later be so popular in Cleveland. The additional $35 bucks or so was good money at that time, especially for a teenager.

The other stations had some terrific talent as well, namely Eddie Meath who previously *owned* the mornings on WHEC, and the late Foster Brooks on WHAM, also on mornings. (Yes, the same "drunken" Foster Brooks from television fame.) Meath and Brooks were my competition, but I hung in well ratings-wise. Gary Smith was another great DJ whom I think is still in the business up there. I also met a fellow named Morty Shapiro who would become one of my best friends in Rochester. We'd hang out together. I always looked forward to feasting on home-cooked meals with Morty, his sister Sandy, and Mom and Dad Shapiro.

Attending Sunday Mass in Rochester introduced me to Father Sundholm at Blessed Sacrament church. Fr. Sundolm, and his associate Fr. Coonen, befriended me largely because they knew I missed Mary Clare. The priests were always there for me to confess how difficult it was to be separated from her. That's one reason that they would make a special effort to invite me to dinner with Fr. Sundholm and his parents during any holiday or special event.

Eating and staying busy were both part of my plan to help time fly by, because Clare and I were engaged to be married and I couldn't wait. Our wedding date was set for June. Since everyone in the wedding party was in Miami (except for me), the job of the wedding preparations fell squarely on our parents. My main contribution was picking out a Rochester "dream pad." My find was a one-bedroom apartment at 103 Bobich Drive that went for

$105 a month. I elegantly furnished our dream pad with an army cot in the living room, a couple of throw pillows, a used card table with two chairs for the kitchen, and a bedroom "suite" that my in-laws had sold me at cost. Our end tables and lamps were courtesy of the Schorrs and the Trenners. That was it. The Holliday "Dream Pad."

The big day finally arrived: On June 21, I married Mary Clare at St. Rose of Lima church in Miami Shores. Mary Clare's cousin, Father Joe Wesley, performed the ceremony. Don Lewis was best man.

Immediately following the reception, Clare and I took a six-hour "red-eye" flight from Miami to Rochester on the old Capitol Airlines. The plane *eventually* landed, and we drove to our first home as man and wife. Clare got a gander of our new digs, army cot and all, after I carried her over the threshold. She thought it was perfect. We were young and had no desire for anything else. We had each other and that was more than good enough for us.

Clare took a job as a dental assistant, so that was another 40 bucks a week income. Upstairs lived a young couple by the name of Dick and Jane Stover, and the four of us soon became good friends. Jane was the first to instruct Mary Clare that you don't BAKE a steak; you broil or grill it. This lesson came right after the Stovers responded to smoke billowing out of our kitchen because of a baked steak episode. Mary Clare had also never experienced snow and found it hard to believe that her feet got so cold waiting for the bus to take her to work each morning. Her helpful coworkers advised her that galoshes were designed to go over the shoes—not to replace them. "Oh, I see," said Mary Clare, a Florida girl through and through.

Arnie remembers Clare as a very religious, proper girl: "John was always so enthusiastic and flying off in all kinds of directions. She was his anchor and kept him grounded. Although she was younger than John, she always seemed more adult. I suspected that she would be making most of the decisions in the family."

Although I was still very green as a professional broadcaster, I began to receive some feelers from other stations. In June of '58, a program director named Clint Churchill from WKBW in nearby Buffalo called me.

Clare and I drove over and met with Clint and his father, Dr. Churchill. His dad not only owned the station but was also a minister heavily involved in the community. The Churchills were planning to change formats at WKBW and wanted me to be part of their exciting new sound, *Futuresonic Radio,* that was set to take off on the 4th of July. They enticed me with a new sound, new disc jockeys, new everything. The money would have been about a hundred and a twenty-five a week—a lot better than I was making at WVRM.

I turned the Buffalo offer down. I really liked my radio family at WRVM. The bottom line was that Clare and I were happy in Rochester. Clint said he was sorry I refused his offer, but he hoped there'd be another time in the years ahead we might hook up. He wished us well as we headed back to Rochester.

Don't think I wasn't intently tuned in on July 4th to hear WKBW's *Futursonic Radio* kick off. Holy smoke. What a sound and what excitement. And *what had I done?* I could have been part of this successful launch. The jocks were fabulous. Perry Allen, Russ "the Moose" Syracuse, Tommy Saunders, Gene Nelson, and Jim Washburn. It took me some time to shake my regret that I didn't sign on when I had the chance.

My time at WVRM continued through February of '59, when Jerry Spinn, the program director of WHK in Cleveland, called me asking whether I'd fly down for a visit. WHK, too, was about to change to Top 40 (the first ever in Cleveland) and Jerry extended an invitation for me to come on board. His offer of $160 dollars a week was too much to turn down this time. It was difficult telling Arnie, the Trenners and the Schorrs—wonderful station owners that I somehow knew then I'd never see again—that I was jumping ship.

> **Arnie:** "By the end of our time together we were like brothers because we had worked together so closely. It was just a matter of time before someone stole him. He was that talented and we all came to realize how good he was. I thought 'God bless him.' Just do well. I kissed him on both cheeks when he left us."

I thought about the first car I bought, a '54 Ford Fairlane, and how Mrs. Trenner had helped me finance it by deducting the payment each week from my paycheck so I could have wheels. The same wheels that would eventually carry Clare and me from Rochester to Cleveland. My life in Rochester had started in August of '57 and ended in January of '59. I left Rochester, and curiously, in all my travels for radio, sports, speaking engagements, and you name it—I would estimate some six million miles to date—I have never been back to Rochester.

Chapter 3

Cleveland's Call

"Hello everybody, good afternoon, welcome into the Johnny Holliday glass cage with the old refugee from the Sunshine State to serve up our cream of the pop crop, here's Bob and Earl, shakin' a tail feather, doin' the Monkey time with 'Harlem Shuffle' on the Fabulous 50 Tunedex tune spot at Number 2... Twenty-eight degrees our street level temperature outside the concrete jungle of Cleveland...on our Wednesday afternoon platter patrol from WHK, Color Channel 14, with your little old Cleveland host who loves you the most, Johnny Holliday till seven o'clock tonight..."

The way I see it, success usually comes from doing what you *really* want to do. Cleveland gave me the opportunity to try it all as a Top 40 disc jockey, theatre performer, sports announcer, commercial spokesman, and television host. Lucky for me, whatever talents I brought to Cleveland found a friendly audience willing to let a 21-year-old newcomer try to get his *acts* together.

It was after midnight when Mary Clare and I arrived from Rochester searching the unfamiliar Cleveland streets for a room. The ritzy Clinic Hotel was too pricey, so we accepted a bargain off Prospect Avenue—our old '54 Ford still packed with our belongings as we settled in.

We discovered that our room had an old-fashioned water closet of a type that we had never even seen before and couldn't easily figure out how to use. More surprises. The feather beds were two feet deep as we sank from view. Somehow we managed to fall asleep.

An hour later I awoke with an odd feeling. A glance out the window revealed a light on in my car and a very busy guy trying to steal our stuff. I immediately surprised myself by chasing this would-be thief down the street. Not sure what I'd do if I caught him, I managed to scare him off and save our goods. Clare phoned the police. When the cop arrived he told us we were in a very rough neighborhood.

"You kids should get out of here soon," he said.

I remember groaning to Clare, "Welcome to Cleveland."

The next morning we woke up to discover that our fellow hotel guests were about 80 years old. Don't ask me why.

"Are we living in a nursing home?" I asked Clare.

We found a fine Warrensville Heights apartment rental and I reported for station duty the following week.

WHK AM 1420 began in 1922, making it the oldest in the city and one of the pioneer radio stations in the country. The WHK studios were in offices attached to the former Bijou Theatre on 5000 Euclid Ave, renamed the WHK Auditorium, and later known as the Disasterdrome, Cleveland's underground answer to the Fillmore East, in the late sixties.

Engineers, protected by their union, sat elevated behind glass, looking down on the jocks. (AFTRA, the American Federation of Television and Radio Artists, equally protected us.) The jocks would play the records and tapes while the engineers ran the volumes. Console in front, big boom microphone, three turntables, and four cart machines. My weekly $160 contract with WHK Color Radio opened the studio door for me. This seemed like all the money in the world to me at the time. I was very excited to be there.

The day I arrived, WHK AM 1420 was eighth in the market, and "no ratings" was the problem. The challenge was to build an audience. Momentum was in our favor. With a change in station ownership, WHK became Cleveland's first official Top 40 rock 'n' roll station.

My first assignment—from 1 to 6 a.m.—was to play my choice of songs as listed on the station's Fabulous 50 Tunedex. My engineer was Paul DeFrancisco, a wonderful guy who still works in Cleveland today. Paul helped WHK (also known as the "World's Happiest Kilocycles") install a new studio reverberation unit. The station dubbed it their new STRAT-O-PHONIC sound.

Our music director, Neil McIntyre, would hold weekly meetings where we could brainstorm ideas and vote on new releases. Everyone got his say— although Cashbox and Billboard mainly set the Top 50. Chaired by our general manager, Harvey Glascock, I remember these meetings as serious and strict but also as a chance to bond with my young fellow deejays. The good-looking WHK crew over the years I was there included Scott Burton, Tom Brown, Pat Fitzgerald, Jerry Healey, Ray Otis, Farrell Smith, Johnny Walters, Keith Morris, Allan Michaels, Eddie Clark, Ron Riley, Bob Friend, Carl Reese, Bob Erwin, and the iconoclastic, legendary Pete "Mad Daddy" Myers.

Pete "Mad Daddy" Myers was the oldest of my fellow radio jocks and without a doubt the most talented and intriguing.

"Welcome, little stinkers, to the land of winky blinkers! Rocking and reeling and hanging from the ceiling. Boiling wavy gravy and distilling the feeling. So hang loose, Mother Goose, here comes the show."

That was "Mad Daddy," and all of my fellow crewmates were in awe of this guy. His off-the-cuff rhyming skills, heavy echo-punctuated maniacal laughter, and original slang were mesmerizing:

"Little Willie peachy keen
Made himself a time machine
But he found it to his sorrow
Much too weak to reach tomorrow
So he turned the knob the other way
And now he's stuck in yesterday."

By day, Pete Myers was a 31-year-old, down-to-earth (and very smooth) radio announcer. We knew he was a graduate of England's Royal Academy of Dramatic Arts and a Californian. His bright pink Pontiac advertised the personality that emerged when he became the "Mad Daddy."

By night, when he donned his black cape and white greasepaint for his 8:00 radio show from "Dracula Hall," as he called the studio, he was all show biz and ready to create a Cleveland radio phenomenon that still carries a cult buzz among radio history buffs.

Neil McIntyre was Pete's best friend. Just two years earlier, Neil, at 16, had been so inspired by "Mad Daddy's" airwave originality that he actually tracked him down at a small station in Akron and offered to be his assistant on the spot. Myers and assistant McIntyre moved from WJW to WHK the next year. By 1959, "Mad Daddy" was the most popular disc jockey in Cleveland.

Pete allowed no one inside the studio to observe him. No visitors. He even covered the windows. Only his personal soundman, Arnie Rosenberg, one of our WHK engineers at that time, was part of the action. Arnie said that "Mad Daddy was all spontaneous, the rhyming throughout the whole show, the sound effects, everything. You'd just sit there in amazement and try to create with him."

I never talked much with Pete about his career. He was so brilliant that I couldn't relate to him. He was living in a different world than I was. If you listen today to a recording of "Mad Daddy" in his prime, his stunning delivery and clever use of slang are remarkable.

Female fans were "the mellow muffins." Horror buffs were "ghoul rockers." Hot rod fans were "throttle jammers." "Mad Daddy" was "your head shrinker's delight." He coined phrases still heard today, like "wavy gravy." He played a mix of rock and roll and rhythm and blues, including offbeat tunes like "The Greasy Chicken" by André Williams and "Ghost Satellite" by Bob & Jerry. He also conjured his commercials in rhyme, especially for Gillette adjustable razors.

One of Meyer's stock bits was called "Zoomerating." He'd run down the alphabet from A (Atom-smashing) through Z (Zoomerating) and free-associate different words to describe his show. Again, with nothing scripted, he would spontaneously blurt out new adjectives each time he did the bit. Always impressive.

"Mad Daddy" once parachuted into a section of Lake Erie. He had planned to fill the lake with Jello, but the FAA nixed that idea. It was his first and only parachute jump. A foolhardy publicity stunt but very "Mad Daddy."

While at WHK, Pete nabbed a "Double Cola" advertisement that ran on Dick Clark's Philly TV show, *American Bandstand*, and word of his talent spread. By the summer of '59, "Mad Daddy" was recruited by New York station, WNEW.

Unfortunately, his persona raised more complaints than fanfare. The "Mad Daddy" show was cancelled after one airing on July 4, 1959. *Billboard* reported that 100 letters of complaint reached the station. For whatever reasons, New York just didn't get him. In search of ratings, station managers successfully toned the "Mad Daddy" down to what became a vanilla "lovable, laughable" version of his former self, the "Mild" Pete Myers, but it never really clicked.

Pete was hired at my next station, WINS, but his career continued to go south. Neil McIntyre had also moved with Pete to New York. Neil says that the final insult was when Pete's friend, Jim Lowe, was switched to midnights when Pete was assigned Lowe's 8 to midnight shift at his next station, WNEW.

Jay Hunt, of Ontario, Canada, is a former Mad Daddy fan who keeps Pete's flame kindled on the Internet these days.

> **Jay Hunt:** "The WINS show was recognizably Mad Daddy, but not as frenetic as in its WHK heyday. The music had changed and so had the times. The Beatles and Ricky Nelson were more likely to be heard than André Williams.
>
> "I grew up in London, Ontario where I listened to the Cleveland radio stations beamed across Lake Erie. Mad Daddy was my favorite DJ from 1957 when I first heard him on WJW through 1959 when he left WHK for NYC.

"I was envious of the Cleveland teenagers who could see him live when he appeared occasionally at the theatre near the station at Midnight after his radio broadcast. I wished I could shop for records at 'The Vous' (Rendezvous Records), buy my girl a 'Goin' Steady Ring' and even get a faster tan with Tanfastic."

"After his shift switch at WNEW, Pete knew this was the beginning of the end of his career," Neil McIntyre explains, "and he was also displacing his good friend to boot. It was a demotion for both of them."

On the morning of Oct. 4, 1968—the day he was to begin his new shift—Pete Myers awoke and dressed sharply in his favorite tweed suit. Selecting a shotgun from his prized gun collection, he walked to the bathroom and used the gun to end his life. A suicide note was found, describing his depression over the change in his radio assignment. He was 40 years old. It was a tragic end to a brilliant talent.

In '59, Cleveland radio was semismoldering in the wake of Alan "Moondog" Freed, credited in '51 with coining the term "rock and roll" on our competitive Cleveland station, WJW. His show was the "Moondog Rock 'n' Roll Party." He'd pound his fist on a telephone book keeping beat to the mostly black rhythm & blues tunes he liked. His 1952 Moondog Coronation Ball at the Cleveland Arena was said to be the first rock and roll concert in the U.S. (I read that nearly 20,000 fans "crashed the gates," causing the show to be cancelled.) An interesting note: in his earliest days Freed was a sportscaster at WKBN in Youngstown, Ohio.

By the time I got to WHK, Freed had moved to New York's WINS, making history not only promoting the Paramount Theater Rock 'n' Roll shows but becoming mired in the payola scandals then twisting the industry. The year 1959 was also the time of the TV quiz show investigations. The media was feeling unfamiliar pressures. Although Freed maintained his innocence, he eventually pleaded guilty to taking $30,000 from six record companies to play their tunes. He was blackballed from radio and died a lonely death in 1965. He's now the only radio DJ—and among the first group of inductees—in Cleveland's Rock and Roll Hall of Fame.

At WHK we felt Freed's legacy in a personal way: The station made us sign affidavits swearing that we had never received "payola" money for promoting records.

I knew that Top 40 was the place to be, and I could handle this new format. We were all young, and I was in on the ground floor. Always a good mixer, I soon understood the staff and the mission. And I was not shy in contributing ideas to grab listener attention.

One of the first clever things we did was contract a new radio jingle from the noteworthy Los Angeles firm, Sande-Green. The lyrics were nothing special (mainly "WHK Color Channel Fourteen" repeated), but the tune was instantly appealing. The station cut an instrumental version—with big brass and strings—and called it "The Pulse of the City." Next, we sneakily distributed it to our competition by promoting it as a regular "new release." Amazingly, the other stations, WERE, WJW, and KYW, all began to play it. When we finally aired our new jingle—complete with the WHK lyrics—the stations realized they'd been had. "Pulse of the City" quickly disappeared from our competition's playlists.

We tried other ideas to build a following. We initiated a WHK "Be Friendly" month, and I'd go with my new WHK pal, Scott Burton—decked out in our bright red WHK blazers—to the lobbies of our rival stations to hand out buttons. Bits like these were good-naturedly accepted then since all the on-air talent shared a sense of camaraderie, regardless of their station allegiance.

Another gimmick was to randomly pick the name of a prominent Cleveland person or someone we thought would generate some publicity. It could be the president of a bank (Joe Anderson) or a local ad man (Mark Wyse). Whoever it was, they would be "the secret word" for 24 hours. I'd pepper my daily dialog with "Today's *secret word* is Mark Wyse." One reason for doing this was to get friends of Mr. Wyse to ask him *why* he was the secret word. A naked ploy to get people talking about him, and more important, talking about WHK.

The "secret word" was also a working idea that the salesmen could use to convince potential advertisers that WHK could be of benefit to them.

"There were tremendous objections by many of the businesses to what they called 'that crap on the radio,'" Neil McIntyre recalls. "We heard slurs like 'Nobody's ever going to be playing THAT music at your wedding.'"

So the sales people would follow up and try to sell ads on WHK to many of the "secret word" businessmen. While they were still amazed at the response from their friends about being the "secret word," the ad guys would call with "I thought you said nobody was listening to that crap?"

We recorded five-year-old Vicky, daughter of Jim Kennedy, my Prudential insurance agent, saying, "My mommy is always listening to WHK. She says it's the thing to do." Great promotion.

We created a WHK High School Hall of Fame with kids nominating their classmate favorites by mail. It was another good promotion for building the teen audience base. Their new Japanese transistor radios helped juice those school promotions along.

Transistor radios made the new music portable. Since this new rock and roll was an affront to the adults, the transistors worked great because the parents didn't have to listen. For those that did we added promos like a "Housewives Hall of Fame," with flowers and candy as prizes.

Many of our promotions were quite involved. I remember feasting with Scott Burton at Cleveland's Sahara Motor Hotel Cafe as Scott underwent the "Luxury Survival Test." This three-day commercial promotion for the hotel's opening was built around the question of "just how much luxury" Scott could stand during his stay. The gag included 24-hour butler service, bubble baths with rose petals, a stretch limousine, and extravagant meals.

I'd be sure to join Scott for the food. The bit concluded when Scott screamed, "I can't stand this much luxury," ran out of the hotel, and "disappeared" for three days. Radio listeners were asked if they'd seen Scott anywhere. There was just *too much luxury* at the Sahara, and Scott couldn't stand it! Today, Scott is a radio consultant in Arizona, and we've kept a sound friendship by phone through the years.

The promotional energy began to pay off. In 22 days, WHK moved to the Hooper-rated number two spot in the market. From my "glass cage in the concrete jungle," I was conducting my "platter patrol" and "clickin' the turnstiles in our wax files."

I was soon promoted to morning drive, and the Hollidays bought a red convertible from Jim Connell Chevrolet. The Ohio Chamber of Commerce then called Cleveland "the best location in the nation," and in my morning drive slot on a number two station, there was no "mistake on the lake" argument from me.

Then, out of left field, the bubble burst. My music stopped.

AFTRA decided to send us out on strike when contract renewal negotiations reached a snag. I was actually scared that I wouldn't get my job back. Nevertheless, I dutifully marched in front of WHK with an "AFTRA Striking WHK" placard around my neck. I remember thinking, "What the hell am I doing? I have a wife, and here I am walking the picket line on the coldest days of Cleveland and me being a Florida boy, *freezing my ass off.*"

Management told the local press that the strike resulted from the "highly exorbitant demands of the employees." *Say what?* I certainly wasn't making any exorbitant demands.

But money really wasn't the issue. It was security. The union felt we deserved some job protection since we were the ones responsible for the success of the new format. Jim Frankel, local columnist for the *Cleveland Press,* sympathized with the staff positions during the strike, noting, "The jockeys at WHK are not name personalities like Bill Randle, Joe Finan, and 'Big' Wilson. They are 'formula' men who must conform to the strict regulations set down by WHK managers. They manipulate their own turntables and are obliged *to stand* for the entire period they are on duty."

Little did he know that I sat on a stool sometimes.

The strike lasted three days, and we successfully regained our personal contracts with some added assurances that future negotiations would be one-on-one with management. I got a $10 hike in my paycheck when the strike was settled. A victory for the station that "Has a Holliday Every Day," as they began to promote me.

After the strike and back on air, I hit upon the promotion idea of which I am proudest: "The Radio Oneders."

Here's what happened: The Wickliffe High School lighting system had failed. A student called and asked if I could host a dance to help raise some money to get the lights fixed. I told him, "I'll do you one better." I could get a team of jocks to come over and play a basketball game against the teachers. The school could charge whatever money they wanted, and we'll just take some sandwiches in return. I called our WHK team the "Radio Oneders"—since we were about to be the number one station. This idea came to me as a reprise of playing baseball in Miami against the newspaper crew. Only this time, I'd turn it into an ongoing charity event for the schools. Believe it or not, it had never been done before.

The first game worked beautifully to promote WHK, and it was a bonus that we won. The gym was standing room only. We had a terrific time, made a lot of money, and the idea mushroomed. We did 23 more games at area high schools that first year.

By the time I left Cleveland we had played almost every high school faculty in Northern Ohio. Sometimes we'd do three games a week. Eventually, we optioned sandwiches against a modest "players' fee" for showing up at the schools. Sometimes we'd split a hundred dollars among the Oneder jocks, or the schools would feed us. The volume of games we played did provide a "side income" for many of the "Swingin' Seven" disk jockeys that participated.

The Oneder game scores were published in the *Cleveland Plain Dealer* newspaper, which was exceptional promo since it was the biggest newspaper in the city. One news article even quoted the kids' reaction to the first game:

Glenn Strandt — "Johnny Holliday does a swell impersonation of Wilt Chamberlain."

Pat Gucciardo — "The Oneders are all right. Wickliffe High School didn't play hard enough."

Jane Kehn —"Johnny Holliday *bothers* me!"

On that last note, my wife took a sharp offense at some kids who were heckling me on court during one game at Orange High School. "He's out there working, making money for your charities," she loudly complained from the stands. The lovely Mary Clare was ready to take on the whole section of agitators—all by herself—that night.

Mary Clare recalls, "When our daughters were old enough to attend the Oneder games, I found them doing the exact same thing when John got the raspberries. Protecting the dad."

Raspberries aside, the real knock on me as a ball player is that I took too many shots. I'd score a lot of them, but many baskets just didn't happen.

If Holliday got the ball, you could expect a shot. This could be a metaphor for my career: If Holliday got a chance he went for it. When it comes to feeling and thinking, I've mostly acted on my feelings first. Thinking usually comes later.

Radio trade publications carried our Oneder success story, and stations across the country soon began to start their own charity teams. Radio staff in other cities called me to ask how I put it together. I'd explain it takes only one guy at your station who likes to play basketball to organize the teams. I sent them contracts showing how I did it. Everybody seemed to jump on the bandwagon.

When the basketball season ended, the Oneders regrouped as a softball team and carried on the charity fundraisers in the sun. The softball was sponsored by Blepp-Coombs, a big sporting goods store located in the front of the WHK building

I used this charity/promotion vehicle for 26 years in Cleveland, San Francisco, and D.C. The Oneders raised almost two million dollars for various charity events.

Other record promoters who played on our WHK Oneder team include my Florida pals, Sal Licata, and Tom Sgro, who also began his record career in Cleveland and later moved from San Francisco and Washington D.C. to Nashville to become one of the top promo men in the country. Other teammates included Marv Helfer, who did independent work, Pat McCoy, Perry Stevens, and Eddie Rosenblatt, who later became the president and CEO of Geffen Records.

Other folks I remember are Bob Skaff, who started his record career in Cleveland then went on to become vice president of Liberty Records. Johnny Musso became president of Scotti Brothers and MCA. Tommy LiPuma produced the hit, "Guantanamara"—that's Tommy doing the narration on the Sandpipers record—and later produced recordings by George Benson and Dianah Krahl. Jack Bratel and Dennis Ganim were successful Cleveland promo guys, along with Allen Mink, who later worked for Mercury, and Chuck Chellman, likewise for Decca. The people I mention here were just outstanding in their field, as evidenced by so many of them going on to take major roles in management positions.

Cleveland is also where I got my start doing commercials. I received one of the first sets of hard contact lenses, created by Dr. Erwin Jay, and did spots (as we refer to commercials in radio land) for this novel product. I also worked with a young Tom Conway from Chagrin Falls, Ohio, to do all the spots for Manners Big Boy restaurants. Tom became *Tim* and went on to comedic fame as Ensign Charles T. Parker on TV's *McHale's Navy* and later on Carol Burnett's CBS variety hour.

Ironically, Ernie Anderson, Carol's announcer and the later voice of TV's *The Love Boat* was one of the jocks originally let go to make room for me at WHK. He and Tim Conway paired to produce some fledgling comedy records. Cleveland fans will also remember Ernie as the popular Ghoulardi character. Ernie passed away several years ago and is kindly remembered as one of the great voice-over talents in broadcasting.

One advertiser with whom I did many commercials early on was Larry Robinson, "The Diamond Man," of JB Robinson's Jewelers. Larry 's first store was at 9th and Euclid, not far from the station. Larry would sit down before we taped the spots and request, "Johnny, one thing I want you to do is mention what a great guy I am. And later in the commercial, maybe you could work in what a terrific guy I am." So I would start the spot off with, "You know, Larry, I don't know how you do it. You're a great guy. How do you get such great diamonds?" He would then humbly respond, "Well, thank you, Johnny, but it's not about being a great guy; it's about the diamonds…" The Diamond Man did have a great voice, and I always kidded him over the years about missing his true (radio) calling.

When I think back about commercials at WHK, I am always wowed by the effectiveness and zeal of our sales staff. The original group at WHK included Joe Zingale, who went on to create the first professional tennis team in the city and ended up owning a piece of the NBA, the Cleveland Cavaliers. Dick Jansen would later be president of Scripps-Howard broadcasting, and Bob Weiss (later joined by Norman Wain) would continue as founders of Nationwide Communications, one of the most successful radio organizations in the business. With neophyte talent like this, it's no wonder WHK's ad revenues were soon soaring.

From '59 through '64, Cleveland was the hottest record town in the country. WHK, WERE, and KYW were stations that could break a record for an artist. There were terrific relationships between the stations and the promotional people who serviced them. Some of the biggest names in the record promo business came out of Cleveland, where they began their careers working for local distributors. My friendships began with these folks, both on a business and personal level, and continue today.

Carl Maduri went on to become one half of Belkin-Maduri Productions (he produced "Play That Funky Music, White Boy" by Wild Cherry and "The Morning After" by Maureen McGovern). Carl brought almost every major show to Cleveland, played on our WHK Radio Oneders softball team, and is godfather to my middle daughter, Tracie. Carl, along with Jimmy Testa, also produced my first "hit" record, "How Sweet it Is," in 1961.

"How Sweet it Is" was a take-off on the classic Jackie Gleason line. Carl recorded an up-tempo vamp with breaks. As each break came up, I would repeat "How Sweet It Is" in different voices, including Ed Sullivan, Walter Brennan, James Cagney, and others. That was the point of the song, or lack of a point as I thought. "Just how in the hell is anyone going to like this?" was my question to Carl at the time.

Amazingly, "How Sweet It Is" was selected by a Toledo radio station as their "Pick of the Week" but it did not go on to gold record status. I think it might have gone "tin."

I called Carl recently to confirm whether the song had sold six or seven copies. Carl guessed seven, but thought we had given five away. Very funny.

Another more auspicious Holliday-Maduri collaboration came much later in 1991 with "Footprints in the Sand." I narrated this Christian poem—written by a 14-year-old Mary Stevensen in 1936—over a spirited gospel chorus. We had some regional success in the Christian market with this one. Carl and I are thinking about reissuing it if this book bombs.

By the end of my first year at WHK, I was in an "afternoon drive time" groove airing the Fabulous Top 50 TUNEDEX—now in chronological order—and averaging 33 percent of the listeners. We routinely beat the competition, including a young, gravel-voiced Casey Kassem just starting out at station WJW. Here's a sample of the "funderful" tunes I was tracking in December 1959. I know they'll bring back memories for many folks:

DECEMBER 28, 1959   Top 50 TUNEDEX

1. Running Bear . . . Johnny Preston
2. Why… Frankie Avalon
3. Handy Man…Jimmy Jones
4. El Paso…Marty Rubbons
5. Down By The Station…The Four Preps
6. Way Down Yonder in New Orleans…Freddy Cannon
7. Go, Jimmy, Go…Jimmy Clanton
8. Where or When…Dion And The Belmonts
9. Heavenly Blue…King Curtis
10. Village of St. Bernadette…Andy Williams
11. Music Man…Danny Valentino
12. Mack the Knife…Bobby Darin
13. It's Time to Cry…Paul Anka
14. First Name Initial…Annette
15. You've Got What It Takes…Marv Johnson
16. Friendly World…Fabian
17. Uh Oh…The Nutty Squirrels
18. Pretty Blue Eyes…Steve Lawrence
19. Little Things Mean a Lot…Joni James
20. I Wanna Be Loved…Ricky Nelson
21. God Bless America…Connie Francis
22. Sandy…Larry Hall
23. Dream Concerto…Ferrante & Teicher

24. Upturn…Eddie Smith
25. Carillon…Compo Verde
26. What a Night…The Chippendales
27. Just Come Home…Hugo And Luigi
28. Ebb Tide…Bobby Freeman
29. Bonnie Came Back…Duane Eddy
30. Danny Boy…Conway Twitty
31. I Can't Say Goodbye…The Fireflies
32. Southern Love…Ronnie Hawkins
33. Shimmy, Shimmy, Ko-Ko-Bop…Little Anthony & The Imperials
34. Not One Minute More…Della Reese
35. How About That…Dee Clark
36. What About Us…The Coasters
37. How Will It End? …Barry Darvell
38. I Really Do…Spector's Three
39. Oh Carol…Neil Sedaka
40. If I Had a Girl…Rod Lauren
41. Whiffenpoof Song…Bob Crewe
42. The Big Hurt…Toni Fisher
43. Teen Angel…Mark Dinning
44. Stairway To Paradise…Pat O'day
45. Smokie…Bill Blacks Combo
46. Every Day, Every Way…Hollywood Flames
47. Do Re Mi… Mitch Miller
48. Why Didn't I Go? …The Curls
49. Harlem Nocturne….Viscounts
50. Clap Your Hands…The Wheels

Feature Album Of The Week: Faithfully…Johnny Mathis

By 1961, WHK was soaring. I've kept a few of my ratings books over the years, and they show I averaged a six share at the station, with my nearest competition, station KYW, managing a 3.9 against me.

But the biggest thing in Cleveland that year was the WHK Listener Appreciation Day at Geauga Lake Park, southeast of Cleveland. It was our way of thanking listeners for making us the number one station. Enormous publicity.

It was a free concert, with Freddie "Boom-Boom" Cannon, Connie Francis, and Fabian playing live sets. Attendance was near 60,000. The city managers and newspapers later complained about the traffic jam, but we thought this was good when Geauga Lake roads were choked with WHK listeners.

I had my own packed crowds when I hosted the "Johnny Holliday Coca-Cola Record Hop" at high schools almost every Friday night. I'd heavily plug these dances during my radio show. The kids were amazing. Up to 1,800 teens crammed into a high school gym was normal.

With this proven popularity, the record promo guys started offering their acts to perform at the hops. Toni Fisher, Tony Orlando, the Brothers Four, Gene Pitney, Johnny Tillotson, and others came out to lip-sync their hits. Johnny Tillotson spent the night in our apartment to save hotel costs. We once wheeled a piano into the gym for newcomer Neil Sedaka's solo performance.

My then closest DJ friend, Scott Burton, remembers Jan and Dean showing up at one of *his* record hops, with Jan hanging behind after the show pestering him to drive Scott's new 1960 Corvette. "I let Jan drive back to the station," Scott recalls, "and he was racing 80 mph most of the way." (Jan Berry suffered brain damage from a car accident in 1967 and never fully recovered.)

I think it was about '62 or so that I started thinking I didn't want to be *only* a Top 40 disc jockey for the rest of my life. Don't get me wrong, I loved the work but I frankly thought I had more to offer. So I started to stretch a bit, to try some different things.

One of my wishes came true when I landed the part of Og, the Leprechaun, in *Finian's Rainbow*. Directed by Ed Ludlum, and staged by Jerry Leonard at the Cain Park Summer Theatre, this would be my first professional theatre role. I felt cozy on the stage and have always felt at home there. Even more than my play-by-play radio personality, I believe the "on stage" Holliday—singing a song especially—is about the closest that I come to sharing who I really am with the world. My family sees this side of my personality all the time.

The headliner in *Finian* was the very glamorous Jenny Smith, from the Steve Allen TV show. Scott Burton, also in the cast, recalls Jenny as "very outgoing." Allen sent a letter when the show closed thanking us for taking such good care of Jenny.

I started to include here a more elaborate description of what a "knockout" she was, but Mary Clare and my daughter, Moira, bluntly reminded me that I don't *really* talk that way and would never utter sexist remarks in this day and age that might offend readers. They are completely right, of course, so I'll just add "bewitching" to my Jenny Smith report and quit while I'm ahead.

The outdoor Cain Park Theatre would be my showcase for the next two years. One fascinating aspect of that Cleveland playhouse: The managers asked big-name talent to come in and perform as leads in shows. Just for Cain Park!

Dion flew in and performed "Wish You Were Here" for two weeks. Bobby Vinton became "Harold Hill" in "The Music Man." I remember interviewing Vinton years later on one of my radio shows and reminiscing about Cain Park. It's a tribute to the Cleveland audience if you think about the time it must have taken Mr. Blue Velvet to memorize all those long singing speeches ("You got trouble my friend...") and realize he did it all just for *two weeks at Cain Park*.

By 1963, I was so thrilling the Cleveland community with my multi-talented, dynamic "Teen Queen's Dream" radio personality that I somehow landed a spot on local television.

And *oh* what a spot it was! The half-hour *Johnny Holliday Show*, produced by Herman Spero, aired Sunday mornings on WEWS, Channel 5, after *Polka Varieties* and before the Gene Carroll show. With a lineup like that, it's a wonder that Channel 5 even stayed on the air. Gene was Cleveland's answer to Lawrence Welk. He was Mr. Cleveland Show Biz at the time. Wonderful man, awful show.

My own TV "spectacle" featured stars like Annette Funicello lip-synching hit records. It wasn't exactly a bandstand—but we did have bleachers. Forty years later, Scott Burton doesn't remember my TV show *at all*, but I have a photo of myself standing next to a TV camera, which proves I was there.

Despite the fact that my TV program wasn't Emmy material, I had worked my way up in Cleveland to feel confident enough to continue to branch out in other directions. Producer Mark Wyse hired me to do the *College Scoreboard* TV show, also on Channel 5, which followed the ABC College Game of the Week every Saturday. Jack Perkins, later with NBC, was the news anchor on WEWS.

College Scoreboard revived my interest in sports broadcasting just in time for my next big break. One of my biggest opportunities came when I heard that the field announcer for the Cleveland Browns football team had passed away. I called the team's new owner, Art Modell, and told him I was a WHK disc jockey (adding "from three to seven" to my pitch) and asked to be his PA announcer. Modell replied, "Well, I've promised the job to someone else, but we're doing a doubleheader football game. Come on down next Saturday."

Indeed, Modell was sponsoring what turned out to be the first doubleheader football game in the NFL history. It was the Redskins vs. the Eagles and the Browns vs. the Giants in '62. Modell wanted me to do the first game, and the other announcer would do the second. The pay was $25.

Arthur B. "Art" Modell was then a 37-year-old former advertising executive—a self-made millionaire—who had purchased a majority share of the Browns team for an astounding $3.9 million the year before. This was an unheard-of sum of money for this kind of deal.

His announcing plan seemed fine. I did my part for the Skins-Eagles game on time. I was announcing from the field, so I had to keep up with the players. Actually, I had to keep up *with the ball*, because wherever the ball would go, that's where I needed to be.

This was in the old Municipal Stadium. After the first game was over, Modell called down to me and said he wanted *me* to do the second game, too. At that moment, I knew I had the permanent job. Capturing a true announcing position with a professional football team was electrifying. I can't recall the other announcer's name, but I do remember his wishing me success and letting me know it was just as well that I got the job. I hoped this was true. The final stats for my first season with the Browns were 7-6-1.

From the sidelines, I was there at the end of the '62 season when Art Modell earned the first major wave of fan resentment with his firing of Coach Paul Brown, who had led the team during its golden era with four consecutive championships in the late '40s. The second fatal blow was struck to Modell's stature when he moved his team to Baltimore in '95 and renamed them the Ravens. The Cleveland fans will *never* forgive him for that move. For years, Modell had sworn he would never take the Browns from Cleveland, and many loyalists believed him. Considering his ties going back to the sixties, I'm sure it was difficult leaving Cleveland.

I sent Mr. Modell a note not too long ago, thanking him for hiring me as PA announcer for $25 a game. I told him, "You can have me today for $30 a game!" I don't know if he got that note, but I always pull for him.

I was elated when his Ravens won the 2001 Super Bowl. He's come a long way from his Brooklyn boyhood, where he hung around old Ebbetts Field, to building a solid football franchise from top to bottom. As for the fans in Baltimore, they are the best.

D.C. journalist Buzz McClain recently asked me who I'd root for if it were the Ravens over the 'Skins. I told him that I don't have a lot of feelings for this Redskins team, because I didn't particularly care for the way owner Dan Snyder handled former general manager Charley Casserly. I think he made a terrible mistake by getting rid of Charley, and that decision has soured me on the current Redskins.

The Cleveland Browns job led to my work with the Oakland Raiders, San Francisco Warriors, Washington Bullets, and other teams. I can tell you that announcing those games has been among the greatest thrills of my life.

Clare always says that versatility has always been my salvation. With my Cleveland Browns job, the radio gig, the Oneders, the record hops, commercials, and TV under my belt, I think I played all that I had to offer and took great advantage of the foundation that Cleveland provided. My talents finally found their feathers. Cleveland was the "airport", and I was flying. I had a fantastic five-year run in the city.

Ben Fong-Torres, former *Rolling Stone* and *San Francisco Chronicle* reporter, and now successful author, published a great book on the history of Top 40 radio. I was very flattered to see that he featured my work in both Cleveland and New York.

When the book arrived, I called sports announcer George Michael to kid him. A longtime reporter on Washington's WRC-TV, and host of the syndicated "Sports Machine," George always tells everyone he was a big rock and roll jock in Philly before coming to D.C. (I know that's true because Maryland basketball coach, Gary Williams, used to listen to George.) Nevertheless, I teased, "Hey, George, if you were so *big* in radio, how come you aren't in Ben's book?"

The following is reprinted with permission from *The Hits Just Keep On Coming*, © Ben Fong-Torres. Published by Backbeat Books, "http://www.backbeatbooks.com". (Thanks Ben!)

You Never Forget Your First Jock

When word first leaked out that Joe Eszterhas had written a screenplay about a disc jockey in Cleveland in the '50s, the assumption was that it would be based on Alan Freed. Surprise. Soon after Telling Lies in America, *an evocative little film about...well, about lying, came out, Johnny Holliday, who lives and works in Washington, D.C., got a clipping of the* New York Times' *review from a friend, who jotted a note: "The only thing he didn't do is mention you by name." Holliday, who specialized in spouting alliterative clichés in a happy, hyped-up, barefooted style, worked at WHK in Cleveland from 1959 to 1964, then moved on to WINS in New York and KYA in San Francisco before fleeing back East to join ABC Sports (where he is today). He is so immersed in jockdom (of the sporting kind) that he didn't even know who Joe Eszterhas was.*

After seeing the clipping, Holliday recalled that a public radio special on the 75th anniversary of WHK had included Eszterhas, "who told about how he raced home every day to listen to me, and what an influence I was on his childhood."

Intrigued, Holliday tracked Eszterhas down. His manager sends word: "Well, fax me your name, your phone number, what questions you'd like to ask Mr. Eszterhas. I can't promise he'll get back to you, but we'll do our best." "So I fax him this letter. I say, 'Dear Joe. I am still every teen queen's dream. I'm still serving up the cream of the top pop crop. I'm elbow deep in the ballad bowl. Fender bender, bumper jumpin', chrome-crackling my way home every day in the boulevard of broken tail lights.' Four days later, I'm at ABC, and I've got a call. It's Joe Eszterhas. So I pick up the phone, and Joe says, 'I cannot believe I'm talking to you.' We talked for 40 minutes."

The Cleveland Plain Dealer *reporter turned* Rolling Stone *writer turned notorious Hollywood scriptwriter told Holliday, "You came to my school; you had a record hop. I came that close to actually reaching out and touching you."*

Eszterhas remembered Holliday's WHK basketball team, the Radio Oneders, which played games to raise money for charities. (Holliday would organize a similar team at KYA.) "I think the night you played, you got a brain concussion," said Joe. "You got hit in the head."

The writer asked an amazed Holliday whether he'd seen Telling Lies in America. *Like most Americans, Holliday hadn't. Within days, he received a tape. "So l watched the movie," the disc jockey reported, "and I was dying, laughing with my wife. I said, 'Man, this is exactly like it was.'"*

A few months after *Telling Lies in America* came out, I received a complimentary movie poster inscribed "To Johnny, For All the Sad Suffering Secretaries, (signed) Joe Eszterhas." That "suffering secretary" line was one I frequently used on WHK, and you can hear it in his film.

A *Cruisin'* series of records was released in the early '70s that featured Top 40 DJs from the late '50s through mid '60s. My WHK work is heard on the *Cruisin' 64* edition. When *Washington Post* music critic Richard Harrington reviewed *Cruisin' 64* as the "best of the series," I phoned Rich to offer my thanks. He replied, "That's you? I thought it was *some other guy* in Cleveland."

One of the better moments on that record was the Kahn's wiener spot. "These wieners are digestible," I guaranteed. "It's the wiener the world has awaited."

There I was, the "potentate from the Sunshine state," pitching a delicious, *digestible* wiener. And what's so comical now is how sincere I was back then. I wasn't kidding. Those wieners really *were* digestible.

I hear that WHK radio today hosts a Christian talk format. Nevertheless, Cleveland still remains a most rockin' sports town. The Rock and Roll Hall of Fame is thriving. The WHK auditorium, under its latest name, the Cleveland Agora, still serves up-and-coming rock acts. The new Browns have a new stadium. If you've never been there, you're missing something. Cleveland is one of a kind. As Cleveland native Drew Carey says, "Cleveland rocks!"

Dave Hughes is a communications industry journalist who has been running DCRTV, a Washington radio and TV web site (http://www.dcrtv.com), since 1997. DCRTV reaches 25,000 unique visitors per weekday. Here's a message posted from one of the radio program directors I worked with in D.C. when news hit that I was working on a book.

Bob Moke: "As a Northern Ohio teen in 1960, I was finding Cleveland radio to be less exciting than it had been in the late '50s. as the crazed Pete "Mad Daddy" Meyers had flown the coop for a gig in NYC, the legendary Bill Randle was no longer a "must-listen" at WERE, and my favorite music station—the mighty KYW—had just been dealt a life-threatening staff-altering blow by the payola police.

"Fortunately I had discovered a station that was in the process of inventing Top 40 radio for the Cleveland market and headed for the top: 'The New WHK, Color Channel 14!' And there was this terrific-sounding jock, just two or three years older than I was, holding down PM Drive, playing those wonderful old long jingles, counting up the brand new "Fabulous 50 Tunedex," and sounding like he was having the time of his life just being there.

"It was with great pleasure a few years back that I suddenly found myself working with Johnny. I wonder if *ALL* of the stories he told me will make it into the book."

I know many remember when WHK *"shot to the tippety-top of the 'ol pop crop,"* and my heartfelt thanks go out to the city and all my former listeners. I'll conclude here with my old Cleveland radio kicker, which makes about as much sense today as it did back then: *"Bye-bye, buy bonds, save chicken fat, and join the Wacs."*

My next career stop was New York City. Up until now, Cleveland was my "big time." NYC would prove to be something altogether different—and not exactly what I had hoped for.

Chapter 4

NYC Forward Motion

NEW YORK'S WINS ADDS TOP CLEVELAND DEEJAY

NEW YORK—Major talent and program changes are taking place at Group W's WINS here, Billboard has learned. The newest addition to the staff soon will be Cleveland's top-rated deejay, Johnny Holliday, a WHK performer for the past five years. Holliday is reported moving into the 10 a.m. to 2 p.m. slot occupied by another WHK alumnus, Pete Meyers. Meyers's "Mad Daddy" character is slated for stripping in the late evening, possibly following Murray the K's Swinging Soirée, thus giving the station a solid evening block of air talent that could prove very big with the younger set.
Billboard, *February 8, 1964*

When 1010-WINS hired Alan Freed in 1957, the station could claim introducing "Rock and Roll" to New York City. In '62 WINS went completely Top 40 and stayed near the tops in ratings until they began featuring more middle of the road music like Frank Sinatra and Andy Williams. Station owner J. Elroy McGraw nabbed a record $10 million when he sold WINS shortly after. The new owner, Group W (Westinghouse) vowed to topple WMCA and WABC in the ratings.

WINS brought in Ed Hider as morning man to "save the station," as Neil McIntyre put it. Neil had moved from WHK to WINS to become Ed Hider's producer/director. This promotion moved him from Pete Myers's assistant to Pete's boss, a somewhat awkward situation as I remember.

McIntyre still thought the station needed more talent. He suggested to the station manager, Joel Chaseman, that I was the guy. Joel sent Neil to

Cleveland to sign me on at WINS. Neil stayed with Clare and me as he pitched the new job repeatedly. I wasn't completely sold on the idea.

Neil McIntyre: "I was there for days trying to convince Johnny. He was very interested in coming, but I understood his reluctance. He had a great reputation with a lot going for him at WHK. At that time John was legitimately one of the top rock and roll DJs in the U.S.—one of the original fast-talking jocks. To come to a new city where he'd be one of 14 million was a major move.

"John didn't have that 'Voice of God' radio delivery like many others did. His was not a big, ballsy voice. Here was a guy who talked as though he was sitting on a block of ice. Initially, John's critics were many of the guys whom he worked with. They thought he talked too fast.

"But once you got with him, you got his rhythm. And the WINS audience really got it. He could spit out all the station information in 30 seconds and move on to the new Elvis Presley record, or what have you. We were all happy that John agreed to come on board at WINS."

"Sunshine and orange juice" is a radio term that describes what management offers when they don't want to pay extra salary. The term originates from when Florida radio stations were trying to lure talent to Miami. ("We can't give you great pay, but you'll have plenty of sunshine and orange juice.") WHK suggested a little "sunshine and orange juice" when they unsuccessfully tried to keep me in Cleveland.

The Cleveland version was "You'll be leaving WHK as number one to go to the third-place Top 40 station in a 50-station market. Stay here where you're already on top."

I relished the excitement of New York City immediately. I loved being on 50,000-watter WINS-1010 with Murray the K just in time for the Beatles' American invasion. I was amazed that I could go to the Warwick Hotel for a haircut by Mr. Rudy and see Steve Lawrence, or some other celebrity, sitting in the chair beside me.

However, the most thrilling New York memory for me has nothing to do with music. Hands down (or gloves up), it's the day I pitched at Yankee Stadium. Here's how it happened:

Just like Cleveland, we started a basketball and softball team at the station shortly after I arrived. The WINS-WINNERS. Singer Adam Wade and pal Sal Licata joined us for basketball, and we had a pretty good softball team that played in Central Park.

One afternoon I received a very official letter in the mail from the New York Yankees. I stared at it for a while before I ripped it open.

"Congratulations, Johnny Holliday. You've been drafted by Phil Rizzuto and his "Totem Homers" as they do battle against Jerry Coleman's "Ale Men." Fill out the enclosed form. Tell us what position you play. Bring your glove and shoes, and we will provide the uniform. Please report to the players' entrance on July 7. (Signed) Phil Rizzuto"

Wow, I thought. I've been drafted into the Yankees. What a thrill for this Yankee fan. I couldn't believe it.

Ballantine beer was sponsoring a celebrity media baseball game at the stadium. They'd split us into two teams—with no particular rhyme or reason—and I was invited to join the "Homers" managed by Phil "Scooter" Rizzuto, one of the best shortstops in baseball, a Hall of Famer, and later a Yankee broadcaster. The other team belonged to Jerry Coleman, a Yankee second baseman, and later broadcaster for the San Diego Padres.

My excitement grew as the Saturday game finally arrived. I walked into the Yankee clubhouse and was handed a uniform with the number held by then Yankee second baseman, Bobby Richardson. *Number one.* A "Totem Homer" patch was plastered over the Yankee insignia. We had the white pinstripes, and the "Ale Men" dressed in the Yankee gray road colors.

I would start as pitcher. I felt pumped and ready. I asked Scooter how he wanted us to play the game.

"Should it be for fun or what?"

"Hell no," he said. "I don't want you to play for fun. I want you to win."

"But Scooter. I'm looking at some of these guys on the other team. There ain't no way they're gonna get a hit off me. You really want me to play seriously?"

"Hell, yes," he said.

So I took the field. The legendary "Voice of the Yankees" and '78 Hall of Famer, Mel Allen, stood behind the plate as umpire. To my left was singer Mimi Benzell, as base umpire. The radio players included Pat Summerall (then at WCBS in New York), William B. Williams and Scott Muni (WABC), Big Wilson (WNBC), Dan Daniels (WMCA), and the "Ace from Outer Space," Douglas "Jocko" Henderson (WLIB). Also representing WINS were Ed Hider and Murray the K. Other celebrities I recall were Kyle Rote, the New York Giants running back, and singer Steve Lawrence, who came with Willie B. Williams and brought his young son David along for an afternoon of baseball.

Watching from the dugout were Yogi Berra, Mickey Mantle, and other real Yankees who traded lots of one-liners with the celebrities. Wish I could remember the jokes, but I was pretty focused on my game.

I pitched for three innings and only gave up one hit. From the batter's box, I was only able to hit a short foul to left field. Awesome wasn't a word we used back then, but that's what the experience was for me. We creamed the "Ale Men."

A week later Mary Clare and I were at home watching *The Tonight Show* with Johnny Carson. Steve Lawrence was a guest. As he walked out, I yelled to Clare, "Turn that up!"

Lawrence sat down on the Carson couch, and Johnny asked him what he'd been up to lately.

"Let me tell you. I just had the biggest thrill of my life playing at Yankee stadium. There I was playing shortstop. Johnny Holliday from WINS was pitching…" This was on national television.

I yelled to Clare, "That's exactly how I felt!"

The following Christmas, Ballantine sent me case of beer with an inscription on each bottle "Brewed especially for Johnny Holliday." I drank all but one.

WINS blasted all over the NYC area. I had to know what was going on in Palisades Park, on Long Island, and in New Jersey, not just Manhattan. I had to be on top of both the popular music and local sports.

I felt ready for what is considered to be the world's greatest radio market. I needed listeners to know they could always call me, get right through, ask me to play something, and I would do it. I enjoyed taking calls on the air. I'd tell the switchboard that if anybody calls for Holliday, then put 'em through. That's the way to build up your fan base. I wanted my audience to know that they were getting an up-tempo show by a guy who was accessible, upbeat, and having a good time. If I was having a good time, then so were my listeners, was my philosophy, and still is. You can't stay isolated in a studio.

I'd keep mental tabs on the various places I mentioned on the air. I'd think, "Well, I haven't connected to New Jersey for awhile," so I'd dedicate a new song by the Beatles to the kids in Newark. These connections helped form my audience.

All the shows we did at WINS, and I can say the same thing for our competition at WABC, and WMCA, had the same positive approach. Nothing negative. Always "up," "bright," and "optimistic." Just a "happy-go-lucky" style all the way.

Monday, February 7, 1964 was my on-air debut at WINS. About an hour into my morning shift, the program director, Joel Chaseman, walked into the studio.

"Johnny, can you do Murray the K's show tonight?" he asked. "He's down in Miami Beach with the Beatles, and he'll be calling in."

"Sure," I said.

So there I was on my first day on New York radio being asked to substitute for the renowned Murray the K. I had yet to meet him.

That evening, just moments before filling in, I heard loud chants of "We want Murray, we want the Beatles" from the studio window. I looked out to see about a hundred kids yelling from behind police barricades.

"Murray's not here. He's in Miami," I yelled back.

As I began to get ready for the show, I turned to Steve Safion, our engineer, with my instructions.

"Coming out of the opening theme, I'd like you to go right into the record."

"Murray doesn't do it that way," Steve said.

"But that's the way I do it," I said.

"It's not your show. It's Murray the K's show, and his way is the way IT WILL BE DONE." Murray's style was to jive talk over the jingle—welcoming people to the show—and lead in with a Sinatra tune.

"Fine, no problem. Let me know what you want me to do." I understood then that I wasn't the big Cleveland jock; I was the new kid on the NYC block.

So I ended up doing Murray's shift for the next three nights besides my own morning work.

On Thursday, I was doing my regular shift from ten to one when I saw a reflection in the glass as the studio door opened. This little guy walks in wearing a Russian fur hat. Nattily attired. Suit and tie.

"Hey, baby, how ya doin'? I'm Murray Kaufman," he purred. "You know I really appreciate your filling in for me while I was down with John, George, Paul, and Ringo."

"Nice to meet you. Glad to do it," I said.

Murray then moved forward and said, "Stick with me and you'll do OK in New York." He spoke in a kind, genuine way.

I thought, this is a real pro. After all, he was *THE* man. He'd been around, and I sensed that he was offering to take me under his wing. Twenty years older than me and enormously successful, I decided to hitch my little wagon to his star right then and there.

My immediate problem was how to address him. Should I say, "Thank you, Murray," or "Thank you, Mr. Kaufman," or "Thank you, Mr. K?"

Looking back, I would say that Murray had already been to the top of the mountain career-wise when I met him. As far as mega-personalities were concerned, Murray had much competition with Cousin Brucie Morrow and Gary Stevens opposite him. They were clearly moving in on his turf. Neil McIntyre would cite Murray's declining ratings. ("He was a better promoter of Murray the K than the station," Neil says.) Some in New York felt that his act had already worn thin.

I did not agree. To me, he was like a Pied Piper, running his live shows at Brooklyn's Fox Theatre. Seeing this 44-year-old entertainer on stage at the Fox—dancing his heart out while the crowd went wild—led me to believe that here was a guy who could still do it with the best of them. A great performer, he was electric and extremely charismatic. He'd come out with that little straw hat on and vee-neck sweater. Tight pants. Beatle boots. Observing him from the wings doing the Mashed Potato or the Watusi, I wished I had that much talent that I could flaunt.

Murray often gave me $100 out of his own pocket to come down and introduce some of the acts like Martha and the Vandellas or Bobby Darin. He knew that this exposure would help build our WINS audiences.

Murray would join me for the WINS-WINNERS games, too. Although he wasn't a great athlete, you could tell that he had played sports. He told me he'd played with the Kansas City Blues, a Yankee farm team.

The people went nuts when Murray showed up. I'd shmooze him with "Murray, you'll be the biggest star on the court," and he loved it. These Oneder games are how we became friends during the WINS years. He certainly didn't have to come out for the games. He was a millionaire at that time.

I also remember a surprise phone call I received from Murray in 1966 after I had moved on to San Francisco.

"Johnny, it's Murray. I'm doing a CBS TV show called *What's Happening, Baby* and I want to fly you to New York to be the announcer. All the proceeds are going to the armed forces," he said.

"But I'm in San Francisco. Why me?" I asked.

"Because you are the perfect guy for this job," he answered.

It was only a one-time special, but it made me realize that what I had done in New York had registered on Murray. It was a professional compliment that I appreciated. So I did it.

In a 1978 interview with Claude Hall, Murray was asked when he got into radio. He told Claude "*It was right after the Giants had won the miracle game against the Dodgers in the playoffs. And Loraine Day, who was married to Leo Durocher, manager of the Giants at that time, she and I did a radio show together.*"

Murray's son, Peter Altschuler, is today a television producer. Peter was in Jerusalem producing a TV show when I contacted him with a request to share the following memories of his famous father and my NYC radio mentor.

> **Peter Altschuler:** "Murray Kaufman was a show biz kid. His mother and aunt played in vaudeville, mom as a pianist, his aunt as a performer, and Murray himself appeared (as one of many child extras) in several Hollywood films of the 1930s. As the only child of a demanding mother, Murray always strove to make her proud, though she had little patience for parenthood and packed him off to a military boarding school.
>
> "When real military service came along, Murray couldn't quite pull off a Section 8 discharge and wound up organizing entertainment for the troops. It was an assignment that gave him a head start at putting

together shows for the resort hotels in New York's Catskill Mountain Borscht Belt.

"In the off season, Murray left the mountains and returned to Manhattan, where he had been born in 1922, and held an assortment of jobs in advertising and music promotion. As a song plugger for Bob Merrill and specifically Merrill's early '50s hit "How Much Is That Doggie In The Window," Murray seemed to have found his stride. By 1953, he was producing late night interview programs from a club on Lexington Avenue. The program was hosted at various times by Eva Gabor, Loraine Day, and Virginia Graham. It was that experience that led to a nightly show of his own, which occupied the two hours before Barry Gray's midnight program and which, in an era when husband-and-wife shows reached the height of their popularity, was frequently cohosted by his 'better half.'

"Murray's antics on the air, on the streets, in the subways, and overhead (broadcasting from Air Force jets), combined with his natural showmanship to earn him a virtual franchise in live events. As the host of personal appearances by hot bands at local movie theatres or as the emcee of four-times-a-year rock 'n' roll shows at the Brooklyn Fox Theatre, Murray developed the first truly multiracial audience. Like Freed before him, Murray Kaufman believed in the talents of black and Latin artists and preferred to play their records rather than the cover versions recorded by white singers. By building preference for a wide variety of music on the air (including Frank Sinatra, whose music opened every show), Murray attracted fans from every stratum to his live shows, and in their passion for the music, tensions had virtually no opportunity to develop.

"Thanks to WINS' nightly 50,000-watt clear channeling, Murray's reputation reached far beyond the boundaries of metro New York. For a while he aired in Toronto, then in Washington and Maryland before returning, in the early 1970s, to a national stint on NBC Monitor and, subsequently, to a regular program on WNBC. That relatively low-key show, which led into Wolfman Jack's late night program, declined along with Murray's health at the start of a long fight with cancer. His last New York gig was in 1975 on the extremely mellow WKTU, a station he willingly left to serve as a consultant on the production of Beatlemania. Following a national promotional tour, Murray left New York for "the Coast" to accompany his soon-to-be sixth wife, a soap opera star whose show relocated to L.A. It put him in an ideal position to host Watermark's syndicated Soundtrack of the '60s, which carried Murray's name and reputation to markets as far away as Australia.

"Yet Kaufman's battle with cancer was a losing one. By the end of one season, he had to withdraw from Soundtrack, giving up his slot to Gary Owens. Within a year, at the age of 60, Murray Kaufman was dead. Yet his legacy lives on through the artists whose careers he advanced (from Bobby Darin and Wayne Newton to Dionne and Little Anthony), the innovations he brought to music broadcasting, and the thundering call of the Submarine Race Watchers: ah bey!"

For the record, it was really Joel Chaseman, along with his associates Mike Hauptman, Bill Rorher, and Neil McIntyre, who connected the Beatles to Murray and WINS.

Hauptman, WINS promotion manager, first alerted Joel about the English group with the prediction that he thought the Beatles would prove to be a big deal. Joel knew nothing about them, but as the hype started building around their U.S. visit, Joel decided that this might be a way to get WINS back in the limelight. It was Joel and his staff who figured out how to make Murray the "fifth Beatle."

"We did everything a station could possibly do to associate with the Beatles. And it worked. We owned the Beatles," Joel says today.

The Beatles taped promo announcements for all the radio staff in '64 from their hotel rooms at the Plaza. "Hi, this is John Lennon, and you are listening to Johnny Holliday on 1010 WINS" was mine.

Murray's popularity was evident when thousands of fans flocked to meet him at our Coca Cola pavilion at the 1964 World's Fair. Each radio station had their day, and the WINS Day at the World's Fair is a great memory for me. My picture was snapped with the U.S. Postmaster General, James Farley.

As I was leaving, a black limousine pulled up. Out stepped Ed Sullivan with his wife, Sylvia. Ed was a small guy, about my size, and it was a blast shaking his hand.

Goldy is a popular DJ on Washington, D.C. "oldies" station WBIG these days. He's always helped me when I needed to promote something, and I genuinely like and respect him, as well as the entire WBIG crew. Goldy's dad was Ed Sullivan's business manager. As a youngster, Goldy had the advantage of seeing all the "big shews" in person. Imagine how exciting that must have been for a teenager.

Back at WINS, the calls soon hit the switchboard with weekend record hop requests. I'd next be all over—from Brooklyn to Connecticut—as guest DJ for high school hops. With artists like Adam Wade or Reparata and the Delrons joining me, and doling out promo records as dance contest prizes, we'd have a ball. The liner notes on the Delrons' first album were mine.

My typical WINS day: From our home in Dumont, New Jersey, I'd grab the 86 bus, take the 8th Ave. subway to 57th St., and there I was at the old dilapidated WINS building at 7 Central Park West—a run-down, three-story building at Columbus circle looking out over Central Park. The studio was on the second floor. The Gulf and Western skyscraper stands there today.

I'd normally get in around 10:30 a.m., type up the show and music format, answer some phone calls and mail, and then go to lunch at Henry Stampler's eatery, about two blocks away. Joining me would be my new WINS buddies or fellow radio pals and music business pros like Don Rubin, then a promo man and now president of EMI, Charlie Koppelman, or Freddy DeMann, a record producer who later worked with Michael Jackson.

After lunch, I'd hit the airwaves and have a super time for four hours.

Everyone worked out of the same small studio. Sandwiched between two turntables, I could activate my microphone, but I needed a special waiver from AFTRA so I could play my own records. Pete Myers was the only other WINS jock allowed this freedom. Otherwise, the engineers ran everything in the heavily unionized shop.

The DJs selected what songs to play from the WINS Winners song list. We followed the music system at the orders of our music director, Julie Ross. We could pick and choose from the list but never add our own choices from outside the list. This rule was a major pain for freewheeling Pete Myers.

Murray, on the other hand, used the playlist restrictions to his advantage. If we heard a Drifters hit tune being repeated on Murray's show, we could usually predict which band would be headlining his weekend Fox shows.

We played 45 and 33 rpm records. Take a song like "Chapel of Love" by the Dixie Cups. I'd manually advance the disc until the first "Go" of the introductory "Going to the Chapel" could be heard. I'd hit a "cue button," as the engineer adjusted the volume. I'd reverse the turntable just before the "Go," and hold the record with my hand, letting the turntable spin underneath. Then I'd be ready to play the song precisely when I wanted to by turning the record loose. We'd fade it out at the end so you never heard the needle skip. That's the way it was done in the ice age.

Here's a note I received from a former listener when I started on this chapter:

> **Terry Morgan:** "It's the 'little things' in life that you remember. In 1964, Johnny had the shift after Ed Hider's morning drive show. I started a small fan club in my neighborhood called the 'Double H Fan Club' for Hider and Holliday. Well, it must have been a Saturday during the summer and I was listening to 1010 WINS. Since they didn't have news on the hour (except during drive), Hider and Johnny were talking at the top of the hour and thanked me over the air. Next Johnny sent me a nice promo picture postcard of himself. I was 13 and was in 7th Heaven!"

Record producer Charlie Koppelman introduced me to his tailor, Mr. Tony, who made custom suits at $120 a pop. Some of the staff started to think I was becoming Mr. Show Business.

I must have been convincing as a genuine rock and roll jock, because I found myself counseling others on how to get into radio. I remember the first intern who asked me, "What's the best advice you can give me?" Just out of college, he was looking to get into sports broadcasting.

I told him, "Just be cool. Be nice. Don't make waves. Don't be controversial. Good things will happen to you." Not the greatest advice in hindsight, but I was trying.

The quizzical intern was Dick Stockton, fresh out of Syracuse University, and now one of the top broadcasters at Fox.

Our rented house in Dumont was at the end of Prospect Ave., directly adjacent to the White Beaches golf club. It was our first house, and a beautiful home. My landlord, Mickey Cullere, was a most interesting guy, and I knew him to be very tight with Yogi Beara, Whitey Ford, and Mickey Mantle. I would be home relaxing on a Sunday when I'd hear Cullere yell, "Hey Holliday," from his golf cart on the green. I'd look out my window and see Cullere with his NY Yankee buddies in tow. That was cool.

I never knew exactly what Mickey Cullere did to make his living. He said he was a "consultant." He had a pencil-thin mustache and drove a Cadillac. He was Italian. Whatever he did, it paid *really* well. Let's just say that I never wanted to cross him. Luckily, he always liked me.

Clare and I joined the parish of St. Mary's. When our pastor, Fr. John Caven, found out I was on the radio, he asked me to bring in some acts for the CYO dances. I saw no problem with "bootlegging" Little Anthony, the Shangri-Las, Lesley Gore, and others to New Jersey so Father Caven could fill the church coffers. He loved me for this. He should. He made all the money.

New York was beginning to be my real home, and in February of '65, I had renewed my WINS contract for another year. I fell ill with the flu shortly after. While sick in bed, I received a call from my boss, Joel Chaseman.

"How are you feeling?" he asked.

"I'm coming along pretty good," I said.

"Well, I have some news that will really make you feel worse," Joel replied.

WINS was about to announce its format switch to all news, and I would soon be out of a job. Fortunately, my boss was reassuring:

"I'm going to get you every dime you have coming on your contract," Joel said. "I brought you to New York. I feel responsible for you and feel very bad about this. We are doing well as a personality station competing with the big guys. We *are* one of the big guys. This was not my decision but rather people above me at Westinghouse. Come April, the station plans to go to news. Don't worry and I'll see you when you come back to work. Get better."

I thought, "Get better?" This news was not helpful.

My first reaction was "Hey, I'm not getting fired." None of the jocks were. We were damned good. The *station* was changing. This wasn't *my* fault, and I knew I could hook up somewhere.

Still, I had started to make a name for myself in the top radio market in the country. And it was all over—just like that.

When the format change was announced, McIntyre's first move was to stop the music director from jumping out the window. Poor Joel Sebastian, the last music jock to join the team, never even had a chance to find a place to live before he was out of a job.

Management's thinking was clear on why "all news" would be a smart move. The new WINS wasn't intending to do a "rip and read" operation, where you just do the straight news off the wire. The goal was to broadcast sound-oriented news from places like the Bronx or Harlem that never before had a voice or presence on the air. The station had already penetrated diverse communities with the rock music, so it made sense.

Joel Chaseman, who first found success as executive producer for Steve Allen's syndicated show when Steve left New York for Hollywood, recalls the WINS experience:

Joel Chaseman: "I inherited a station which was going downhill and had been confused by ownership, not by talent. It was a rock station that the ownership wanted to be less rock. It's not possible to do a station like that. You either had to commit to it or not.

"When the owners made a decision to water it down, it confused the talent and everybody else, including the listeners. Pete Myers was caught in that dilemma.

"Westinghouse was not comfortable running a rock station in those days. Rock was relatively new and not well accepted by the intellectuals and the media buyers and planners. Rock was looked on as coarse and just for kids. All the prejudices—which I think had to do with race and class—came out. This highbrow outfit, Westinghouse, owned a rock station in New York and didn't know how to deal with it.

"Coincidentally, a newspaper strike in NYC came along. Westinghouse decided they would use their deserved reputation among intellectuals to capitalize on the strike by interspersing frequent newscasts between the music. They added news analysis. The people who tuned in for music got really confused and evacuated the premises in short order.

"The all-news format was a good marketing ploy and it played to Westinghouse's strength. All we had to do was invent the format, which was the hard part.

"One of the hardest speeches I had to give was to the WINS staff to tell them we'd be doing all news and wouldn't need them. Awful.

"After the speech, Stan Z. Burns, one of the DJs and a real character around the station, came bounding into my office. He just leaped in, spread his arms out in a vaudeville pose, and announced, 'You're looking at the World's Greatest Newsman.' This cracked me up. He ended up reading news for WINS."

Stan continued with WINS, covering many of the top stories like the NYC blackout and transit strike, until his death in 1990 at the age of 63.

"Give us 22 minutes and we give you the world" was the new WINS slogan. Insiders thought this was a clever approach because Arbitron measured listeners in 15-minute quarters. If listeners tuned in for 22 minutes, the station would capture the entire half-hour ratings.

On April 18, 1965, each of the WINS jocks took their turn saying goodbye to their listeners. I spun the final rock and roll song before WINS switched formats. It was "Out in the Street," by the Shangri-Las.

Chapter 5

San Francisco High Ball

"So strong are the personalities at KYA, the leading Hot 100 station here, that Johnny Holliday once out-Pulsed a baseball game in audience ratings. His real strength at being able to influence his teenage listeners also cropped up in Billboard's latest Radio Response Rating survey of the market. He was leading air personality at influencing sales of singles records with 42 percent of the votes of record dealers, distributors, one-stop operators, and local and national record company executives.
Billboard, March 26, 1966

My agreement with Westinghouse had me tied up so I couldn't work within 100 miles of New York. That's how tight the contracts were back then. With ten months remaining on my WINS contract I knew I'd have some money coming my way to hold me over until I found a new job.

The Westinghouse plan was to send me to one of their other stations. My options were Boston, Pittsburgh, Fort Wayne, Chicago, or station KYW in Cleveland. I knew I didn't want to return to Cleveland and go up against my beloved WHK.

Before I left WHK for New York, my general manager, Jack Thayer, had promised the door "would always be open" if I ever needed work. Now, without a job, I did consider Jack's invitation.

However, I knew in my heart that I couldn't recapture the excitement of what I had accomplished at WHK. I really couldn't go back. All Cleveland options were dead on arrival as far as I was concerned.

My next call came from Clint Churchill, owner of San Francisco's KYA, and the same guy who had tried unsuccessfully to hire me in Buffalo. I answered the phone, and Clint boomed, "Now I gotcha!"

"Yeah, it's a good chance that you do," I answered.

Clint flew to New York and we discussed his job offer over dinner.

"I can't pay you a lot of money, but I can get you what you came to New York for. You can work for me at KYA," he told me.

It sounded pretty great to me. I knew little about KYA, and I had never been to San Francisco, but I took his word for it and agreed to the job.

Clare and I packed up the house, our two girls, and our English pug, "Toasty the Wonder Dog," and flew to the city by the bay. Bill Gavin, with his wife, Janet, met us at the airport. Bill Gavin and Clint Churchill were the only people we knew in San Francisco, which was fine by me since Gavin was the most powerful man in the music business.

Fifteen years earlier, *Billboard* magazine had published an "Honor Roll of Hits," the Top 30 best-selling single records in America each week. Bill Gavin took that list and turned it into a radio show on station KNBC. The first of his real genius moves was when he thought to write disc jockeys across the country and ask them to send him *their* Top Ten record lists. "Mad Daddy" Myers was one of Gavin's earliest contributors.

Radio stations began to ask Bill if he would help them program their own formats around this "Top Ten" approach. Next, Gavin developed a rotation scheme where new records would be added once an hour. He first marketed this programming service to KYA and San Diego's KCBQ. Bill added a report three times a week on what songs he thought should be played and the tunes that other stations were tracking. This became the "Bill Gavin Record Report." It was the radio programmer's Bible.

KYA put us up in style at the Sheraton for the next four weeks. Clare and I went house hunting and found a beautiful stone home on Geldert Drive in Tiburon, overlooking the Golden Gate Bridge, one of three homes designed by French architect Anthony Dinola. Down the street was the dock, so I could take the ferry to work. The price was $50,000. Joel Chaseman had delivered on his promise to get my contract buyout money. His check for $20,000 went toward our downpayment on the new digs.

Joel went on to become president of *Post-Newsweek* and is now retired. He lives not far from my Kensington home and we often get together for lunch. The Hollidays can thank Joel for that wonderful home in Marin County, a home I often wish we *still* owned.

Four years ago I was in Sacramento with the University of Maryland playing in the NCAA Tournament when I took a nostalgic visit to see the old Tiburon house. While I parked in front of the house reminiscing, the owner came out and asked if he could help me. After I identified myself he invited me in for a drink. It turned out that he was the fellow who had bought the house from us.

"I don't remember you, but I do recall the lady," the owner said. "She had two little girls and an English pug."

He was right. I was in Washington, D.C. when Clare closed the deal. As we talked, I noticed Clare's original curtains were still up in the rooms— *25 years later.* The owner casually mentioned that we gave him a good deal on the house. He recalled paying us $69,000. I asked him what it was worth today.

"One point two million," he replied.

KYA was the "Boss of the Bay" and yours truly became the "Baron of the Bay." The small studio, high above Nob Hill at Pine and Mason, was nested in the rear of the elegant Hotel Mark Hopkins. Clint Churchill was in his mid-30s, not much older than his staff. With "The Boss" emblazoned on the back of his basketball jersey, Clint was involved in everything at KYA. We'd even see him in the station late at night splicing tape—uncommon behavior for a station owner. He lived and loved radio.

Clint hired me for the 2:00 to 6:00 afternoon shift. The KYA team was Tommy Saunders, Jim Washburn, Gene Nelson, and Russ "The Moose" Syracuse.

These were the same guys I could have worked with seven years earlier had I grabbed Churchill's offer at WKBW. Clint brought the whole group from Buffalo intact. It was an exciting time, as KYA owned the market. (KFRC —which would later become the powerhouse in the area—wasn't even in existence then.)

My KYA starting salary was $27,000 a year, the same salary I had going in New York. My base salary had more than doubled from the $11,600 I earned at WHK. This wasn't bad. When you add in the promotional fees and commercial revenues, I was earning $44,000 in just my first year at New York, a boatload of money back then.

For the record, I have never had an agent. Clare has been the only financial planner in my life. At KYA, I continued to get even more heavily involved in commercial work. Tower Records started in San Francisco, and I did their very first spots.

KYA was involved with whatever was happening musically in the city. We sponsored shows at the Cow Palace and other local venues. One of the first big shows I emceed featured the Rolling Stones, the Byrds, the Beau Brummels, Paul Revere and the Raiders, and the Vejtables (sic), at the Civic Auditorium on May 14, '65. I think "Satisfaction" by the Stones had just been released.

"Captain" Bill Stauch, of Walnut Creek, CA, became my traffic reporter. Bill had a regular nonradio job. He'd drive through the Caldecott tunnel in Oakland every morning and phone in his "tunnel report" when he got to his office. Capt. Bill's "exclusive tunnel reports" were mostly the same each day: "Well, things are pretty good this morning. No apparent tie-ups."

Sadly, Bill died in January 2002. Bill and his wife, Patti, became two of our closest friends in the Bay area.

I took off once on the weekend with the "KYA Air Force." This was one small airplane that we landed at different airports around the Bay area and invited listeners to meet us for prizes. I'd hop out of the plane in a base-ball cap and a red scarf around my neck, meet the fans, give out a few records, hop back in the plane, and off to the wild blue yonder I'd go. Some of those flights in windy San Francisco were uneasy at best. *Really* rockin' and rollin'!

The most sweeping promotion I ever did at KYA was a Principal of the Year election where kids voted for their favorite school leader. The winning principal would receive a $1,000 wardrobe and a free concert at their campus featuring the Lettermen and a young, unknown Neil Diamond.

I knew Neil from New York before he hit. As a favor, he once pur-chased a pair of Beatle Boots for me in Manhattan and brought them with him on a flight to San Francisco so I could wear them when I hosted a Beatles concert.

The principal contest went right through the roof. Since there were no entry restrictions, the winning all-girl Catholic high school duplicated votes around the clock and delivered over *nine million* votes for their principal. Clint commented that "We knew the contest was serious when they began to bring the votes down in trucks."

I found the newspaper account in my attic. Here's what the *San Francisco Examiner* carried on their front page:

St. Paul's Principal "Election" Winner - 9.75 Million Votes

"Students gathered in the street in front of St. Paul's High School in the Mission District danced and cheered and gathered round their youthful principal, Sister Mary Joanette. They began to gather excitedly last night only moments after KYA radio announced Sister Mary Joanette had tallied 9,757,586 votes to win the radio station's Principal of the Year election.

"In all, 56,244,867 votes were cast in the two weeks the contest ran. The votes came from some 300 high schools in nine Bay Area counties...

One of the most talented jocks in the city was Sylvester Stewart, also known as "Sly" Stone, working at KSOL (K-Soul") a 1000 watts day/250 watts night station. KSOL programmed to the city's black audience. I'd listen to Sly with guests like Billy Preston who'd drop by and jam with him on the air. Sly had a great set of pipes and a soothing radio style. It was Sly's idea to add tunes by the Beatles and Bob Dylan to the KSOL play list.

After I became friendly with him, we cooked up an idea to put a tele-vision show together. Sly would be the "black guy" and I'd be the "white guy," and we'd call our show *Salt and Pepper*.

We met at the Mark Hopkins coffee shop one afternoon to brainstorm the plan. Sly was in his flamboyant hippie clothes and we were both aware of the heads turning as we entered the hotel shop. We got a kick out of guessing what other people might have thought *we* were doing together.

Salt and Pepper would be a variety show with audience participation and guest musicians from the Bay area. I think Sly was looking to create a show that would be equally popular with black and white audiences. The show never got off the ground, but we had fun dreaming it up.

Sly was a compelling DJ and a really good guy. Although he later got involved with drugs, he was pretty sharp when I knew him. Sly produced Bobby Freeman's hit "C'mon and Swim" and later songs by local bands, the Beau Brummels and the Mojo Men. By February of '67, he was performing locally with his own group, The Family Stone. A benefit show at Bill Graham's Fillmore for the Council for Civic Unity was one of their first gigs, but it took only a year before 'Dance to the Music' was a Top 10 single in the USA. By 1969, Sly and the Family Stone was world famous.

Every year, Bill Gavin would name his *Radiomen of the Year* awards. I had been an honorable mention since 1962 against folks like B. Mitchell Reed, Dan Ingram, Joe Niagara, and the "Real" Don Steele. I was absolutely blown away when Gavin named me as the *Americas' Number One Top 40 DJ* in 1965. In no way did I think I was in the same league as my competitors for that honor.

Sometimes I've joked, "What a coincidence! Both Gavin and I lived in San Francisco, and Bill's daughters babysat for my young girls." However, Gavin's credentials and integrity were impeccable and he played no favorites. Nobody could convince or sway him to do anything that he didn't want to do. Clare's reaction to my winning this award was sort of "Big deal; when is your next basketball game?"

Here's our Top 20 play list from October 9 in my year as number one DJ in the U.S.:

1. Yesterday…The Beatles
2. Lover's Concerto…The Toys
3. Eve of Destruction…Barry Mcguire
4. Help…The Beatles
5. Treat Her Right…Roy Head
6. Keep On Dancin'…The Gentrys
7. Mohair Sam…Charlie Rich
8. The "In" Crowd…Ramsey Lewis Trio
9. Hang On Sloopy…The Mccoys
10. I Still Love You…The Vejtables
11. Catch Us If You Can…Dave Clark Five

12. Do You Believe In Magic...Lovin' Spoonful
13. Steppin Out...Paul Revere And The Raiders
14, There But For Fortune...Joan Baez
15. Ride Away...Roy Orbison
16. Like a Rolling Stone...Bob Dylan
17. I Live For the Sun ...The Sunrays
18, I Got You Babe...Sonny And Cher
19. Houston...Dean Martin
20. Everyone's Gone to the Moon...Jonathan King

During my four years at KYA, we experienced a fundamental, historic change in radio programming. I had started in Top 40 AM personality radio, and next came "flower power" music, the underground movement of the newly emerging FM format, pioneered by Tom Donohue at station KMPX. (Donohue had worked at Washington D.C.'s WINX in the very early '60s.)

San Francisco quickly became the heart of the new hippie music movement in America. Local promoter Bill Graham took over managing the Carousel Ballroom, renaming it the Fillmore West. Neighborhood bands like Sopwith Camel, Blue Cheer, Moby Grape, Jook Savages, Quicksilver Messenger Service, and the Warlocks played their mix of pop and blues, there and throughout the city. The Warlocks changed their name to The Grateful Dead and slowly began to build a devout following.

As the FM format began to attract listeners, KYA tried to adapt. Our new format became less structured. We had more freedom to try new things. The spirit was to talk more and express our personalities. The regimentation that I had experienced in Cleveland and New York eventually evaporated at KYA.

Billboard Magazine profiled my own changing approach to radio programming on July 29, 1967:

KYA Plays List Flexible Way

San Francisco—There has long been friction between two schools of thought in programming a rock and roll station—on one side the program director with a playlist of records shorter than a miniskirt, on the other the program director who stretches his playlist like last summer's fishing story. Johnny Holliday is one of those program directors who can't resist playing a good record. The playlist of (San Francisco's) KYA expands as the occasion demands...

Holliday believes there are other ways you can knock off a tight playlist station. "It's a wonder stations don't get wise in the ways you can knock off a screaming tight playlist operation. This can be done through creative radio. I think the day of the screamer is gone. You have to be more creative as a personality today ... you have to relate to the audience; deejays can not

*merely play the music, saying the same things…" KYA has been able to air
10 to 12 records exclusively and Holliday feels it lends excitement to Hot
100 format radio by playing potential hits first. On this, he'll listen to the
advice of his deejays; it was Tony Bigg who discovered "Oogum Boogum"
and brought it to Holliday's attention…*

Does anyone remember "Oogum Boogum?"

Our AM station had a 24-hour open-door policy for the local musicians in an effort to to compete with the new FM format of our competitor,
KMPX. I came to expect musicians like the Lovin' Spoonful, the Beau
Brummels, and other up-and-coming groups joining us in the studio, or to
see members of the Grateful Dead fan club hanging out in the lobby.

I once interviewed Janis Joplin (with her group, Big Brother and the
Holding Company) and she appeared happy, although her entrance was pre-
ceded by a telltale odor. It wasn't exactly BO, but rather the smells of the
Fillmore, as I liked to call it. Alcohol, weed, and perspiration. It certainly
wasn't the aroma of Saks Fifth Avenue, or even the lobby of the Mark Hopkins
Hotel.

One of the KYA jocks balked at a group photo with Big Brother because he thought they were "too filthy." Some of the other guests who visited
KYA around then were Dionne Warwick, Dave Clark Five, Spencer Davis
Group, Vanilla Fudge, the Four Seasons, and Bobbie Gentry. Linda Ronstadt
once called in to thank me for playing "Different Drum" by her first group,
the Stone Poneys.

Marijuana was increasingly becoming trendy and prevalent among the
musicians, the fans, and many of the KYA staff. Longtime Bay area record
promoter Walt Callaway, who also played with the KYA Oneders, offered me
a joint after one of our softball games. I've never smoked cigarettes, so I wasn't
sure what to do with it. I took some puffs, choked, and handed it back to
Walt. Nothing happened. (Just like Bill Clinton, I didn't inhale.)

Honestly it didn't bother me at the time that so many around me were
smoking their pot. They were doing their thing, and my take on it was "to
each his own." I was out there taking jump shots at charity basketball games,
hitting into double plays in softball, and performing in theater. That was
where I got *my* kicks.

I did get a big kick out of Grace Slick once when I introduced her
Jefferson Airplane band from a flatbed truck in a shopping center parking
lot. "Let's bring on the Jefferson Airplane," I roared over the crowd, where-
upon Grace grabbed the microphone from my hand and howled, "Johnny
Holliday — *Friggin' A*!" (Only she didn't say "Friggin'".)

I also did a national promotional spot with the Airplane hawking Levi-
Strauss jeans. Today Grace lives in Malibu. She remembers our Levis spot as

a goofy commercial that we probably did at Golden State recording studios. Looking back she says, "I never listened to the radio. When a band member first told me we were number one, I thought he was talking about a sports team because I only listened to records back then."

I recall that a short time after my marijuana initiation, Gene Cornish, guitarist with the Young Rascals, joined me in the studio. Just a half dozen on-air announcements that Gene would be there produced thousands of young fans standing in the KYA parking lot, with another hundred milling inside the lobby. These numbers were reported in the local news. I preceded the interview by playing the Rascals' then current hit, "Groovin'," and follow-up, "How Can I Be Sure."

Gene talked about the foolhardiness of young people experimenting with drugs and came out squarely against LSD and marijuana. I seconded Gene's comments by adding that there was no good reason to jeopardize your health and reputation for meaningless kicks. This interview was published in our radio's weekly newspaper, *The KYA Beat.*

Going public against recreational drug use in the "Summer of Love" era was a lot like being against pie at a bakers' convention.

Another big change for me came in '67 when Churchill sold KYA to AVCO Broadcasting. Personnel changes would soon follow. Tony Bigg joined the on-air staff, doing nights. Tony later changed his name to Tony *Pigg* and is now Regis Philbin's TV announcer. Ed Hider came on board from New York. Mike Cleary (who recently retired with a brilliant radio career resume as one of the top morning men), Tom Campbell, Gary Schaefer, and Chris Edwards rounded out the new team. It was almost a complete personnel change. Gene "The Emperor" Nelson, and yours truly, the "Baron of the Bay" were the only talent they kept after the ownership change.

Our new KYA general manager, Howard Kester, was noticeably different from the other radio staff. Many of us at the time wondered what Kester had done—what his background had been—to earn this plum job at KYA. Some of us still wonder. He had to have done something good to become the new KYA boss. After KYA, he went on to be the executive director of the Northern California Broadcasters Association. He passed away in 1989.

Kester was an immaculate dresser, but he had two annoying features: a constant blink and a nose sniffle. He'd say, "Hi, Johnny," followed by a blink and a sniff. I'd look at this guy and want to laugh.

Kester added "Program Director" to my duties. Immediately, I disliked the pressure of being the KYA PD. I tried to refuse the job, but he was a big imposing figure and the boss.

When I moved to mornings, Kester would often call first thing at 6:05 a.m.

"KYA," I'd answer.

"Who is this?"

"It's Johnny Holliday."

"Yes, Johnny, this is Howard (sniff). I'd like to talk with you when I come in this morning. I have a few ideas."

"Sure, Howard, no problem."

Then I'd get another call at 6:20.

Howard would ask, "Who is this?"

"It's still me. It's Johnny Holliday."

These repeated calls would go on until my shift ended. Kester would usually have an urgent need to read me something he'd written, or share a contest idea. His mind was always running—just like his nose.

Ed Hider followed Gene Nelson in the mornings. Hider used scores of voice tracks and sound effects. A typical Hider bit was a loud voice repeating, "I hate washing dishes! I hate washing dishes!" His act was just wild and crazy on the air from nine until noon. I think Ed guessed that Kester didn't like some of his looseness, so Ed would talk back to the voices sometimes just to drive Howard nuts.

Kester finally told me to fire Ed—*while Hider was on the air.* I pleaded, "Howard, Ed Hider is a wonderful, talented personality. You don't want to get rid of him."

"I don't like the things he's doing," said Kester. "I want him fired now."

I refused to do it.

After the shift, Ed Hider and Howard Kester parted company, and that firing—by Kester—was one of the biggest mistakes KYA ever made.

Really, it was an AVCO decision to fire Hider, since AVCO had hired Kester in the first place. AVCO had purchased stations in Cincinnati, San Antonio, Dayton, Columbus, and even my next home, WWDC-AM, in Washington, D.C.

In fairness, I am sure that Kester felt the strain of running a station that was losing its dominance. KYA suddenly had competition after KFRC and KMPX climbed on the scene. Kester's responsibility was to insure that KYA keep up with the times, which were a' changin'.

The music scene was fluid and moving unpredictably—especially after the Beatles' "Sgt. Pepper's Lonely Hearts Club Band" was released in the 1967 "Summer of Love." To be honest, I didn't think much of "Sgt. Pepper's" when it hit. I was so much into Top 40, and the songs were so different that I remember thinking it was weird. I guess I was wrong.

After holding down the programming job for about a year, I finally—and firmly— told Kester I didn't want to do it anymore. I was much better on the air and had problems disciplining guys I was working with, all friends of mine.

For example, we had a format for the station identification at the top of the clock. You were supposed to come out of your record and hit the station ID and go right to the next record. Don't say anything else, just sweep across the hour.

I was sitting at home one night as eight o'clock rolled around. I hear Tony Bigg get out of one record, start another one, and talk over it as he announced the time and station ID.

"Hey, Tony, you're not supposed to do that," I told him the next day, "Don't do it that way."

"Yeah, man. You're right, Johnny," he agreed.

Of course, Tony made the same mistake the following night. He didn't care about any format. When they coined the phrase "laid back," they were thinking of Tony Bigg.

I had to laugh. I couldn't get mad at him. This is one of many examples where I really didn't have the energy or disposition to be a strict PD. So Dick Starr was brought in from Miami as the new program director. I went back to focusing on my radio show.

At KYA, Clint had commanded everything, but he also listened to us. He cared about what his employees thought and felt. I'm sure his religious upbringing gave him an added understanding of how best to deal with people, since his father had been a minister in Buffalo. At one time Clint's dad owned almost all the radio stations up there.

Kester, however, annoyed us all.

For instance, he nagged us to let him play softball with the Oneders. We reluctantly agreed. The first game out, he slid into base with such force that he almost broke the third baseman's leg. This was unnecessary. It was a public relations event, for God's sake, and he was out there getting everyone all riled up. The fans were ready to charge the field and *throw things* at our general manager.

He was constantly on us—picking and pushing. You can't do that and expect to get a good performance out of your talent. I really blame Kester's clueless management style for much of why KYA eventually went down the tubes in ratings.

On a positive note, Ed Hider and I became friends. I was proud to watch him go on to become a top comedy writer for folks like Cindy Williams, Soupy Sales, and Joan Rivers. He's a funny, funny man and has done very well for himself.

Ed and I shared a great practical joke we started in New York and continued at KYA. To this day, I keep a photo of a topless dancer in my briefcase to remind me of this gag. Here's how Ed tells the story:

> **Ed Hider:** "There was a fan Johnny and I befriended in New York who stalked us at every public appearance we made. No matter where we appeared, there she was waving at us to come over and autograph whatever she was wearing. Since she was always there we would introduce her to the crowd and to any celebrity we were with at the time. We took a picture of her, and this picture served as the focal point of a

running joke that began in the mid '60s at WINS New York right on through the late '60s at KYA.

"The main purpose of the running joke was to pass the picture back and forth in any unusual way we could think of. First, Johnny hired a Fed Ex driver to deliver the photo to me in a giant envelope while I was in the lobby of the station. Next, I tipped a waiter from the Mark Hopkins Hotel to wheel a serving cart with a full place setting and the picture under a covered dish to Johnny at the station.

"Next at one of our KYA Radio Oneders basketball games, Johnny had a teacher approach me on court and slip the picture inside my shorts. I countered when we were having lunch and I had a waiter slip the picture inside a cheeseburger Johnny ordered at Burger King. Next, Johnny sent in an ice cream cone when I was on the air. It was a regular ice cream cone except for the cone, which was actually the famous picture with ice cream inside it.

"John cleaned up the picture and gave it to a policeman friend of mine who pulled me over to the curb near the station and when he started writing up the ticket, handed me the picture.

"KYA held a Principal of the Year contest that was won by a nun at a nearby Catholic high school. All of the KYA DJs showed up for the awards ceremony. After we were there for a while, the nun handed me a Bible. I opened it up and, you guessed it, there was the picture. The nun gave me a kneeling ovation.

"Not to be outdone, I contacted a friend of mine who worked at the San Francisco Zoo. I asked him to "rent" an elephant, scotch tape an enlarged picture of the fan on the elephant's butt and take the animal to Johnny's house. I was turned down by both the zoo and the elephant who got tired of working for peanuts.

"Finally, when all else failed, I went to a local strip club and hired a beautiful blonde to come to the station when Johnny was on the air doing his show. When the microphone went on and Johnny was reading a commercial, I quickly brought the stripper into the studio. She took off the raincoat she was wearing and had nothing on from the waist up except for the picture of Johnny, the fan, and me taped between her boobs.

"Being the pro he is, Johnny kept right on reading the commercial, never missing a beat.

"Over the years, I never knew whatever happened to the stripper or the fan, but I have kept track of Johnny's career, and I am quite sure that even to this day, at ABC radio, he's again working with a couple of boobs."

Ed was with me when KYA brought the Beatles to Candlestick Park in 1966, the group's last tour and concert. The tickets cost $5, $6 and $7 bucks, available by mail from KYA, No. 1 Nob Hill Circle, San Francisco.

I vividly remember cutting the promo spots about how the "Beatles' new sound system" would make sure everybody heard the Fab Four. (It didn't.)

But it wasn't until the author faxed me a *San Francisco Chronicle* article written by my friend, Ben Fong-Torres, listing me as an emcee that I remembered taking part in the show.

Wow. How could I forget that? It would be the Beatles' last concert on their last tour, although nobody knew that then. It still baffles me that I initially had such a hard time remembering the concert. Ed Hider recalls, "Oh yeah, you were there all right." Luckily the memories have returned in time for this chapter.

Gene Nelson and I came out on stage and exchanged a few wisecracks. I announced the first act, The Remains. (I wonder where *they* are these days?) They kicked off the evening with "Hang On Sloopy." Bobby "Sunny" Hebb was next in line and dedicated "I Left My Heart in San Francisco" to Joan Baez, who was there with her sisters Pauline and Mimi. The Cyrkle and Ronnettes, minus Ronnie Spector, did brief sets before the moment everyone was waiting for erupted. It was Gene who actually announced the Beatles, and they calmly walked from the dugout, in double-breasted Edwardian suits, and launched into "She's a Woman." I remember that George Harrison wore white socks.

Of course, fans were there more to see the Beatles than listen. (Fong-Torres reported, "The San Francisco show was a relative flop for the group...25,000 seats sold out of a possible 30,000...and a money-loser for its promoters." "The wind was so strong that it blew the sound towards the East Bay," Gene recalls.

Knowing the way I operate, the reason the memory of this Beatles concert was diminished is because Gene was the king of the station, or at least he thought he was. I was probably disappointed that he—and not I—had been selected to lead the Beatles introduction. I was most likely wishing I were playing in a Oneders game rather than being stuck playing second banana on a windy night in friggin' Candlestick Park. So I blocked it all out.

Whenever I hear from a listener who remembers me at that last Beatles concert, I find I've made a new "best friend" for life. Ed Hider tells me that the Beatles escaped the park that night in an armored car with a police escort. I can almost remember that.

On June 16-18, 1967, the first and only Monterey International Pop Festival took place. Clare and I attended the shows, climbing over bodies sprawled around the Monterey County fairgrounds.

KYA heavily promoted it. Big Brother and the Holding Company, the Airplane, the Paupers, the Grateful Dead, and other local San Francisco artists performed with national acts like Simon and Garfunkel, Otis Redding, Johnny Rivers, the Byrds, and Lou Rawls. Along with Janis Joplin's debut (she got her first recording contract right after that performance), Jimi Hendrix delivered the most spectacular coming-out set. Ed Hider says he introduced Lou Rawls. If you listen to the recordings, however, you'll find that various rock stars did the introductions. So much for our memories. Ed did take home movies of the shows, which he still has. Every performer, except Ravi Shankar, appeared at the festival for free.

The concert proceeds were distributed to charities like the UCLA Children's Hospital and the LA Free Clinic. Never before Monterey had over 30 rock bands played together at one event. I certainly didn't realize at the time how important these shows would turn out to be.

Heck, it was San Francisco. I thought *this was the way it was supposed to be.*

Chapter 6

Hullabaloos and Hollywood

"It's Hullabaloo. Tonight's guests: Chuck Berry. The Byrds. Sonny and Cher. The Miracles. Vicky Carr. And guest host, Michael Landon. Brought to you by Carnation Evaporated Milk—now VELVETIZED for Better Cooking! And by Clearasil, to fight today's surface blemishes and the excess oil that might cause tomorrow's blemishes! And by Betty Crocker's Cake Mixes, Goodness with a Capital G!"

While still at WINS, I received an unexpected call from TV producer Gary Smith.

"We've got a show called *Hullabaloo* on NBC, and we want you to be the announcer, " he told me. The announcer they started with "wasn't working out."

I first thought "sure," but then I had doubts. This would be *network* broadcasting. People were going to hear me *all across the country*. Honestly, I was a little scared.

On the other hand, I knew I was doing well, and hoped there would be more to accomplish. I made it to New York, *but so what?* A lot of guys make it to New York. So I said yes to *Hullabaloo*.

When I arrived at Studio 8-H, the same studio now used for *Saturday Night Live*, I found out how they did the show. We had one taped rehearsal with a full audience. My job was to "warm up" the crowd and let them know who the host and guests were, and encourage them to scream, whistle, shout, and applaud.

With Peter Matz's live orchestra (which later became the *Carol Burnett Show* band), we'd tape the rehearsal. After they cleared the studio and brought in another crowd, we'd do a second taping. The producers would pick the best of both shows for the final aired *Hullabaloo* on Monday nights. The show went from a half-hour format initially to a full hour in the second season.

Hullabaloo, along with ABC's competing show, *Shindig*, were the first network evening shows devoted to rock music. *Hullabaloo* ran from January '65 to August '66. The first 12 shows included a segment from London hosted by the Beatles' manager, Brian Epstein.

The *Hullabaloo* dancers, choreographed by David Wintem, were a big part of the show. They often got more camera time than the singers, which was fine by me. One *Hullabaloo* dancer, Donna McKechnie, went on to fame in Broadway's *A Chorus Line*. Donna sure could swim, jerk, shake, and shimmy. When I wasn't announcing, I'd sometimes sit at one of the tables in the fake "Go Go" club, or turn up in a segment when a crowd scene was needed.

One of the first serious blunders I nearly made was when Sammy Davis Jr. hosted. I recognized his wife, May Britt, sitting in the front row. May was white and in the center of a then controversy about Sammy's "mixed marriage."

I was about to introduce her, but I had May mentally mixed up with Frank Sinatra's new bride, Mia Farrow. I came within a few seconds of announcing, "Ladies and gentlemen, let's give a warm welcome to Sammy's lovely wife, *Mia Farrow.* "

Fortunately, a distraction gave me the chance to mention to our producer that I would be introducing Sammy's wife, *Mia.*

The producer said, "That's *May Britt.*"

I said, "*Oh Shit!*"

Hullabaloo had a lot going for it. The acts mostly sang their hits live, although their backing tracks were prerecorded. Each show would feature a medley spot in the middle where the acts would perform other artists' then current hit songs. I thought this segment was the most spontaneous and interesting.

My favorite highlights were Marvin Gaye's *Ain't That Peculiar*, the Miracles' *Going to a Go Go*, Martha & The Vandellas' *Nowhere To Run*, and Chuck Berry's *Johnny B. Goode*. Berry played live guitar on that one.

My favorite guest host was the comedian Alan King. Here was one really nice guy. He took time to make everyone feel comfortable. A real old-show biz pro, as I remember.

Many guest hosts who recognized me from WINS were surprised to see me at Studio 8-H for *Hullabaloo*. For the ones who didn't know me, I would make sure to introduce myself as Murray the K's friend, the one who works with Murray the K at WINS.

When I moved to KYA I continued doing *Hullabaloo*. This meant I'd leave San Francisco at 8 a.m., arrive in NYC at 4 something with a car waiting, and then head to NBC. We'd tape two shows. I'd be back on a flight to San Francisco at 11 that night. I did this every week except when we did the show from NBC Burbank a few times. I would be sure to tell my KYA listeners all about the show the next day.

Hullabaloo is available in eight volumes on VHS and DVD. Talk about some laughs. My youngest daughter, Moira, was approaching 21 when I first played her some of these tapes. She could not believe the outfits the dancers wore. I told her those were special times when good ole Dad was a hotshot DJ. She still finds it hard to believe I did *Hullabaloo*, since all she's ever been familiar with is my sports career.

Years ago I received a surprise residual check for $37.50 and learned that *Hullabaloo* had been rerun in Argentina.

Gary Smith—still one of the best TV producers around—next signed me as announcer for the new Roger Miller TV show. With a string of hits, Roger had proved his TV likeability with guest spots on the Andy Williams show. Gary flew me up and down the coast as the show was taped in the NBC Burbank studios. I really liked Roger's songs and his laid back, casual style. Nobody sounded quite like him.

Roger had an alleged romance with the grape during the period I was there. His reputation as a drinker was confirmed on one particular night. Roger was supposed to open the show standing on top of a railroad boxcar singing his hit, "Engine, Engine Number Nine". Yankees manager Casey Stengel was the guest star that night.

However, Roger was very much "under the weather" when the taping was set to start. The studio audience waited for over an hour while the producers made sure that Roger was sober enough to balance himself on top of the boxcar. A tipsy Miller falling off the railroad car and breaking his neck was not in the script. He got through the taping eventually, but he wasn't at his best that night.

For my part, I was mostly right on the money. Here's one of my typical openings:

> "Tonight ... Tarryton, the charcoal tip cigarettes with the taste worth fighting for, and the Dodge Rebellion present the Roger Miller show with tonight's guest, The Doodletown Pipers, and tonight's special guest, Soupy Sales... Ladies and Gentlemen, Roger Miller."

It's too bad that the Roger Miller show was not a success and lasted only 13 weeks, because he continued to impress me with his talent. He is the only country artist to win Broadway's Tony award. This was for his hit show *Big River*. Diagnosed with lung cancer in 1991, he died a year later at the age of 56.

Around this time, promoter Don Graham sent me out on a U.S. tour with the Monkees and Boyce and Hart. I did the introductions, and the crowds were enormous. I know it is hard to believe, but the *only thing* I remember from this tour was how intelligent and cordial Monkee Mike Nesmith was. He was my favorite by far.

In '67, one of the funniest guys to come out of San Francisco was Ronnie Schell, whom I met at KYA. His break was landing the lead in a TV sitcom called *Good Morning World*. Newcomer Goldie Hawn also made her TV debut on the show. The talented Billy De Wolf, then known for his many guest shots on Carson's *Tonight Show*, played the station general manager.

My own TV acting debut came when Ronnie asked me to appear for a one-shot gag. They wrote a part for me as "Andy McChesny." Andy was a new hire at the station as the newsreader. We rehearsed for one day.

Billy De Wolf had just returned from London where he played J.B. Bigley in *How to Succeed in Business…* Since I was then in rehearsal for the same show set to open at the Woodminister Theatre in Oakland, I decided it might be a perfect time to ask Mr. De Wolf about his experiences.

My shot came while waiting for the final taping to begin. Standing behind him, I started to ask him about his London show when he quickly turned around to me and said in his trademark prim and proper manner, "Mr. Holliday. Never speak to Mr. De Wolf when Mr. De Wolf is waiting to go on."

If there had been a nearby hole to crawl into, I would have done it in a second.

He twisted around again and smiled, "Got you, didn't I?" He had been pulling my chain, and I fell for it. He turned out to be marvelous. He was supportive of my theatre goals and told me that he thought my role as J. Pierpont Finch was "perfect casting." I invited him to attend the Oakland production, but he later sent me a handwritten note saying his schedule wouldn't permit flying up to Frisco. "Please pass my best to the cast. I know it will be a smash," he wrote. From that day on I was always happy to see Mr. De Wolf on TV.

My big moment on *Good Morning World* aired. Andy McChesny is introduced at the beginning of the show appearing naïve and uncertain. The radio station crew is apprehensive. Can Andy cut it as the newsreader? The tension is set by the end of the program when Andy has to step up to the mic and deliver. Is Andy going to make the grade, or choke?

Then I went into my most confident David Brinkley impression, and the audience cracked up. That was the joke.

It's a little ironic that I would be hired 30 years later as the voice-over announcer for the final year of ABC's "*This Week with David Brinkley.*"

Chapter 7

Warriors and Oneders

"I gave up a prime year of my life—when I could have gone ahead and been playing NBA basketball—to play for the KYA Radio Oneders. I look back and say, 'What the heck was I thinking about?'"
– **Rick Barry**, *Basketball Hall of Famer*

Today, there is an increasing number of men and women who can participate in sports broadcasting. Back in 1967, it was a much smaller circle. There weren't as many teams. Cable didn't exist, and fewer games were televised. To be among players and coaches was exhilarating, and I wanted to be there.

So when I was finally settled at KYA, I contacted Scotty Sterling, the public relations director for the Oakland Raiders, to see whether they needed a PA announcer.

"Funny you should call. Yeah, we can use you," he told me. Scotty is now a NBA scout, and I still run into him on the road, most recently at a tournament in Maui.

I later spoke with one of the San Francisco Warriors PR guys and landed a job as their announcer as well. The Holliday luck continued. I was on a roll.

Working the microphone for the NBA Warriors' and AFL Raiders was a huge opportunity for me. I got to call the games, introductions, statistics, and note the players who scored. The perks that came with PA announcing were enormous. Number one, I was seeing every game—the top of the NBA and the best of the AFL before the football leagues merged—night in and night out. My press pass gave me access to meeting people that the average Joe couldn't meet. Talking with—and about—the athletes, getting close to them, and becoming part of that magic circle of sports was gratifying. I was a member of a very special fraternity. I also had one of the best seats in the house.

I soon got friendly with all the officials. One referee, Joe Gushue, once strolled over just before a Warriors-Houston Rockets game. Elvin Hayes was a Houston rookie then and at 28 points per game led the NBA in scoring. Gushue placed a five-dollar bill on the table and said, "Hey, Holliday, five bucks say you won't get through the opening without blowing something."

"You're on," I said, as I matched his bet. I started the introductions flawlessly until I got to Elvin Hayes.

"At 6' 9" and 230 pounds, Elvin *Jones*," I announced.

Jazz drummer Jones had just played a gig at the *Hungry I*. Still that was no excuse. Elvin Hayes glared intensely at me from the court upon hearing my very loud error. I felt like jumping under the table. A broad grin stretched Gushue's lips as he grabbed the two fives and put them in his pocket.

Once during a Warriors-Lakers game, the officiating was so bad in the first half that the Warriors' owner, Franklin Mieulli, sent me a note asking me to apologize to the fans. He wanted me to offer them a free ticket to the next game because of the terrible calls the refs were making. I feared there would be a riot in the arena if I read his note, but I also knew that Mieulli wasn't kidding. I ignored his request that time. You really couldn't do something like that back then, and you certainly can't offer a refund for bad calls in today's sports world. The sports economy would collapse.

Speaking of the Lakers, my old Cleveland pal and fellow WHK DJ, Johnny Walters, had told me many stories about the eccentric Lakers owner, Jack Kent Cooke. Prior to WHK, Walters worked for Cooke's radio station in Toronto. During a halftime break, I took liberty to introduce myself to Mr. Cooke, who was sitting directly behind me.

"Mr. Cooke, my name is Johnny Holliday and I worked with Johnny Walters in Cleveland. I just wanted to say hello."

"What a fine lad Johnny Walters is," Cooke replied. "Is that you 'on the box' announcing this game, Johnny?"

"Yes, sir," I confirmed.

"Well, you're a *God-damned cheerleader* for the Warriors, Johnny," Cooke bellowed. "How about giving my team a little credit, for God's sake? You're a God-damned cheerleader."

Cooke was exactly as Johnny Walters had described him. I called Walters that night and we had a big laugh over my introduction to the droll Mr. Cooke.

In 1965, the Warriors signed Rick Barry as their first draft pick in the second round. Barry had led the country in scoring during his All-American senior season with the University of Miami Hurricanes, and following his first season with the Warriors, he triumphed as NBA Rookie of the Year.

Barry had played two seasons for the Warriors before he sat out a year in order to jump to the newly formed American Basketball Association. Meanwhile, Oakland TV station Channel 2 asked me if I'd do play-by-play for their Saturday night University of California Game of the Week.

Rick recalls, "Since I wasn't playing professionally, Johnny told the producer, Bud Weiner, that I might be available to do the color analysis for the games. So we had the opportunity to work together on TV."

This turned out to be Barry's first TV broadcasting experience and my own play-by-play debut as a TV sportscaster. Rick and I eye-witnessed some spectacular games in those Frisco days. We were covering the University of California at Berkeley every week against the likes of players like Lew Alcindor (later Hall of Famer Kareem-Abdul Jabarr) at UCLA. The six-foot-seven Barry and I became good friends then, a friendship that continues today.

Coincidentally, Dr. Dan Mote, now the President of the University of Maryland, was on the Cal faculty then. I was reminiscing with Dan recently about all the great players from that era.

Dr. Dan Mote: "When I first came to Maryland, Johnny and I renewed our contact from when he was a disc jockey in San Francisco and Cal's sports announcer. He is just as lively, just as exciting now as he was then. His delivery is captivating. The voice is the same; only the address is different."

The American Basketball Association was formed in '87, and Oakland landed a team. The ABA knew that if they could get some big-time NBA players to jump leagues, they'd have instant credibility. One way to do this was to hire Rick Barry's father-in-law, Bruce Hale, to coach the new Oakland Oaks. Hale had coached Rick when he was at the University of Miami.

Rick wanted to play for his father-in-law, and ultimately the Warriors didn't offer Barry enough money to stay. So Rick sat out a year so he could join the ABA, and that's when he asked me if he could play with the KYA Oneders. Just to keep in shape. I said sure, we'll take an All-Pro player from the NBA.

Rick Barry: "Johnny was the 'Baron of the Bay' on KYA. Somehow we met, hit it off, and got to be friendly. He's the godfather of my son, Scooter.

"Johnny was always performing like a stand-up comic. I'd have lunch with him, and he'd make up a complete comedy routine on the spot involving the salt and pepper shakers and the ashtrays. He was always on.

"The year before I sat out of the NBA, I was the scoring leader in my league in my second year and two times All Pro. We almost won the championship. We came within two plays of beating a team that everyone talks about nowadays as being one of the greatest teams in NBA history, if not the greatest. And I didn't have a good time. For the first time in my life, basketball wasn't fun for me. Well, not for the first time, really, because in high school I had a coach that I didn't like. Anyway, I had to give some serious thought to what I wanted to do.

"The opportunity was there with my father-in-law, Bruce Hale, to go over to the ABA. He coached me that first year.

"Contrary to what people said then, I did feel loyalty to the Warriors. I told them, 'Look, give me your best deal, your best offer.' They didn't do that. They told the press they offered me something [good], but that's not true. The Warriors' offer was so much lower than what the Oakland team offered. It was a very difficult decision for me to make. I remember actually having tears in my eyes and crying when I left [Warriors owner] Frank Meulli's office telling him I was leaving the team, though I knew I would play for my father-in-law, who was like a second father to me and helped me so much in my college days.

"Again, had the Warriors given me the offer that they told everyone they gave me initially, I would have stayed. I would have felt I owed it to them.

"I wanted to keep in shape, so I wound up playing with the KYA Oneders. I played point guard. Johnny should have been the point guard, but he wasn't known to be a passer. I used to feed Johnny, so he could take his 40 shots per game.

"Of course, if I hadn't left the Warriors, Johnny Holliday would have never had the wonderful experience of being able to score so many points for the KYA Oneder team. You can see that everything worked out for the best.

"That old cliché really fits Johnny. He never saw a shot he didn't like. He fired up more shots than Heinz has pickles. The Oneders was fun, and I enjoyed playing. It gave me a chance to work on my ball handling. I'd get a rebound, or penetrate, and throw it out to Johnny, and he'd fire them up there.

"Johnny put the team together, and he really was the number-one personality on KYA. We gave him carte blanche and let him get away with his shooting. I'd bust his chops about it, but he had some big scoring games. Of course, when you're taking that many shots, you should score.

"The only down side was when I played faculty who were trying to prove something by playing against me. I had to be careful. I didn't want to get hurt. It was all for a good cause and we raised money. We had some unbelievable characters on the Oneders team. Bud O'Shea later had a great career in the music business. Ed Hider was a short, heavyset guy who was off-the-wall funny. Some of the team couldn't play very well. Johnny would bring in some ringers. Our 'officials' would be there to make sure things didn't get too out of hand. It was a lot of fun.

"Unfortunately, for me, I gave up a prime year of my life—when I could have gone ahead and been playing NBA basketball—to play for the KYA Radio Oneders. (Laughs.) I look back and say, 'What the heck was I thinking about?'

"But everything in life happens for a reason, and we did have a good time. It was a chance to raise money for a worthy cause. And they got me for cheap.

"Once after the game we had a party in the locker room, and I caught Johnny off guard with a camera. I took a picture of him–stark naked, frontal view. I kidded him that we needed a magnifying glass to see whether he was one of the guys. Like the Seinfeld episode, it was probably the cold water from the shower."

I was elated when the KYA Radio Oneders featured a turbo-charged star like Rick Barry (whom I remembered driving a turbo-charged Porsche until Rick corrected this chapter with the comment, "No, it was just a regular old Porsche 911. I wish I could still afford to drive a Porsche these days").

Having Rick on the team would be like getting a pro of Shaquille O'Neil's caliber to join me today for a local high school fundraiser. Imagine the excitement these charity games sparked with Barry on board. The intensity really shot up.

Intense is a good word to describe my friend Rick. During one early Warriors game I remember an agitated Barry slam-bouncing the ball in frustration as he unsuccessfully engaged the late Mendy Rudolf. The referee immediately yelled to Barry, "If the ball comes down, you've got a technical foul."

At times he'd lash out at his teammates because they weren't playing the way he thought they should—which was all out, 100 percent all the time. He wanted everyone to have the same competitive juices and focus that he had. This was almost impossible for them to do because Rick was such a great player.

Some opposing players despised him. Mike Riordan, the owner of Riordan's waterfront restaurant in Annapolis, was a Bullet when he played against Barry's Warriors in the '75 championship game. Riordan was one of the hardest, toughest defensive players to play in the NBA. I once mentioned to Mike that Rick's a good friend of mine. Riordan replied, "I'm sorry to hear that." There's no love between those two.

Rick would moan and groan when a call went against him, and he'd let the officials know about it. John McEnroe looks like a puppy dog compared to Rick.

I've always stood with Rick and defended him. I've felt that Barry was very much misunderstood as a player. As a friend, I found Rick totally different from how the press portrayed him. He wasn't a "cry baby" when I was his teammate. I never had to sit him out for insubordination when he was a Radio Oneder. If he wanted to play, he played.

He's still the all-time leading free-throw shooter in the history of the NBA and the only player in history to lead in scoring for the NACC, ABA, and NBA. Did he care about his scoring, about his "reputation?" Here's Rick on Rick:

> "I didn't care about scoring. I've found that when you try to go out there and look to score is when you usually wind up having a lousy game. You usually score your most points when scoring is far from your mind. That just happened to be a part of what I did. I was out there to win. I was asked to go to the Rockets, and the Rockets didn't ask me to score, and I didn't shoot the ball very much. I accepted that role, and it probably shortened my career. I probably should have demanded that I shoot more. The thing is that I never did that. I did what the team wanted me to do. It just so happens that scoring was one of the things that I did well, and it would have been rather foolish for a team not to utilize that, as the Rockets didn't do.
>
> "I played to win. I didn't go out there to make friends, and that probably hurt my chances for getting coaching jobs. The managers and presidents of teams are all your former players. I was out there to kick their ass, not to make friends with them.
>
> "Cliff Ray, my old teammate, would say, 'B (he always called me 'B'), you obviously did a really good job of that.'
>
> "The thing is that they didn't like me when I was a ball player, but they allowed that to affect their feelings about me as a person. And they didn't know me as a person.
>
> "As for Johnny, I can't remember ever having a disagreement with him. We got along well, and I miss not getting the chance to see him as much as I used to, because we always had a lot of fun together. Johnny is one of the most honest and nicest 'straight shooters' I've known.
>
> "Unfortunately, he didn't shoot straight on the basketball court. Despite that, I have great respect and admiration for his many and diverse talents, and I'm proud to call him my friend."

In '69, the Oakland Oaks franchise moved to Washington, D.C. to become the Capitals, a pretty good team. Rick and Larry Brown, now the coach for the Philadelphia 76ers, rented an apartment in Chevy Chase, and they let me stay with them whenever I wanted the first six months after I had moved to DC to work at WWDC. Mary Clare was still settling the household move in Frisco, so there I was, a bachelor for a while with Rick and Larry.

Rick went to the Houston Rockets when the ABA folded and ended his excellent career back with the Warriors, beating the Bullets in 1975 for the championship. Rick would be a 12-time All-Star when he was elected to the Hall of Fame in 1987.

When Rick was in town for those later Warriors games, he'd come over to dinner with Mary Clare and me and sometimes bring his laundry. Clare would toss a load in the washer, and we'd go to see the game.

Today, Rick hosts a sports talk show on KNBR, the top sports station in San Francisco. As always, he's quick, knowledgeable, and outspoken.

Rick phones me often. I know it's Rick as soon as I pick up the phone. He tries to throw me off, but he has an unmistakable voice with that great New Jersey accent.

"Is this the Prince of the Potomac? Is this the Baron of the Bay? Is this the King of the Concrete Jungle?" he asks. It's Rick calling from the airport on his way to visit his son, Scooter, who also plays basketball, most recently in Italy.

Rick never seems to fail in trying to sell me on some hotshot money making scheme he's involved with. The most recent call was a stock deal, which would include investing my money into something that he "feels very strongly" will succeed. Since it's always a sizable amount of my cash, I turn the "investment opportunity" over to my financial advisor, Mary Clare. I'm still waiting to get a response from her on his latest offer. This leads one to believe that "this too shall pass," as have other offers that Rick has pitched me.

The KYA-Oneders evolved considerably in San Francisco; the station provided us with custom-made uniforms and our own cheerleaders. We rode first class in our own Greyhound bus, piloted by Darryl, the bus driver. The late Owen Kashaveroff, a teacher from El Camino High, and Mike Orlich, a football coach from Jefferson High in Daly City, were our official referees. (Orlich was also John Madden's high school football coach). Two other high school coaches, Don Delbon from Terra Nova High and Don Novitsky from Oceana High, played every game with the Oneders for five years.

Record promo guys also joined us on the team. These included "Bashful" Bud O'Shea, "Charming" Chuck Becker, Marty Goldrod, Lou Galiani, and "Dashing" Dick Forrester, whom we nicknamed "The Whale," since he was not missing many meals in those days.

We even had our own PA announcer, Steve Somers. Six-feet-seven Joe Durenberger and Dan Carlson were friends who also joined us on the court, and a couple of guys who helped out were Breck McClaren, just out of the College of San Mateo, and Don Robbs, a KYA newsman who went on to become the Johnny Carson of Hawaii. Robbs had a little goatee. I think those whiskers may have prevented him from scoring. We could see that his future was not in basketball.

Other radio promotional staff who regularly attended the games and frequently brought their artists with them were Chuck Gregory, Denny Zeitler, Guy Haines, Don Graham, Bill Keane, Chris Chris, Pete Marino, and Jerry Huff.

Once, Bill Harrah flew the team to his Lake Tahoe resort to play a team of baseball All-Stars and put us up at his hotel with free gambling chits. What a deal. At times like those we really felt like a professional team.

Our public address announcer for the KYA team was a young man named Steve Somers. He attended San Francisco State. Steve called me up asking if we needed a PA announcer for all our games. He was more than willing since he was a communications major and this would be good experience.

Thus began the first step for Steve Somers on his rise to the top of the broadcasting business. Steve did such a good job for us that our KYA general manager tapped him as a KYA "high school reporter." From KYA, Steve moved on to KPIX TV as weekend sports anchor, backing up the lead, Barry Thompkins. (Barry would later be my roommate in Sarajevo when we covered the 1984 Winter Olympics for ABC Radio.)

Steve Somers landed TV jobs in Los Angeles, Sacramento, and Atlanta before he finally found his "home" as one of the first sports hosts on New York City's WFAN in 1987. Steve is still there and is the last of the original guys at the Fan. His success makes me proud that I played a small part in getting him his first job in the biz.

The secret of the Oneders was to get the school to recruit as many teachers as they could to play. The kids loved to see their teachers in that different light: playing against us. That was the success behind the early games in Cleveland and New York because the faculty would be as big a drawing card as the disc jockeys. As far as competition on the court, we didn't have to worry much about the regular faculty. But I soon found that most of the faculty coaches were passionate to show their student body what *they* could do against us.

When we started getting professional athletes like Sal Bando, Joe Theismann, and Rick Barry on board, the basketball coach wanted to show that he could shut down Rick Barry. The football coach wanted to show the student body that he could handle Joe Theismann. The baseball coach was determined to shut out Sal Bando. Added pressure on the faculty came from their students. The kids would knock them all week with predictions that they were going to get killed by the Oneders come game time. The students would light the competitive fire. This made for some very rough games.

Classic case: The Oneders were playing the Palo Alto High School faculty. Standing room only. One of the coaches kept repeatedly undercutting Barry as he drove to the hoop. Enough was enough, and Rick pulled him aside and said, "Look, I'm here helping you raise money. My career is in the professionals. I don't have to be here. And I know that you are trying to impress your students that you can play basketball. But the next time you undercut me, I am going to take your ass and throw it in the tenth row." That took care of that.

Another time, Sal Bando was with the Oneders and we played the Redwood High faculty from Marin County, north of San Francisco. We had a 20-game winning streak going, but Redwood loaded up on us by bringing in some outside people. Bando fouled out and some heated words were exchanged, falling just short of thrown punches

The closest I came to a brawl on the basketball court was in La Plata High School in Maryland. I started bitching and moaning about a faculty opponent twice my size who kept flattening me. But the officials—not ours, mind you—were calling the fouls on *me*. Finally, this guy started to go after me with fists clenched. Four of my teammates—Art Monk, Terry Metcalf, Monte Coleman, and Tony Peters, all Washington Redskins—stepped in front of him and said, "If you want Holliday, you'll have to go through us." But I still got tossed out of the game.

My college play-by-play led to more TV work in San Francisco. I hosted the Giants' pregame show, a 15-minute interview taped with players (for road games) or live from the ballpark (before home contests). These were the days of McCovey and Mays. I consider my worst interview ever to be a painfully dismal and embarrassing chat with Jim Bunning, who had just come from the American to the National League, traded to the Phillies. Bunning, now a U.S. Senator from Kentucky, was a big guy, 6'3", and a great sidearm pitcher. Bunning would be the first pitcher since Cy Young to win over 100 games or to strike out over 1,000 players in each league. He retired second only to Walter Johnson with 2,885 career strikeouts. I got Bunning lined up to be my guest.

Unfortunately, Bunning didn't want to be interviewed. I stood (at 5'8") stretching the mic up to Bunning as he reluctantly answered in one word "yeps" and "nopes," or "whatever you think, Johnny." It was frustrating. The 15-minute interview felt like 30 minutes. We were both relieved when the nonconversation finally ended. This episode reminds me of a quote by Edward R. Murrow: "Just because you put a microphone in front of a fellow doesn't make him a genius."

One real coup for my radio show was landing St. Louis Cardinals pitcher Steve Carlton for an interview. Even then, the very eccentric Carlton was noted for his reluctance to do interviews. Elected to the Hall of Fame in 1994 in his first year of eligibility, Carlton and I attended the same North Miami High School (he's about ten years my junior), and we pitched for the same baseball coach, Jack Clark.

I had phoned Coach Clark for help in contacting Carlton for an interview. Sure enough, the phone rang on my KYA show and it was Carlton. I put him on the air, and I also asked him if he'd do my TV show. He said, "Sure, no problem." Indeed, one of the last interviews he did before breaking off all relationships with the media was on my Giants pregame TV spot. His closing remark to me was, "Anybody who played for Jack Clark can't be all that bad, because Jack was a pretty tough coach."

Once when I was playing baseball against Key West High, one of the guys was late getting back to our motel room, so we waited with glasses of water. Jack Clark, our coach, walked in instead, and he was not happy getting drenched.

Jack Clark and his wife Pat retired to the mountains of North Carolina, and we'd get together whenever Maryland played Clemson. I'd kid him by saying, "Hey, Coach, besides Steve Carlton, who's the best pitcher you ever had?" He'd never say me.

I was having dinner once with the coach and some buddies, including Georgia State athletic director, Greg Manning, when I finally pleaded, "Coach, for the sake of my friends here, can't you just say that I was one of your best pitchers?" But no way. He would never give me this credit.

Sadly, the coach passed away a few years ago. I know he contributed a great deal to generations of athletes. I'd still like to think I was one of his best pitchers.

Another extracurricular activity that I added to my San Francisco resume was coaching some youngsters in the Bay area. Here's how Art Thompson, my assistant coach (and now baseball scout for the Padres), remembers it:

Art Thompson: "I was already a fan of KYA and particularly liked the morning man, Johnny Holliday. I heard him one morning explaining that he was going to coach a Marin County youth baseball team that consisted of players between the ages of 13 – 15. Johnny then said that he needed an assistant coach to help him with the team.

"I had played ball through high school and had helped coach a Pony League team in Hampton, Virginia while I was in the navy. I gave Johnny a call, told him of my background, and set up an appointment to meet with him. We got along just fine and thus started our adventures with the Marin County version of the 'Bad News Bears.'

"These kids came from a very affluent area of Marin County called Tiburon and would play in the Mill Valley Babe Ruth League. These kids were also the leftovers from the league draft. The kids nobody wanted…the last kids picked in the neighborhood pickup games.

"I cannot remember if we won a game or not. Our job turned out to be much more rudimentary than trying to win games. Talk about baby steps, we were teaching the kids how to put on a uniform and how to walk off the mound after striking out the batter for the last out of an inning. They were a great bunch of kids, and I had more laughs and good times than at any other time in what would turn out to be 16 years of coaching.

"Billy Schwartz was our only pitcher. He knew where the pitcher's mound was located. His family owned a meat packing and distribution company, Schwartz Sausage. Billy, fortunately, wore braces. I say fortunately because we ultimately had to employ the braces as a defensive strategy. Billy became our 'secret weapon.' When he wasn't pitching, he would play a position in the field. We would line him up so that the sun would reflect off his braces into the batter's eyes, distracting the batter. We were never sure of the effectiveness of this strategy, but we needed all the help that we could get.

"Johnny would tell the stories of the game on his radio show the next morning. The kids loved it and so did I.

"One time when Billy struck out the final batter of an inning (with runners on base…there were always runners on base), he was so elated he was bouncing off the mound. Both Johnny and I thought Billy should have displayed a little more style when coming off the mound after such an impressive performance. We gave him 10 minutes of instructions on how to strut off the mound to show that he was in complete control of the game. By the time we had finished demonstrating the correct walk, Johnny was in tears laughing."

By 1969, KYA began to slip in the ratings. I could feel that we were not going to be the number one station much longer. Deciding to bail, I applied for a job as sports anchor on KTVU Channel Two's 10 o'clock news and was hired. This seemed at the time to be a good career move. I could keep the Oakland Raiders announcing job and work on television.

The first problem arose when I tried to keep control of the Oneders. After all, this was my baby. Howard Kester insisted the team stay with KYA, so we got into a pissing match, and I lost.

When I got to KTVU and began my evening sports reports, it took about two weeks to realize I had made a big mistake. I found myself bored waiting all day just to do six minutes on the nightly news. Sometimes I'd get bumped. When city or world news broke, the first ones they took a camera crew away from were the sports. I really missed radio.

I called Kester and told him that I wanted to come back to KYA. I wasn't surprised when he said, "Sorry, all staff positions are filled." I knew I had burned my bridge with him. Kester did promise to contact AVCO on my behalf and tell them I was looking for another radio job. AVCO owned WWDC in Washingon, D.C.

Up until I quit KYA, I felt like either I had done everything right or that my good luck had handed me winning directions. Now, however, I knew I had made my own career decision and it was a bad one. Doing the nightly sports report was a drag and no fun. I had to get back into radio.

Kester came through for me. The next thing I knew I was off to the nation's capital.

Chapter 8

Washington DC's Capital Acts

*"A listener once called in to ask how I was able to do so many things in
the course of a single day. I told her that I simply prerecorded the first two
hours of my WWDC radio show and in fact I was on tape right then as we
spoke.*

"'Oh, I see,' said the caller, apparently satisfied with my explanation."

When I arrived in Washington in 1969 and throughout my years at
WWDC, Frank Harden and Jackson Weaver were the guys my bosses wanted
me to beat in the ratings. WMAL's Harden and Weaver were number one in
the market and would continue on top for 25 years until their retirement. I
told them the following when they published their own memoirs, *On the
Radio*, in 1983. It's my side of the story, and I'm sticking to it.

"While I was breaking in at WWDC, I worked the afternoons for a
while so I had a chance to listen to Harden and Weaver in the mornings. I was
pretty confident after hearing them that it shouldn't take me too long to beat
them out. After all, the two stations were doing basically the same thing—
both were middle-of-the-road stations. We had the helicopter and the heavy
emphasis on news and sports. We had Washington Senators baseball and community involvement, and as for Jackson Weaver's voices (he was "Smokey the
Bear" for the National Park Service), hell, I had 27 different characters, and I
did a lot of outside speaking engagements. I thought it would be just a matter
of time before I caught up with them…"

My character impressions were what I hoped would win over audiences. "Celebrities" like Ed "out of work" Sullivan and Howard "speaking of
sports and telling it like it is" Cosell were always close by. I invented a slew of
originals, too. Ralph Ferhling, the "boss's assistant," delivered angry reports
about the graffiti he'd find on the executive washroom walls.

The World Famous Answer Man could never be stumped. He may not be right, but he always gave you an answer.

I did a running gag about the fictitious Nome University and its star athlete, "Easy Ed" Hartley. Dr. Graham Cracker, a send-up of Rev. Billy Graham, was always selling things. "Guido Guido," the Mafia legman, read the daily horoscopes.

My most popular character was William W. "Billy" Bicep, a six-foot-four, 98-pound. muscleman. Billy was a prissy do-gooder. The teacher's pet.

Taking my cues from the news, my characters would reflect the trends of the day. When streaking was a fad, Billy Biceps became a streaker. Imagine this tall, skinny character streaking, wearing only a pair of argyle socks and a smile.

Then there were the phone calls. I once got through to Col. Harlan Sanders on his birthday, and the sly colonel used my bit to plug his Kentucky Fried chicken. I also tried to phone Fidel Castro once, but I got bogged down when the overseas operator wanted his address. ("Uh, I think it's the Presidential Palace. No, I don't know his middle initial".)

The WWDC 1260-AM studio was in an old house on Brookeville Road, in Silver Spring, Maryland. Out back was where "Captain Dan" Rosenson, the best damn traffic reporter in Washington history, would set down his helicopter each day between his morning and afternoon reports. Dan paved the way, or should I say scraped the sky, for Walt Starling, Andy Parks, Bob Marburgh, and all the others who followed in copters and planes. No one has ever come close to matching Dan's popularity and accuracy.

Dan would literally drop in and have some coffee and doughnuts with yours truly, along with news director Dick Stapleton and many of the fine news staff who played a major role in making WWDC relevant. Peter Gamble, Rudolf Brewington, Tina Gulland, Ross Simpson, and Larry Mathews were top news staff. Ross is on the air these days with Westwood One.

Larry Matthews went on to an award-winning journalism career until 1998, when he was arrested and jailed for child pornography trafficking. Larry claimed he was investigating the porn industry for a radio report. At the time of Larry's trial, I was quoted as saying, "Matthews doesn't just report a story. If he was going to do something, he tried to get into it as much as he could. I've known him now for 30 years, and I'd be shocked if he were doing child pornography for any other reason than to do a professional report."

Unfortunately for Larry, the judge didn't rule in his favor. For the record, I still stand by Larry.

Our radio staff was outstanding. Tony Roberts handled sports. I think Tony is the best play-by-play voice on radio. Period. You can catch him today as the voice of Notre Dame football.

Tony Roberts: "Johnny and I have had parallel careers. I've been broadcasting for Notre Dame for 23 years, and he and I started at WWDC. Johnny and my wife, Shirley, also went to the same high school, North Miami, although at different times.

"People gravitate to Johnny because he's extremely likeable. He's very professional, but you can have a lot of fun with him. In the 32 years I've known him I have never heard a derogatory word said about him from anyone. For a guy who has accomplished as much as he has, Johnny's very humble. I don't want to make it sound like Johnny is one of the apostles of Jesus, but he would have been accepted.

"This idea that nice guys finish last is a crock. Nice guys finish first, and no matter what endeavor he's set out to do, Johnny has succeeded. There's a great sentiment about him and for the people he knows and cares for. I'm surprised that some con man hasn't gotten to John by now, because he really has a heart of gold and will literally give you the shirt off his back. I think not many people really know all that he does for others. There's never any publicity. He doesn't ask for thanks. The guy is mush, pure and simple.

"I played on his Oneders team along with a good many Washington Senators and several Redskins. In those days the players were more visible in the community. Under Coach George Allen, the Redskin players seemed to be more involved in community than players today.

"One thing about the Oneders games; we all knew that if we passed the ball to Johnny, we'd never get it back. I think he had several surgeries in his right elbow from shooting so much. That's a joke, but you can say I said it.

"On his golf game I can tell you that he shoots disgustingly straight, but Mary Clare can out-drive him.

"One funny story happened when I was broadcasting for the Senators before they left Washington. They didn't leave because of me, mind you, but we were in spring training down in Florida one time.

"Unbeknownst to me, Johnny had set up a practical joke with the hotel operator. John called my room directly, but the operator got on the line pretending she was a woman staying with me. They go through this long diatribe insinuating that I'm having some kind of affair on the road."

Tony tried to get me back by shipping a pair of lacy black women's panties to Mary Clare. The gag was supposed to be that I somehow left the underwear at my hotel room, and he was "doing me a favor" by sending them to my house. I recognized Tony's extravagant handwriting on the shipping label immediately. Nice try, Tony.

Bill Sanders was my first GM (general manager). Pat Whitley was our PD (program director), followed by Gloris Gibson when Pat moved on. Larry Kirby followed Sanders as GM. Larry still reminds me of the winner of the Roy Clark lookalike contest.

Larry Kirby: "Johnny once tracked the truck driver delivering the White House Christmas tree from Minnesota. Each day our 'driver' had another 'mishap.' He got lost, drunk on eggnog, and was arrested. Johnny kept hoping he'd make it in time for the 'lighting.' Of course, it was one of his buddies, calling from a pay phone with made-up scenarios.

"He once read a tear-jerker letter from a distraught new husband who had to leave on an extended trip right after his wedding and begged Johnny to call his new wife and tell her how much he loved her. This tugged at Johnny's heartstrings, so he called the lonely bride at 7:15 a.m. as requested. A man answered.

"Johnny left it right there.

"Everyone on the staff was peppered with questions. 'Did you hear that phone call? Do you believe that? Was that a real person?' Johnny's stock answer was 'What do you think?'"

Kirby was a great golfer with a fine sales staff: Barry Alentuck, Eddie Sachs, Fred Goodman, Gene Thompson, Tom Walker, John Marshall, Tom Bresnahan, and Lenny Klompus. Klompus put together the first network to televise Maryland basketball games with his company, Metro Communications. Tom would later be my boss at WMAL.

Neither Tom nor Lenny could hit that well when they joined our WWDC softball team. I still kid them that they were better salesmen than ball players. Adman Jim Walczy, attorney Jack Quinn, and Dave Dupree, now of USA Today, also came on board, as did pro players Jim Hannan, Tom Brown, and Bob Windsor.

My old Cleveland buddy, Scott Burton, joined the WWDC crew of Fred Knight, Dick Hemby, "Tiger" Bob Raleigh, Ron Starr, and Earl Robbin. Even Murray the K was with us for a short time.

Fred Gale was doing a controversial late-night show when I first came to the station. Fred Fiske took over his time slot, reinvented the show in his own classy style, and became prominent at the station almost immediately.

Fiske had been a child actor, journalist, radio soap opera veteran, straight man in the Catskills for Danny Kaye, and top-rated music deejay.

He started in radio in 1936 at age 15. The native New Yorker became a regular on network radio's "Theatre Guild of the Air" with stars like Ronald Coleman and William Holden. A graduate from Columbia College with a major in speech, Fred enlisted in the Air Force and became a radio gunner on a B-24 just in time to fly 30 missions over France and Germany. His squadron leader was Col. Jimmy Stewart. I think Fred has led a charmed life, and I doubt there's ever been a nicer guy in broadcasting.

He nearly lost that life in a WWII bombing mission. After an encounter with 150 Focke-Wulf 190 fighter planes over Germany, only one of the 34 aircraft in his group made it back to home base. Fred's plane crash-landed in France.

After WWDC, Fred went on to host the premiere nighttime talk show in D.C. for 16 years on WAMU-FM 88.5. Fred interviewed thousands of politicians and celebrities from Averill Harriman and Richard Nixon to Raquel Welch, until his retirement from the airways in 1987.

WWDC also gave me the chance to get my daughters into the act. I'd spend many midnights at home writing parody introductions for our traffic reporter, Capt. Dan. The intros were longer than Dan's actual traffic reports. I'd start off with a song like "June is Busting Out All Over" and teach these old show tunes to my girls Kellie (age 11), and Tracie (age 8). We'd go into the studio and twist it into:

> *"Capt. Dan is here each morning and do not forget the afternoon*
> *Yes he tells it as he sees it, when he sees it, then he yells it*
> *You can bet that he's right here with us each day.*
> *Capt. Dan you are my favorite. The kids, moms and dads depend on*
> *you.*
> *On the Beltway, in the District, from Virginia, in the copter, it's your*
> *job to get us there and right on time.*
> *Dan, Dan, Dan, Dan, Dan, Dan, Dan, Dan, Dan,*
> *Capt. Dan from 12-6-0."*

Or to the tune of 'Hello Dolly' sung as a duet with Scott Burton:

> *"Hello Danny, yes Hello Danny*
> *It's so nice to have you over us each day.*
> *You're looking down, Captain, on each car, Captain*
> *With a traffic tip and safety word for all of us to hear*
> *The guys and gals, Danny, hear each word, Danny*
> *And we marvel at the way you do your thing, so—*
> *Flash us that smile, Captain*
> *As we sit and wait, Captain*
> *Frannie's may be the place for you*
> *But in our hearts you'll always do*
> *Captain Dan in copter 12-6-0."*

Here's a third with me singing to a country tune:

"Time to get up. Better get a move on. Start another day.
Breakfast cookin', coffee is a' perkin', Get up! Bounce on your way.
We got the news. We got the best in music. And don't forget up in the
sky.
You've got some troubles drivin' on the highway. Look up! And Dan's
the guy.
Grab the papers, a second cup of coffee. Hear the news reports.
Ross and Rudy typing in the newsroom. Shelby workin' sports.
So start your day with good ole 1260, DC from six to nine.
Ooh, it's mighty fine."

You're lucky to get only three examples. I have about 40 of these on tape.

The police had a maintenance yard near the radio station where they'd gas up and get snacks. The yard's proximity to WWDC helped them get to us. My on-air, freewheeling patter seemed to appeal to many of the cops who were young and just starting out. The Holliday show became a police favorite.

My interest in law enforcement began in Cleveland. Elliott Ness had been Chief Public Safety Officer there following his crime-busting heroics in Chicago. I heard that he died in debt to the tune of nine grand in '57, shortly after writing his memoirs. The first *Untouchables* aired on TV a month after we arrived in Cleveland.

But when Scott Burton talks about my "police fetish," he's a little off base. It's true I've always admired the cops. Frequently, I was invited to ride in the police cruisers on their beats, especially on the weekends. These rides were intriguing, especially for a broadcaster. It was also a way to relax and get away from the radio grind, if you can believe someone could relax in a police cruiser.

One close police buddy during my WWCD days was Larry Pagley, a Montgomery County, MD policeman. His nickname was the "Snake." I'd often join him on his midnight shift.

As a gag, the Snake and I once hid around the corner from the station, waiting for Scott Burton to come off his radio shift. We followed Scott for a few miles until he turned on to Highway 270 toward Gaithersburg, MD. Pagley turned on the siren and pulled him over. I crouched down in the patrol car seat while the Snake hassled him a bit. Burton was about to come unglued when Pagley let him off the hook by pointing over to the patrol car. I popped up laughing.

Once the tables were turned on me. My morning commute to WWDC was well timed. I'd leave the house at 5:40 a.m. and arrive at the WWDC studio, ready to hit the airwaves at 6:05.

My trip took me through the Walter Reed medical complex. On one otherwise normal commute, I got pulled over by a Walter Reed MP. I knew something was up when the patrolman took my license and said "Mr. Holliday, you've got to take it easy, because the speed limit around here is 15 mph and you were exceeding it."

Wait a minute, I thought. My license says "Bobbitt," not Holliday. That's when I knew the Snake was behind this one. I took some shots at the Walter Reed police when I finally got on the air. I was mad and nearly late for work.

Another time, one of the Snake's cop cronies, Ted Parker, quietly walked in and handcuffed me to my studio chair and walked out. I continued the show. Listeners never knew what had happened. Officer Parker came back later and released me. I think he was either disappointed or impressed that I could still do my radio act in handcuffs.

Reader takes note: these gags were funny only when we did them to somebody else.

I liked to play radio excerpts from *The Lone Ranger* on my show. I thought they were funny, and listeners liked them, too. One morning, newsmen Larry Matthews, Peter Gamble, and Tony Roberts called me into the newsroom. "You've got to come outside and see this," they said.

In the semicircle outside WWDC, there were *ten* Montgomery County police—with handkerchiefs on their faces—standing alongside their patrol cars. They were chanting loudly, "We want more Lone Ranger." The only thing missing were outstretched arms pointing their guns at me. I'll never forget that one.

Doug Hill was another policeman whom I first met when he visited the station armed with some public service announcements (PSAs) he'd written and produced.

Today, Doug is an award-winning weather man on WJLA-TV Channel Seven in Washington. I asked Doug to fill in the blanks (police, guns, blanks ... get it?) about how we met. I'm flattered by his contribution and proud to call him one of my dependable, daffy, doppler-radar friends.

Doug Hill: "I was a big Johnny Holliday fan when he was doing his morning show at WWDC. I was also a radiophile. My oldest brother was a disc jockey and newsman in Baltimore for years, so I was bitten by the radio bug from about six years old. When I joined the police department, and after a few years on the street, I got involved in producing public service announcements and made my way to every radio station in the area trying to peddle these spots to get them aired. They were fairly clichéd and corny, but what the heck. Example: "Beware of scam mail that seems too good to be true, because they probably are. The police remind you that crime prevention begins at home."

"When I got to WWDC I met Johnny and asked him if he'd play some of my promos. We had chatted for a few minutes when he told me he thought I was pretty sharp on my feet for a cop. I think what he meant was that most cops speak police language and don't speak English. I had also been interviewed as a representative for the police for various police events, so I think John had an idea of who I was before we met.

"When I got around to telling him about my interest in broadcasting, he was very giving and full of encouragement and information. I asked him if I could come back and sit in on the show to observe how he did it. There was no hesitation. 'Absolutely,' he told me.

"I returned frequently as he showed me how the control board worked, how to use the turntables, how he did his voices, where he got his ideas, and so on. Although I was very much captivated by his personality, I was most impressed about what a genuinely warm human being he was. By that time, I had been around enough media people to know that many had problems. My oldest brother, whom I adored, would warn me to stay away from some of them. He told me to never get into broadcasting. It was a terrible business. I was always hearing wild stories about the jocks.

"So here comes Johnny—a pro in the business. Well-known. Multi-talented. And one of the nicest people in the world to talk to and get guidance from. For a person like me who had an interest in broadcasting, it was like a dream come true. John became a hero and an idol for me.

"After I had produced my DJ demo tape, I first took it over to John for his critique. He told me that even though big, booming voices weren't necessary in radio anymore, I would have to lose my Baltimore dialect. 'You still need to be crisp and clean,' he said, 'so lose the dialect.'

"At John's suggestion, I promptly enrolled in speech and articulation courses at Maryland University for a couple of semesters, tutored by Dr. Sandra Elliott, specifically to improve my diction. One year later I broke into broadcasting.

"At every key point in my life where something really important has happened, there has always been somebody there to make a difference for me. This is my personal opinion, but I think that God places people and uses them in certain situations to do His stuff, and, for me, I really feel John was that person."

While at WWDC I began noticing and listening to The Joy Boys at WRC-AM. Ed Walker (known as "Eddie" to his many pals) and Willard Scott had established the Joy Boys act as one of the best and funniest radio teams in the city. Their theme song, "We are the Joy Boys of Radio, we chase electrons to and fro…" (sung to the tune of the old circus song "Billboard March") still cracks me up.

When asked how the Joy Boys got together, Willard once cracked, "Eddie's monkey died and I was out of pencils." Actually, Eddie, Willard, and college friend, Roger Gordon, met at American University in the '50s. There, they helped relaunch the campus radio station, WAMU, a year after it had been destroyed by a fire.

Eddie Walker: "Roger and I and a few other fellows began fiddling around with this college station. I'd do my show, which I called "Ed Walker's Waxworks." I'd bring my own records in and play them; someone else might bring in Gregorian chants. You never knew. Roger would read the news and sports right out of the *Evening Star* newspaper.

"The campus station slowly gained support from the university administration. WAMU was then what was known as a carrier current. Instead of using an antenna, the signal was fed into the power lines. The first remote transmission we did was a talent show out of the girls' gymnasium. I knew that the girls' dormitory had a switchboard, so we patched in our microphone at the station to the remote at the gym through the girls dorm switchboard. We used miles of telephone wire. It worked. I was a big hero because I had figured this out.

The legend told in Eddie Walker's family is that the first complete sentence he spoke was "Turn on the radio." His mother would swear it was true. The legendary yet true story of Eddie's radio career is that he was born blind and became one of the best radiomen around.

"I knew it was going to be hard when I went into broadcasting," Eddie confesses. "In the early days I wasn't making much money. The commercials and copy had to be put into Braille, and the only way I could get that done was to do it myself. My father would read for me, and I'd type the Braille."

Eddie kept his blindness secret from his listeners for many of his early years. It wasn't because he was ashamed of it.

"I felt that if were going to attain success, I wanted to do it on my merit as a performer," he explains.

Listeners seldom knew or didn't mind that he was blind since Eddie handled the radio controls masterfully and had them laughing with his quick wit and great voices, especially his character of "Baltimore Benny." This character finds its roots in Eddie's childhood days when he rode the bus from his D.C. house on Euclid Street to the Maryland School for the Blind in Baltimore. He'd listen to the voices of the other students, and his abilities as a mimic grew from these experiences.

"I couldn't look at the scenery, so I'd listen to people talk and pick up their accents. I was certainly more aware of how they sounded than how they looked," he laughs. "Baltimore Benny" uses that special lingo where "payment" means "street" and "zinc" refers to the kitchen sink.

Several years after Eddie established himself on the radio, he heard that some of his former teachers had been saying that it was very kind that the radio stations let Eddie hang around and do broadcasts. Eddie was sure that the teachers had no idea he was being paid—and making a pretty good living—for his work.

"I should say, however, that I had some memorable teachers who gave much more than nine to five," Eddie recalls. "We had competitions in sports like wrestling, which is great for blind people because it's a contact sport. We also used to put on plays at school, and to do that is more difficult when you're blind. We needed to have the stage set up long before the show, because we'd have to memorize the stage along with learning our lines."

I first met Eddie and Willard on a freelance session, a big production commercial. I have an early picture of Willard tossing a cream pie in my face in the parking lot of WWDC. When I ask Eddie today what that was all about, he jokes, "It was because Willard didn't like you." I think it was a bet that I lost.

Eddie and I have since done hundreds of jobs together over the years, including a series of spots for the "Fantastic" Kroger cakes that ran recently in the Ohio area. Eddie adds, "We'd always make fun of the client, but never their product. We'd often treat the clients like schmucks."

WRC-AM eventually went all news and the Joy Boys were out of a job after a great run. I decided to phone in on their last day and invite them over to join me for a week on WWDC. The Joy Boys said, "How nice. We'll be there."

Eddie recalls "Signing off on our last show at WRC, we could say 'look for us on Monday on the Johnny Holliday show at WWDC.' Lee Sherwood, the WRC programming director, hated that."

During their week with me, we skipped most of the music and just laughed each day from 6 to 10 with voices and bits. Our station manager, Bill Sanders, gave us carte blanche. I think that initially Bill was trying to capitalize on the Joy Boys' popularity by letting them guest on my show, but he was so overwhelmed by the listener response we got that he said, "Hey, I've got to find a spot for these guys." WWDC hired them after their guest week on my show, and the Joy Boys returned to afternoon radio. Willard was also doing the TV weather on local WRC-TV.

Willard was tapped to be the weatherman on NBC's *The Today Show.* Uncle Willard's success story is well known. He began as a 16-year-old NBC page and moved through his early "Bozo the Clown" gig, established The Joy

Boys, created the first "Ronald McDonald" character, and finally became America's favorite weatherman. Today he owns more homes than Motel 6, Eddie says.

> **Willard Scott:** "Every time I worked with Johnny it was a 'Holliday.' He gave the Joy Boys a break when we really needed it and we'll never forget it. We laughed so hard when we guest-starred on Johnny's show that I don't think we played one record. It was especially hard to do commercials with John because you can't keep from laughing."

In 1975, Eddie cohosted *AM Washington*, a local show that aired on WJLA-TV. His partner was Ruth Hudgens, who had begun her career as a secretary at the station. She graduated to a public affairs show covering the urban community. They were a good team.

Eddie worked from notes in Braille on a clipboard in his lap. He could read the notes without having to look down. The director of the show, Charlie Stopak, gave him directions through an earpiece. It all worked great.

Eddie and his wife, Nancy, whom he met in college, live in nearby Bethesda. Over the years Eddie and I have both made names among the ad agencies in D.C. as "the guys who can do impressions." Eddie has that deep radio voice that is pitch-perfect for his characterizations of Humphrey Bogart or William F. Buckley, for example. He also really knows the studios. If even a chair is moved, Eddie will walk in and notice it.

After 32 years, I am proud to call Eddie one of my closest friends.

At WWDC, the station management thought they could generate some strong publicity by hiring my old mentor, Murray the K. The mistake that Murray made when he took the job was that he never related to the local audience. All he wanted to do was tell his listeners about his New York adventures. "Hey baby, I just came back from the Big Apple and had lunch with Tom Jones—and he sends you his love."

Murray's ratings suggested that Washington listeners didn't give a damn about his schmoozing with Tom Jones or his weekend parties in New York. I also resented this because Murray wasn't broadcasting for D.C. He was trying to impress the local listeners with his New York name-dropping.

So Murray the K never caught on at WWDC. He later jumped to D.C.'s pioneer alternative music station, WHFS, but he didn't do well there either. He finally made his way back to New York and regained his career at station WOR, until throat cancer claimed his voice and his life.

Thinking about Murray again conjures up memories of Beatlemania. In Washington, tales of Beatlemania eventually lead to Carroll James.

The day I arrived, I received a telegram from Carroll wishing me success at my new job at WWDC. Carroll had previously hosted "CJ and Company" in afternoon drive time before he was let go. I remember thinking what a classy gesture this was, especially since I was one of his replacements.

Carroll earned a place in music history when he became the first disc jockey to play the Beatles in America. And it all started on WWDC.

Carroll had received a letter from Marsha Albert, a local 15-year-old junior high student, requesting that he play a song by an English group called the Beatles. Marsha had seen them on Walter Cronkite's CBS News (30 seconds briefly describing how British fans were mobbing this new group). Carroll went to one of the WWDC staff, Jo Wilson, and asked her how he could obtain an English recording by this foreign band. Jo knew a representative for British Overseas Airways. After a phone call, a stewardess brought it over on a flight the next day.

Carroll and Fred Fiske listened to this just-released record. Carroll thought it was interesting, but Fred didn't like it at all. Carroll then called Marsha Albert and asked her to come quickly to the studio to introduce the song.

"Marsha was scared to death," Carroll recalled, so he wrote out an introduction for her, and at 5:15 p.m., December 17, 1963, Marsha said, "Ladies and gentlemen, for the first time in America, the Beatles singing 'I Want to Hold your Hand.' "

"The switchboard lit up like the proverbial Christmas tree," Carroll said.

"The listeners just went wild. It was spontaneous combustion."

He played the record every day for a week, fading it down in the middle to say, "This is a Carroll James exclusive," so the other stations wouldn't steal it.

Executives at Capitol Records in New York, who had signed the Beatles to a contract, were planning to release 200,000 copies of "I Want to Hold Your Hand" to the American market early in 1964.

News of the record's success in Washington reached New York, and Capitol moved the release date up to December 26. The company arranged for three production plants—Capitol's own and those of RCA and CBS—to work through the Christmas and New Year's holidays in order to press one million copies of the soon-to-be hit.

By the time the Beatles arrived in America, on February 7, 1964, to appear on Ed Sullivan's TV variety show, Sullivan had received 50,000 requests for the 700 available seats for the debut. Carroll James and his wife, Betty, were invited to attend. Betty sat with John Lennon's first wife, Cynthia, and remembers her as completely overwhelmed by the unprecedented fanfare for her husband's band.

After the show, Sullivan greeted Carroll backstage by saying, "You're the guy who's been saying he discovered the Beatles. Well, you can forget that because I've had them booked since October." Maybe so, but Carroll James and WWDC were the first to play the Beatles publicly, and D.C. audiences were the first to acclaim them.

Carroll was always a class act and a very nice man. He died a few years ago from a rare spine disorder and is greatly missed by his family and many friends in Washington.

I also helped break a record at WWDC. It was a tune called "Playground of My Mind," written by Paul Vance, whom I had known from my WINS days in the Big Apple. Clint Holmes, an excellent talent just waiting to be discovered, recorded it. Clint had found his local audience at Mr. Day's in Georgetown and various other D.C. nightspots. When Clint's record promoter dropped the single off at WWDC, we just jumped all over it. It became a hit overnight.

Clint is the sort of fellow you just automatically like the first time you meet him. He and I played tennis at Candy Cane Park in Silver Spring and shot a ton of hoops together. He's a good athlete.

I couldn't be prouder of what Clint has accomplished in his career. After "Playground" hit, he became Joan Rivers's sideman on her short-lived late night show on Fox, and then he got his own TV gig on WOR-TV in NYC.

Today Clint Holmes is one of the hottest performers in Las Vegas. One of the first things you see when you step off a plane at McLaren airport is a gigantic billboard proclaiming Clint as "the next Sammy Davis, Jr." Clint's reply is "Yeah, could be. But I'm not certain that I can dance like Sammy."

Mary Clare and I, along with Capt. Dan, Larry the Snake, and their wives (all of whom are now retired in Sin City), recently caught Clint's shows at Harrah's. It's one of the tougher tickets in Vegas. Was he ever dynamite! Good things happen to good people, and Clint is one of the best.

When Tony Roberts departed WWDC for greener pastures at WRC, I was offered the play-by-play job for Navy football. Man, talk about some big shoes to fill.

Pete Larsen, the pride and joy of Cornell University, stayed on as analyst. Pete was what you'd call a student of the game. His NFL experience included the NY Giants and the Redskins, so I naturally thought he'd know football as well as anybody. This turned out to be the case. I was lucky to find such a compatible partner.

Probably the coldest day of my life was spent with Pete in the old open-air broadcast booth at Syracuse. This was before they built the Carrier Dome. With temperatures in the low 20s, and a fierce wind blowing directly in our faces, we had a time of it keeping our papers from flying off in every direction. Then came the rain, followed by snow. It was a frostbiting experience for this old Floridian.

Art Monk was the key to the Orangemen attack on that cold afternoon. Art would later join the Redskins, and he once told me that he remembers that game as if it were yesterday.

Discipline was the key to Navy football. Head Coach George Welsh was not a good loser by any stretch, and not the easiest of interviews. Coming off of a loss, he was a man of very few words. I had to be certain I was prepared with plenty of questions when we taped our pregame show. Joe Krivak was on Welsh's staff then. Joe moved to Maryland as assistant and finally head coach of the Terrapins.

Commander Jack Fellowes was the officers' rep for the Navy team. If any midshipman had a problem then Jack would sit down with them and get it sorted out. I'll bet that none of the players could ever convince Jack that their problems were bigger than what the Commander had endured in Vietnam.

Jack was shot out of the sky while piloting his A-10 attack bomber from the *U.S.S. Constellation* and was captured by the Viet Cong on August 27, 1966. For the next seven years he was a POW.

When I think I have problems in my work or at home, I have to think of what Jack must have gone through in that Vietnamese prison. Instantly, my life seems quite nice and comfortable.

Fellowes had a great sense of humor. I'm sure that helped him get through those seven years in a hellhole. On our flights to Navy games, Tom Bates, the Navy sports information director, would assign seats for the passengers, including Pete, Jack, and me. Fellowes would always try to mess up Tom's "system" by sitting in the wrong seat, just to upset Bates as he went through his checklist to see if everyone was present and accounted for in the plane. We lost Tom this year after a long battle with cancer.

Jack was also there on the sidelines for every game, pacing back and forth. Pete and I started to keep track of his "pacing yardage" during the games, and would mention on air how many yards he had racked up. I recall his best game was 250 yards, which still stands today as most yards gained by an officers' rep pacing.

I spent just one season with Navy, but what an awesome time it was. I especially remember the Army-Navy game in Philadelphia and the home opener at Navy Marine Corp Memorial Stadium in Annapolis, with the Brigade marching onto the field as jets soared overhead.

And let's not forget the media luncheons held at the Academy's boathouse each weekend. Navy spared no expense with those mighty feasts of steak, potatoes, salads, and a wide array of desserts. They were the best meals of my life, and I wonder if they still serve those smorgasbords today.

This all happened some 26 years ago, and I thank Capt. Bo Coppedge, Coach Welsh, Commander Jack, Tom, and Pete for that very special time. And to think that it would have never happened had not Tony Roberts left for another job.

Jerry St. James, today the popular one-half of San Diego's STAR 100.7 FM's "Jeff and Jer," is a University of Maryland grad. Jerry sent along his memory of listening to my WWDC act:

> **Jerry St. James:** "Maryland had an outstanding campus car-rier current radio station, WMUC, when I was there. It won count-less awards and was 'college station of the year' many times. It was 100 percent student run with minimal faculty interference. My first semester, I auditioned for and got the midnight and 1 a.m. news-casts on the station! From there, I learned enough about radio to get my own, once-a-week, really, really bad show.
>
> "But I listened to Johnny every morning and tried like crazy to understand how he did it. How to be like him. It took me 15 years in radio to accomplish that. Being 'yourself' on the air is the most difficult thing to learn and pretty much impossible to teach. Most radio talent put on their air 'personalities' like a shirt when they enter the studio. Johnny was always himself. I knew that if I walked into his house and had a beer with him, he'd be exactly what I heard every morning on the air."

By 1978 WWDC had begun its ratings decline. It was really slipping. My show was the only live program they were airing as the station gradually moved to using automated, syndicated programs. I knew it wasn't going to survive at the top of the ratings.

My eye was still on WMAL-AM 63, the station that still owned the town. WMAL was the dominant station for music, sports, everything; but the lineup there seemed permanently anchored with no openings in sight.

Around this time I somehow met Geoff Lebahr, who ran WJMD-94.7. Geoff is probably best remembered in Washington as the guy who later fired Howard Stern from WWDC's FM sister station, DC-101.

Geoff pushed to hire me to bolster their mornings. WJMD's music format was MOR (middle-of-the-road) pop with Barbra Streisand, The Beatles, Neil Diamond, and the like. This would work for me. Also, the station was at 5520 Wisconsin Ave, north of Georgetown, right across from Sak's Fifth Av-enue and not far from my home. I decided to take his offer of $75,000 a year—the fattest paycheck of my career at that point and about 40K more than I'd been making at WWDC. I eagerly signed on as their new morning man from 6 to 9 and bid goodbye to WWDC.

A few weeks after I began at WJMD I started to realize that the move was a mistake. I liked Lebahr when he was up-front with me, but the operations manager, Andy Bitsco, began giving me problems immediately.

"These characters like Billy Bicep that you used at WWDC will not work here," Andy informed me.

"Wait a minute," I protested. "I thought this is why I was hired. The characters are all part of the shtick that I do."

Bitsco and I couldn't see eye to eye. Next, WJMD moved me to a mid-morning time slot. Then it became a classic case of the old bait and switch (and yes, I'm implying deliberate dishonesty here). The unexpected switch was to a "beautiful music" format. The former "King of the Concrete Jungle" was stuck playing tapes from nine to noon. I was making a lot of money, but I was very unhappy.

"Geoff, I can't stand this," I told him.

"Don't worry," he said. "You've got a job for life here, especially if you can adjust to *not having to do anything*."

"But I want to work. I don't want to just sit here and play tapes."

Goeff actually suggested that I bring books into the studio and read while the beautiful music flowed. The fact that I had also landed a play-by-play job with George Washington University football probably gave me sufficient reason to stick it out for a year at WJMD. Eventually, enough was enough.

Geoff Lebahr couldn't believe I would just walk away from 75K. (Neither could Mary Clare.) I got through to him when I finally said, 'It's not working. I've given WJMD a year, and I know it's a lot of money—more money that I've ever made before—but money can't buy you happiness. I'm going nuts here. This job is killing me."

With no real prospects for a job on the horizon, I quit WJMD on Friday, Feb. 5, 1979, the same week my youngest daughter, Moira, was born.

Chapter 9

Sports Segue

"For anyone under the age of 32 living in the Washington, D.C. area, the local sports scene has never been without Johnny Holliday. He's a perpetual personality, an inescapable fixture, as ubiquitous as faded Redskins bumper stickers. He's always been there.
    Buzz McClain, SportsFan Magazine

I drove to Pittsburgh to cover a weekend George Washington basketball game right after I quit WJMD. At Sunday Mass, I noticed a prayer card in the pew guaranteeing something good would happen if I said the prayer for seven days straight. With no regular job and a new baby in the house, I recited that prayer faithfully.

Sure enough, on the seventh day a call came from the president and general manager of WMAL, Andy Ocherhausen. "Let's meet and talk about you coming to work for WMAL," he said.

Andy, along with operations manager Jim Gallant, offered me swing shifts and weekend work. They didn't know about my sports background. After some discussion they decided I'd be good for the Maryland basketball and football games.

That's how I arrived at WMAL to begin a 24-year association with the University of Maryland sports programs. I also did a Sunday afternoon show and substituted for the regular staff when they were away. These fill-ins kept my hands and ears in the music scene.

Andy was the perfect general manager. Everyone in the community knew him. He *was* WMAL. I always felt comfortable bugging him with phone calls or pitching him ideas for the station.

He always prefaced remarks about me as "my guy Holliday." I figured he thought the world of me until I realized he called everybody "my guy." Andy went on to run Channel 50 for a while and eventually went to Home Team Sports, now known as Comcast.

While at WWDC, I always thought that it was just a matter of time before I beat Harden and Weaver. But it came down to the old cliché: "If you can't beat them, join them." I became their sports reporter for 12 years, doing two sports reports an hour from 6-10 a.m., five days a week.

Working closely with Frank and Jackson in the studio, I came to have a much deeper appreciation for their gifts. Both were true gentlemen and went out of their way to make me feel at home. I discovered what really made them so magical. They were there for their listeners every single day. With nothing foul, off color, vulgar, or suggestive, they were a couple of nice guys having a good time. They did the same stuff every day, but it was funny. You could depend on them. I, like thousands of others, miss that comfort zone of having them with us each morning.

Frank had me as his guest at the Kenwood country club to play golf. I especially remember our golf days because Frank had a keen eye and could always locate both of our balls *off* the fairway.

Jackson was one of the funniest human beings and always in a good mood. He'd always stop by the old country store on Old Georgetown road for coffee on his way to work each day. I can still hear him saying "Good morning, *Mr. Holloway,*" in that little old lady voice of his.

"He' such a nice young man, that *Mr. Holloway*," Jacskon would comically comment after my sports reports.

Frank corrected him, *"That's Holliday."*

"Yes," said Jackson. "I saw *Mr. Holloway* in that musical, *38th Street.*

"That's *42nd Street.*"

"Whatever," Jackson agreed. "I still like that *Mr. Jimmy Holloway.*"

Eddie Walker and I would fill in for them when they took vacation, but I had to be careful. I couldn't go in with bells and whistles and 28 different voices, although I was still wishing I could have been in Harden and Weaver's shoes from time to time.

But Harden and Weaver never considered me a threat. That's one of the reasons we got along so well.

On my final show, they dedicated the last hour to me. This was a big deal. Normally when you leave a station, people don't realize it for weeks.

Toward the end of Jackson's life I returned from vacation to learn that he was in Holy Cross Hospital. I paid a visit, and his wife said, "Jackson, look who's here."

Critically ill, he gazed up and asked, "Where have you been? I thought you died." And he was laughing.

WMAL had a terrific news department backing up Harden and Weaver. Ed Meyer, Bud Steele, Carole Preston, Marge Kumacki, Bob Kneiser, Milagros Ardin, Wes Moore, Larry Mathews, J.J. Greene, and Karen Leggett, with commentaries by Joseph McCaffery, made a big difference in the quality and substance of the WMAL programs. They really helped keep Harden and Weaver, and the rest of the lineup, on top of the ratings.

Len Deibert was WMAL news director then. Len was one of best bosses I have ever had. Len related so well to everything we were doing. He cared about every newsperson and every newscast. Len was always complimenting us on the fine job we were doing. Nothing negative. Everything was positive. Today, Len is the managing editor for *Business Now*, a nationally syndicated TV news magazine.

Len Deibert: "I only knew of Johnny before from listening to him on WWDC. He was a strong, dominant air personality. But he needed to show me he could do sports. And he did. During the next several years at WMAL, he showed me a full range of abilities.

"We did a boxing match with Sugar Ray Leonard defending his title at the Capital Center one year. I don't think John had ever done boxing before, or since, but when I asked him if he could do play-by-play for the match, John said sure. And he did a hell of a job.

"The funny part is that we had sold the show for the full 15 rounds, but Sugar Ray knocked his opponent out in an early round. I was scrambling to make sure we could stretch the time to get all the commercials in, and John just did it. He got his friends from the audience, like Pete Wysocki, and did interviews, and filled the time—for something like 10 rounds—so we could get all the spots aired.

"One of the reasons I have so much respect and affection for the guy is because if there was a breaking news conference or event that we'd need to cover locally, and I needed him, he'd be there. Sometimes I'd call him at home and say, 'Johnny, I need you.' He was always there for us. I can't recall an instance where he was unavailable. That endeared him to me tremendously because I knew I could always count on him.

"Johnny would also volunteer to fill in for other broadcasters so they could, for example, see their own kids play sports. He always has that willingness to help people. That's the Johnny Holliday I know and like so much.

"I think the thing that disappointed him was that he was never given the chance to do Redskins play-by-play. John was the senior guy at WMAL, but the station had this idea that if they got someone who was in the television arena, then they'd get more bang for their buck in terms of cross promotion. So Frank Herzog was hired, and he's been there ever since.

"There's always humor in Johnny's broadcasts, but I've only heard him break up on air once where he couldn't continue. In 1984 we were doing a USFL game with the Washington Federals versus the Tampa Bay Bandits, then coached by Steve Spurrier. Johnny was doing play-by-play with his color guy, Ken McQuilkin. Spurrier called a triple reverse play, and Holliday was describing it. He said something like, 'I haven't seen that play since I played in high school.'

"Ken replied, 'Yeah, back when they wore leather helmets.'

"Johnny never recovered. It was one continuous howl of laughter. He just completely broke up."

Another great staffer was Robin Vierbuchen, who began her career as a desk assistant in the newsroom. She married one of the engineers that I worked with, Dave Sproul, who is still at WMAL.

Today, Robin Sproul handles the prominent and demanding job of Bureau Chief with ABC News in Washington.

WMAL had a rock 'em, sock 'em two-man sports department: Ken Beatrice and me. We shared the same office as I settled into doing the morning sports. Ken took listener sports calls at night.

The station always had a presence with anything involving sports. They'd send either Ken or me out to handle the assignments. I took over covering Maryland games as well as the Masters, the USFL, and major championship boxing matches, mostly involving Sugar Ray Leonard.

Beatrice was one of the most unforgettable sportscasters I've ever met. I realized early on that sports were his whole life. He had absolutely no other interests. Just sports. He was a walking encyclopedia of sports statistics.

By contrast, my main interest is in basketball, football, baseball, boxing, golf, and some track and field.

But Ken knew something about *every* sport. If he didn't, he made it up. I'd tell him that it was OK if he made a mistake once in a while. He didn't have to know everything. Nobody can do that.

For many years his show was the only sports talk in town. He was always nice to listeners and kids and never blew anyone off. I admired him for that. It took a special person to sit in the studio every night and do what he did. I knew I couldn't do it.

When Tony Roberts's young son, Lance, was hoping to get into broadcasting, Ken took him on as an intern. Tony told me how helpful Ken was in teaching Lance the ropes. Lance is now working at a San Diego marketing firm and making a pretty good living.

Ken's ratings were always super. Once the phone rang at WMAL at 5 p.m. and the caller had a question for Ken. When informed that Ken's show didn't start until two hours later at 7:05, the caller said, "But I can't get through then. Just keep me on hold."

Our former boss, Len Deibert adds, "Like Johnny, Ken was always supportive of what WMAL was trying to do, and he'd go anywhere, and talk with anyone, anytime. There may have been sports talk on Washington radio before Ken, but he set the standard."

Beatrice would brag to me about the number of phone calls he received in his office. (Make that "our" office, since we shared it.) He'd especially stress his number of requests for speaking engagements. I figured out a way to gently annoy him. I took to asking him how many calls he was getting, and then waited for him to give me a number.

"There were 46 calls last night before I went on the air."

"Really, Ken? I had 56 calls this morning," I'd reply.

Or I'd hear him complaining about being overextended with both a luncheon and a dinner engagement the same day. (You see? He'd already given me a number.) I'd sympathize with him.

"I know how you feel, Ken. I have three gigs today. A breakfast, lunch, *and* dinner engagement."

At some point he probably caught on to my game, because he quit giving me numbers.

What he never quit doing was going overboard in trying to impress listeners with his wisdom. He didn't have to do that. Eventually, people began to call in with phony questions. Ken, in turn, would give elaborate answers to their queries, not realizing that the listeners were putting him on.

A classic case was the night sportswriter Morrie Segal phoned in as "Joe from Bethesda." Morrie sounded like he had several drinks under his belt when he asked Ken what he thought about a linebacker with South Dakota State Community College. Ken went on to describe the player and share what he liked and didn't like about the South Dakota team.

The problem was no such linebacker existed because there was no South Dakota State Community College.

On another occasion, I was driving back from RFK stadium following a WMAL play-by-play broadcast of a Washington Federals USFL game. My color analyst, Ken McQuilken, a former Redskins quarterback, was in the passenger seat. Ken and I tuned in to Beatrice's show. Ken was already analyzing the game. His commentary sounded like he had been *at* the stadium.

McQuilken and I started to get really ticked off, because we understood that everything Beatrice was saying had come from our broadcast because the game wasn't televised. Beatrice had been stuck in his studio. And he wasn't giving us any credit.

I called Ken later and asked, "Did you ever think to give us some acknowledgment? That would have been the decent thing to do."

Beatrice told me he thought he had done so, but I wasn't buying it. He didn't have to pretend that he saw every game. How could he be in a radio studio every night and expect people to believe he was at all the games?

Pretty soon I'd start to hear folks doing Ken Beatrice impressions—much like folks would do Howard Cosell—mimicking Ken's high, clipped, very Boston "Good evening," or "Beyond belief." The Beatrice voice got to be a local in joke, especially at many of the area bars where the media folks would hang their tabs.

Finally, Tony Kornheiser wrote an expose in the *Washington Post,* and the joke was over. His piece left Ken badly shaken.

> **An excerpt:** *"The story people at WMAL tell about Beatrice concerns an alleged scouting trip he made a few years ago to a Wisconsin-Illinois football game.*
>
> *"Beatrice allegedly told someone he was going to Madison, Wis., to see the game, that some of his scouts would join him there. On Monday, two days after the game, Beatrice was asked how he'd enjoyed Madison and the game, and he, as the story goes, said both were great.*
>
> *"In fact, the game was played in Illinois."*

By the way, I had the pleasure of helping Tony break into radio when we cohosted some Redskins pregame shows together. Management broke us up because they felt we weren't taking the job seriously enough. Tony can see something funny in almost everything. It was a good move splitting us up. Look where he is today: Doing nationally syndicated shows on ESPN radio and television and writing best-selling books. His latest is *Back for More Cash.*

After Tony's expose, WMAL suggested that Beatrice take six weeks off to try and get it together. Mary Clare suggested that we invite the Beatrices over for dinner.

"For what?" I asked.

"Just to be nice," Clare said.

So I called him up. "Ken, we'd like to invite you and your wife over to sit around and B.S. Just a quiet evening for dinner and relaxation."

He declined because he said he had too many speaking engagements.

I ended up feeling sorry for him. The saddest thing is that he really was a great entertainer. He knew his stuff and had flair.

Ken recently came out of retirement to do a Redskins review on station WBIG, "Big 100." I'm glad for him. This town will never see another Ken Beatrice.

It is a pleasure to recall the other talented staff I came to know during my 12 years at WMAL. Bill Mayhugh, for example, really stands out in my mind. It seemed like everybody listened to Bill's overnight music show. He was just about as smooth as they came. I was always amazed that he could do so many things with so little sleep.

For example, Bill would sign off just before 6:00 a.m., and do a luncheon at noon for the Red Cross. He'd return that evening after midnight and tell his listeners not only about the luncheon but also about his afternoon golf game with the Shah of Iran, or whoever else happened to be in town that day. I took pride in doing a lot of things, but Bill's schedule, by comparison, made it look like I wasn't doing anything at all.

Tom Gauger, who is now my coworker at ABC News, was one of the best radio personalities in Washington. He was just as good at playing the hits as he was handling his 11:45 a.m. feature about area theatre events.

Mac MacGarry, the longtime host of TV's *It's Academic*, a high school quiz show, was at WMAL on Sundays playing big band music. Eddie Walker jokes that Mac "always did the first hour of his show standing up," as a funny reference to his *It's Academic* pose. Eddie did his popular "Play it Again, Ed" show from eight to one on Sundays. Eddie's format of big band music and radio nostalgia was the highest rated weekend show at WMAL for many years.

Another fine WMAL personality was John Lyon. The city was grief-stricken in 1975 when John's young daughters disappeared while walking to a suburban shopping center. They vanished and were never found. I was always amazed at how strong John and his wife, Mary, were during this tragedy. Everybody admired how John and Mary held up during this ordeal. I don't know how they did it. Today, John heads up a support group in Montgomery County, Maryland, for others who have lost family members.

I would say that WMAL was the last of the great Washington radio stations. Today, many of the shows are syndicated. Andy Parks, Charlie Warren, and Chris Core continue the local programming tradition.

Chris Core: "Over the years I had a chance to work with Johnny as he filled in for Bill Trumbull a couple of times, and he let me do a walk-on part at the Harlequin dinner theater. I also got a short tryout with the Radio Oneders until he realized I am just terrible at softball.

"Which brings me to this point: how can it be that a guy who is as athletic as Johnny can be as terrible as he is at golf? He might be the only guy I can beat.

"It has been a great honor to work with Johnny over the years. I guess I will always remember him coming into the station in the afternoon to do his ABC sports reports with his daughter Moira. She was about five then, and cute as a button. The love for her was so obvious in Johnny's eye. One day years later when I was ushering my own five-year-old daughter around the station, I stopped for a second to think: 'Ah, this is what it felt like to Johnny back then.'

"Rock? Ok. Jock? Sure. But Dad first."

I think that if Eddie Walker, Bill Trumble, Tom Gauger, Bill Mayhugh, John Lyon, and I were on a station like WMAL today, the station would be successful. We might not be number one, two, or three, but the owners would make money.

Why? Because you'd have highly identifiable personalities who had deeply integrated into the community. It is the community identity that is sorely lacking on many of the stations today. You hear a voice but not a personality.

And what about the audience over 40? They shouldn't just drop off the end of the earth. I tell Eddie Walker that it will happen. He'll be back.

Wait a minute. He is back. Ed hosts that Big Broadcast on WAMU 88.5 on Sunday nights.

A very short time after I arrived at WMAL, Andy pulled me aside to let me know they were thinking about changing the evening lineup. It seemed that Felix Grant's long-running "Album Jazz" show was slipping in the ratings. Andy thought I might be a good replacement.

However, audience feedback was passionately negative when word went out that WMAL was planning to retire Felix Grant. It turned into a community uproar. "What are you doing?" listeners phoned in. "Felix Grant is a legend. You cannot replace him. Has WMAL lost its mind?" Letters poured in. The local newspapers strongly endorsed Felix.

Some suspected that people who never even listened to Felix were determined to keep him on the air. His legacy was that strong.

I watched the situation for a week. The backlash was so intense that I told Andy, "Look, I'd rather wait. It's OK with me not to do this evening show. I'll bide my time. I don't want to be the guy who's in there trying to take the place of Felix Grant."

Luckily, the listeners weren't taking shots at me. They were taking shots at the station for even thinking of replacing Felix. I told Andy to change his mind. "You'll make some friends by reversing this decision." The station agreed and backed down.

When Felix started his first job at $37.50 a week for WWDC in the 1940s, everything was live. Tape didn't exist, and only the music was recorded. All the commercials were scripted. For sports, there were no actualities to go to. No other sounds but the announcer's dominant voice. This is one of the reasons for the need for different kinds of voices early on.

Felix was the complete professional. I almost wanted to call him "Mr. Grant" as I was so awed in his presence. He had a smooth, distinctive voice that was heard on D.C. airwaves for over 45 years—30 of which were on his "Album Sound" jazz show at WMAL. He drove a red Thunderbird convertible and was always dapper, dressed in suit and tie. Someone at the station once joked that Felix was so suave that he farted Old Spice.

He was also meticulous with his impressive personal collection of jazz records, now housed at the University of the District of Columbia. He's been credited for introducing bossa nova and reggae music to American audiences. He'd wheel the records he selected for airplay into the studio in a small grocery cart. Sometimes I'd find records in my box that he thought I'd like.

The engineers were always getting lectures on the proper way to handle his prized discs. One engineer got fed up with the nagging and took one of Grant's more valuable records and secretly replaced it with an old public service announcement disc. When Felix turned to cue the song, the engineer "accidentally" dropped it on the floor and rolled his chair over it. Felix nearly had a hemorrhage.

Anyone who knew Felix well will tell you he was a loner. He had an apartment with his wife in the Watergate. Some tenants thought the floor might cave in from the weight of his record collection. Felix came and went each night with his little grocery cart and rarely socialized with the radio crew.

In 1983, my coauthor, Steve, sat in with Felix during his show and taped the following candid conversation. The single interview question was "How did you get started, and what is Felix Grant all about?" Never before published, it's the most personal account of his life that I've seen:

> **Felix Grant:** "I first saw Washington, D.C. during World War II. I was in naval boot camp in Baltimore and got a 17-hour pass. I hopped a train on a Sunday morning and walked the concourse out of Union Station, and there was the Capitol. I couldn't believe it. There was no television in those days, so you didn't see the kinds of pictures of Washington that people are very used to today. I walked the Mall and took in the Washington monument, the Lincoln Memorial, and ended up in a little beer joint called Brownlees.
>
> "The second visit was in 1944, but by that time I had spent a few years at sea in a couple of hair-raising war adventures including getting sunk by a torpedo in the Pacific. The navy had chosen me to give speeches for the War Plan Tour, as they considered me one of their war heroes. It seemed that many of the folks working in the plants were getting bored in what looked like dead-end jobs. Many were drinking and losing faith that their work was meaningful. Collectively, they were slowing down the war effort. So I went out with some other war survivors to give some evidence, some incentive that they shouldn't quit. It was effective.
>
> "My commander was Jack Egan. Jack had been a road manager for the Tommy Dorsey Band, a former editor for *Downbeat Magazine*, and had lots of public relations experience. He befriended me and helped me do a miniscule amount of radio work for a Coast Guard service program on WWDC.

"Then the war abruptly ended. We heard about the 'Adem' bomb. That's how I thought it was spelled—A-D-E-M—but I couldn't conceive of what they were talking about. I had all the points I needed to get out of the service, and with a cheek in the door of radio, I decided to try for a job and made the rounds of the six stations in D.C. I got an offer at the old WINX—part-time—for $19 a week. Here was a job I wanted more than anything else in the world, but I had to turn it down. It was physically impossible to live in Washington on $19 a week. It really hurt me to give that one up.

"My mother had a big apartment in New York City, so I had a place to go and to sleep. It wouldn't cost me anything, so I was packing my things in my rooming house on a Friday morning, getting ready to head to NYC, when the phone started ringing. In rooming houses in those days the phone always seemed to be on another floor from where your room was. It kept ringing, so I thought I might as well go downstairs and answer it, although it won't be for me.

"But it was. WWDC was asking me if I was still looking for a job. I got palpitations as the guy wanted to know when I could start? He said come on over in the morning—Saturday—and we'll assign you something. I couldn't believe it. That phone call really changed my life, and changed the life, I guess, of a lot of other people who have listened to the music on my radio shows over the years.

"WWDC got me off on the right foot. I became more interested in jazz and could take in the shows at the Capitol and Howard theatres, or in the many jazz clubs sprouting up on U Street. I found I loved the entertainment and the lifestyle. In a matter of six months everybody in town knew me because there were only six radio stations. I was so pleased with working in Washington that I never applied for any jobs in New York City throughout my career.

"I worked at WWDC until 1953 and then came over to WMAL, primarily because they also had a new TV studio, and it seemed to me that they had more potential than the other stations. I even took a salary cut—from $120 to $60 a week—to make the switch. I was sure that I'd make out better in the long run, and it turned out to be the smartest move I ever made.

"*The Evening Star* newspaper owned WMAL, and it took me awhile to figure out that the *Star* management was very paternalistic. And I don't mean that negatively. They felt an employee was an integral part of the whole structure of the organization, and they didn't put any super pressures on me. When I wanted to do something different, they'd give me enough rope to disappear over the horizon before they would ever cut it. And even then they'd have reservations—like maybe he's 'out of sight.'

"When I started doing [my jazz program] in 1955, I would play Ray Charles, Dinah Washington, and lots of acts that had never before been played on Washington radio. There were some serious questions raised. I got more crap from rednecks calling me on the phone and complaining. Before my show, WMAL listeners had not been in the habit of hearing Billy Holliday and Louis Armstrong. Many didn't want those voices in their homes. But I never mentioned any of this on the air. I didn't share the criticisms with my listeners. I ran a one-man show and have continued for so long that I just felt I'm responsible for what I play, and so be it.

"Playing jazz on the radio is not the easiest thing in the world. You're always looked on as the oddball. Also the thing that has confused a lot of people is that I always spoke English. I always hated the flip, finger-snapping kind of radio jargon, like 'hey man, what's happening?' One of the guys here at the station tells the story about me—a story that never happened. He said, 'Yeah, I heard Felix introduce the song "It Does Not Mean a Thing if It Does Not Have that Swing."' When I heard that story it made me sound like some kind of prig or ass in some respects. I didn't like the comment.

"A woman once wrote to me that she wasn't really very fond of the music I played, but she loved listening to my show. I thought, 'Gee, imagine listening every night to something you don't particularly like.' That was kind of interesting.

"I have to be very careful so that the radio management doesn't misunderstand me, or that it looks like they have no control over what I say or play. It's their radio station and they allow me to be on the air. They tried to fire me four years ago, but it backfired on them. They thought they would withstand the flack, but the outcry at the time was so strong that they gave in. The public relations and the media made it look sensational. But if they really wanted me off, they would do it. Everybody can be replaced." (Oct 25, 1983)

WMAL did replace Felix Grant with John Lyon and Eddie Walker a year later. Eddie recalls, "I wouldn't have done it unless Felix was permanently fired. They were grooming John and me for the morning team, because we thought Harden and Weaver were going to retire. But the station was sold, and Andy Ockershausen went instead. So that never happened."

Some of the most enjoyable things I've done at WMAL were the Christmas Eve broadcasts from the Kennedy Center. These were free concerts with all the station personalities taking part. Joining us were local choirs and hometown performers. Tom Gauger started the tradition as emcee. John Lyon picked it up after Tom left WMAL and I did the hosting in my last years at the station.

Moira Holliday and her first grade class from the Stone Ridge Country Day School of the Sacred Heart in Bethesda, Maryland performed with me at the first concert. We did the shows together for the following six years. WABC in New York would pick the shows up as well.

WMAL started inviting me back a few years ago. Moira and I brought out all five grandsons, JT Smaldore, 12, his brother Devin, 7, and the three Rolle brothers, Christopher, 9, Nicholas, 7, and Jack, 4. Their bit was to sing the refrain "Merry Christmas to you." I told the audience that the last time I performed here we only had one grandson.

Last Christmas, Chris Core hosted the Kennedy Center show. "Pop" Holliday returned with his grandsons singing, "Do You Hear What I Hear?" It's no surprise the kids totally upstaged me. Next year I'll include my newest grandson, Anthony Vincent, Kellie's third, born April 7, 2002.

Michael Terrance is my pianist for personal performances like these. Mary Clare heard Michael play at a brunch at the Hyatt in Bethesda years ago and asked him to play for our daughters' weddings. We've been together ever since. You can probably best catch Terrance at the Le Canard in Vienna Virginia. He's very good.

Every time I go to the Kennedy Center I run into Bobby Lewis. Now he's the stage manager there, but I knew Bobby long before that job.

Bobby was a senior with the North Carolina Tar Heels when they made the Final Four in 1967. He scored 31 points in the championship game, losing to Dayton. Lewis was a first-round pick for the San Francisco Warriors. I was the PA announcer for the Warriors when Bobby turned Pro in 1967.

In 1977, I began a two-year association with the George Washington University Colonials basketball program. The GW games were broadcast on WINX-AM, not the best outlet, but at least we were on the air. One of the station personalities on the air at the time was Bruce Allen, now a top-flight news anchor on D.C.'s all-news station, WTOP.

GW assistant athletic director Bernie Swain was my color analyst for the first year, followed by Brian Magid, a standout player who had transferred from Maryland. Magid had been one of the best players to come out of Montgomery Blair High School. He was known for his long-range shots and could light 'em up from anywhere on court. GW's head coach was Bob Tallent, who was one of the all-time leading scorers at GW in his senior year. Bob averaged 28 points a game.

Tallent had been a WWDC Oneder, so I was among friends at GW. One of his biggest Colonial victories came against the Terps at Cole Field House in 1976. GW beat them 86-76 in a game that saw John Holloran score 38 points against Lefty Dreisell's team.

The next year GW knocked off the Terrapins 101-90 at GW's Smith Center. John Holoran would later suit up for our WMAL Radio Oneders.

After Andy Ockershausen left the station, WMAL started lopping off all their good talent. Then they dropped Maryland University sports after 22 years. WMAL was ending its association with the Terps.

Evidently, the station management couldn't come to terms with Jefferson Pilot, the outfit that syndicated the Maryland games. WRC picked up the Maryland contract for three years, and WMAL signed a one-year agreement with Navy. I had a decision to make.

Sugar Ray Leonard's advisor and attorney, Mike Trainer, agreed to negotiate a package for me with Maryland.

I took a lunch meeting with Jack Lengle, athletic director at the Naval Academy, and Jim Gallant. WMAL had informed Lengle that I would be doing Navy games. This made me uncomfortable, since I hadn't reached a decision. Still, Lengle was pleased that I might be doing Navy.

After the lunch, I called him.

"Jack, I need to be honest with you. I've been thinking about this, and there's a chance I may be leaving WMAL. Don't put out a press release yet."

I had a vacation planned so I left for Florida. The vacation was less than enjoyable because I had this dilemma hanging over my head. Should I stay at the best radio station in the city, but be without my favorite activity, Maryland University sports? Or do I leave WMAL and give up 12 years built in? Either way I'd keep my freelance commercial and theatre work.

I went back and forth on this for days. On a Monday I was convinced I should remain at WMAL and be part of Navy's very classy organization. The next day, I'd think no way. I have to leave WMAL and continue doing the Maryland games. It was back and forth throughout the week.

Then Maryland athletic director Andy Geiger let me know that Maryland wanted to keep their association with me. Bingo. That did it. I could work *for* the University of Maryland and continue my sports shows on ABC. Then and there, the right choice was obvious.

Mike Trainer gave me good advice. "If you're going to resign WMAL, just walk in and do it. Don't hang around, because they'll try to talk you into staying."

When I handed in my resignation letter to Tom Bresnahan, I added at the bottom:

"PS—Please get some new typewriters for your people, will you?"

Leonard Shapiro at the *Washington Post* noted the event on July 11, 1991:

> *"Sportscaster Johnny Holliday will end his 12-year association with WMAL Radio today with a letter of resignation that will allow him to continue as the voice of University of Maryland athletics. 'It's been 12 great years,' Holliday said last night. 'I'm leaving to pursue other radio and television opportunities, but the association with Maryland is the bottom line here. They wanted me to stay with them, and I wanted to stay too.'"*

Years later Tom Bresnahan welcomed Maryland sports back on WMAL. Tom was there when they bounced us, and he was there to bring us back. What goes around comes around.

Chapter 10

Fear the Turtle

"Johnny and I are friends first, and then he's the announcer and I'm the coach. I've been with John for 13 years, and he gives the program an identifiable voice that many people depend on for access to Maryland basketball. I think that people like the idea that they have a 'name' that was famous around Washington before he did Maryland basketball. You want everything to be first class anytime you run a basketball program at this level. Johnny certainly gives us that first-class announcer connection."
Coach Gary Williams, *University Of Maryland*

Big sports have changed during my career. That's for sure. There's too much emphasis today on the money. The bucks are so big it's ridiculous. Big corporations run it all now. They're going to price themselves right out of business one of these days. And the fans are the ones getting the shaft when you figure the ticket prices, the parking, the food, and the souvenirs. The average family of four can't afford to do it. The fans have to foot the bill for the enormous salaries these players are getting. I know that nothing ever remains the same, but I'd like to see them play more for the love of the game. Fortunately, some of them do, but the 13th man on the bench doesn't have to worry much about the game if he's getting a million bucks just to sit there.

This is why I like and prefer the college games. Families can afford to go out and enjoy the contests. It's not going to bust you for one night. College games are the best entertainment value for your dollar, as they are almost always exciting and unpredictable.

For me, October couldn't come quick enough in the 2001-02 season. Although it would mark the final games at historical Cole Field House before moving to the new Comcast center, I knew this Maryland team wanted to finish at Cole undefeated. And that's exactly what they did. A perfect 15-0 season.

The 2000-01 basketball season had ended March 31 in Minneapolis with a heartbreaking loss to Duke in the Terps' first Final Four appearance. I shared the same feeling of helplessness with every other Maryland supporter. I wished there was something I could have done to help Gary and his team get to that Monday night championship game.

"You are only as good as your last game" is something Gary Williams has always preached to his players. "What have you done for me now?" is how Gary puts it to his team. Gary was extremely disappointed to have lost the opportunity to play that championship game, but, on the other hand, very proud of what his players did accomplish.

Gary had a great comment after the 2001 Duke loss when he said that if Maryland couldn't do it, he was glad a team from our conference could. All of this points out how difficult it is to win an ACC championship. It shows what a strong league the Atlantic Coast Conference really is.

However, each player who returned for the 2001-02 season made it their goal to not only return to the Final Four, but to win it.

Not only did the Terrapins win, they did so in an impressive fashion with teamwork, dedication, and a sense of purpose that I've never experienced in the 22 Maryland teams I've covered. Seniors Juan Dixon, Lonny Baxter, Byron Mouton, Earl Badu led by example, and Steve Blake, Taj Holden, Drew Nicholas, Chris Wilcox, and Calvin McCall had gotten their taste of the Final Four and wanted desperately to win it the second time around. Newcomers Ryan Randle, Mike Grinnon, and Andre Collins would be fortunate enough to share the amazing journey.

For the first time ever, the Maryland Terrapins advanced to the NCAA Tournament in 2002 as the number-one seed. The Terps opened up at Washington, D.C.'s MCI Center with victories over Sienna and Wisconsin, and then it was on to Atlanta, site of the Final Four, for a second consecutive year. Maryland was also the only team in the nation to advance to the Elite Eight for their past two seasons.

In the semifinals, the Terps defeated Kansas 97-88 behind a career-high 33 points from senior Juan Dixon. I've witnessed some outstanding individual efforts from players over the years, but I'm hardpressed to come up with a better showing that Juan put on that night in the Georgia Dome.

On Monday night, April 1, the Terrapins showed the world they weren't fooling around when they took the floor with a school record of 31 victories to face an Indiana team that surprised the experts by beating Oklahoma.

As the final seconds ticked off in the Terps' 64-52 victory over the Hoosiers, I found it very difficult to deal with the emotions of broadcasting a championship game. After all, it doesn't happen that often, and many broadcasters never experience this thrill. I thought of the many coaches and players who had gone before us, paving the way along the road we had traveled this season. Gary Williams's coach at Maryland, Bud Millikan, and coaches Frank Fellows and Lefty Driesell. Players such as Gene Shue, Len Elmore, John Lucas, Tom McMillan, Joe Smith, Walt Williams, Len Bias, Keith Booth, Steve Francis, Greg Manning, Buck Williams, Albert King, Ernest Graham, and Adrian Branch. None of these had experienced a Final Four.

But nine players, Coach Williams, and I had the thrill of back-to-back Final Four appearances in basketball and football seasons that saw Maryland become the first school in history to earn outright ACC championships in both sports. And to top that off, Gary Williams and Juan Dixon *and* Ralph Freidgen and E.J. Henderson swept the Coach and Player of the Year awards in both sports, as well. Wow.

The impact of this will be felt for years to come. I heard from colleagues from all over the country. One in particular was Bob Harris, the long-time voice of the Duke Blue Devils. Harris had been to the top with Duke and I had always wondered what it felt like. My partner, Chris Knoche, and I certainly found out. And you know what? I like it. It's a feeling I want to have again and again.

Then there was the welcome-home celebration at Cole the day we arrived back from Atlanta. Twelve thousand fans showed up to salute their new champions. To emcee that event was so special, and it was difficult for all of us to control our emotions. The look on the players' faces was priceless. How do you describe happiness and exhaustion all rolled up into one package?

For Gary Williams the long road to a national championship had ended. It took him 24 years at the collegiate level—13 at his alma mater—but he made it. He had accomplished something that no other basketball coach at Maryland had done.

Gary Williams grew up in Collingswood, New Jersey, where he lettered four years straight in high school basketball and baseball (and he also listened to WRC sports announcer George Michael, when George was a rock jock on WFIL in Philadelphia). Gary lettered again at Maryland as point guard and captain under head coach Bud Millikin.

Up against South Carolina in '66, Gary was a perfect 8 for 8 from the field, and it was during his college days that he developed his preference for the full-court pressure defenses that his Terrapins now bring into play. The swift-breaking offense that you see in today's Maryland team is not unlike the offense that Vic Bubas's Duke teams used against the Terps when Gary was competing on the court.

I first met Gary in 1980 when he coached some remarkable teams at American University. I remember him as extremely enthusiastic on the sidelines. He was really into the game and completely pumped up every time his team took the court. From AU he went off to coach Boston College and from there to Ohio State University.

June 13, 1989 was the day the turnaround really began for the Maryland basketball program. That's the day Gary was hired to come back to his Alma mater to coach the Terrapins. Gary was at a university dinner event when I approached his table with my congratulations, telling him how excited I thought everybody was to see him return to Maryland to get the program back on track.

I immediately knew that Gary Williams would restore the Terrapins to respectability. He was as intense and competitive as ever. His desire to win was extremely high. Everything just pointed toward success.

Gary's record certainly speaks for itself. He has done two things that no other coach in the history of Maryland basketball could do, and that is to take his team to the Final Four and follow up the next year with an NCAA championship. Maryland basketball is finally on top under Williams's guidance.

He took a team that had been suffering after Lefty Driesell was let go. A team that was put on probation for violations and couldn't appear on television when Bob Wade took over for a couple of years. And, from there, consecutive NCAA appearances, the first Final Four ever in the school's history, and the 2002 NCAA championship—all because of Gary Williams.

Former Maryland sports information director Jack Zane walked into Cole early one day just after Gary was hired. Jack saw Gary leaning up against the rail looking down at the court.

"Are you reminiscing about the old days?" asked Jack.

"No," said Gary. "I'm just concentrating on the things we have to do."

For the past 13 years I've been with Gary on radio and television shows each week. And what a run it's been. I could have written this entire book on what Gary has done for the program—his wins, his presence, his leadership, and how he has so favorably represented the University of Maryland.

There's something else I've noticed about Gary: He always gives great credit to his assistant coaches. Billy Hahn, for example, had been with him for 12 years before he took the head coaching job at LaSalle. Former Terp Matt Kovarak took Hahn's place on the staff. Jimmy Patsos, a three-year varsity letter winner in his own playing days at Catholic University, has been an assistant coach at Maryland for 10 years, and Dave Dickerson, a '89 Maryland alum, has also been with Gary for seven years. Director of basketball operations Troy Wainwright is also in his seventh year. Basketball trainer J.J. Bush has been at Maryland for 28 years, as Gary's trainer for 13. Strength coach Kurtis Shultz played for Gary in '95 and has done one tremendous job keeping the Terps in tip-top shape.

Gary also gives credit to a couple of players who really helped turn the program around when Maryland was struggling. Walt Williams, now in the NBA, stuck around for his senior year when he could have gone to the Pros a year earlier, to play for Gary. The school has noted Walt's loyalty to the program as one reason Maryland was able to recruit competitive teams during his playing days. Walt would go on to the Sacramento Kings upon graduation, in the first round of the college draft.

Another NBA player, Tony Massenburg, stayed with the Terps as well. These are just two guys who decided they could get better under Gary. He's produced All-Americans like Joe Smith, Steve Francis, and Michael Adams, who played at Boston College with Gary. The list goes on.

In person or on TV, most people see a coach who puts every ounce of energy into the game he's coaching. They see a man with disheveled hair in a suit soaked with perspiration, roving the sidelines, defending his players to the officials, questioning calls, and getting on his players when they aren't performing to his expectations. That's the picture most people have of Gary.

I see that side of him, but I also see a guy who loves his university, loves his players, and is loyal to a fault to those around him. Frankly, I find a coach who is hard to believe. Sensitive. Compassionate. His whole life and personality are wrapped up around the basketball program.

What's his down side? I've seen him get mad at other people. Some members of the media have experienced his wrath. If anything has hurt him over the years, it has been some articles in the local media about Gary not being able to get his team to the Sweet Sixteen. Well, he proved them all wrong.

Gary also has a great sense of humor. If Gary Williams doesn't want you around, or if he is not a big fan of yours, then he won't trade one-liners and jokes with you. But he is always accommodating to everybody. From the folks in the smallest city on the map of Maryland, to those at the highest level, Gary is gracious to all of them. He was typically generous when I asked him for the following contribution about our relationship when I first began this book.

Gary Williams: "You like to think that you will improve over time as a coach, and I'm sure it's the same with announcers. Johnny works at this. He knows me, the players, and our style of play. For our fans it's a very comfortable thing because they know Johnny is very thorough and he prepares. Fans know he's the Maryland announcer, but they also know he's not a 'homer' and that every call against the Terps won't be reported as a 'bad call.' Although I don't get a chance to listen to his broadcasts, obviously, I do know that many of my friends turn the radio on when they watch the games on TV and listen to John's play-by-play.

"Working with Johnny on my TV show makes my life a lot easier, because it is during the season and a very hectic time when we tape the show [right after the games]. Johnny is very relaxed. He can wing it really well. He asks questions that draw me into the discussion and take me to the things I want to talk about.

"In all the time we have worked together we have never had a blow-up or disagreement. We both understand that we have to do certain things as coach and announcer. So we have been able to maintain that professional relationship, as well as our close personal friendship. For the TV show, we are comfortable now, so we can kid around but still get to the main business at hand. This is where his radio background serves us so well. He has a great sense of timing. I never have to worry about talking too long, because he'll give me a look, and I know it's time to cut it off.

"In the early basketball season, he's still doing the football games, but he's never missed a broadcast even with his amazing schedule. Sometimes we'll be flying back from a road game and won't arrive at Cole Field House until 2:00 a.m., but then John is in the ABC studios at 5:00 a.m. doing his sports broadcasts. I'm sure he gets tired sometimes, but he seems to thrive on it. Johnny likes the action. He's so well rounded with the other things he does, like the summer stock theatre—and I do kid John about his rock and roll days—but I believe that the sports part of his life keeps him in tune with the times. As we all get older this is a nice thing to have when you're dealing with the younger players. It's a good way to keep current.

"The basketball players can talk to him. Many people lose that ability to relate to young kids, but Johnny has it. They really like 'Mr. Holliday.' He also does some funny things with them, especially around Christmas time. For example, he asked Chris Wilcox on the air what he was planning to give me for Christmas. Chris replied, 'I don't know, but I wish the coach would give me his car.'

"The biggest thing about Johnny, in both the TV show and doing the games, is that he is a very positive person. He doesn't criticize other players or coaches, but he does give an accurate account. You feel that he isn't out to hurt anybody. He doesn't have a personal agenda. And he's always there for us."

Gary doesn't head straight for the locker room when the games are over like previous coaches. He wants to talk to the fans—right at courtside—after the game. At the new Comcast Center, as was the case at Cole Field House, our postgame conversations are carried—not only on the radio—but also to the thousands of fans in the arena. Fans who stick around hear what he'll have to say. No other broadcasters in the ACC, and very few in the nation, do live interviews with the coach—with the sound piped into the arena—immediately after a game.

This immediacy can be a problem, because when you lose, it's hard. It amazes me that sometimes he's at his best after a difficult game—win or lose. Of course, I have the good sense not to ask him ridiculous, off-the-wall questions, like "What happened?" or "Why did you lose?" After so many years now with Gary, I think I've learned when I can push him for information and when I should back off.

Usually, I'll give him a setup line. For example, if Maryland got beat by four points, and they led to the last minute and then let it slip away, I'll open the conversation with, "Hey, Gary, man, this was a tough one," and let Gary take it and go on from there.

"Yes, John, it was tough, but we're going to learn something…"

I suggested to Gary some years ago that if it were possible, we should get a player on the postgame show after a win? "Absolutely," he said. So now after Maryland victories, Gary will have the featured player on first.

We tape our coach's TV shows every Thursday morning from the center of the arena. Comcast SportsNet airs the show the following Saturday at 11:00 a.m. Gary doesn't know what I'm going to say before the show, and neither do I. Sometimes if we're having a good time, we can talk about anything. If you have a satellite dish, you can see the show all over the country.

We do make sure that all the players get a chance to be on during the season at least once. Gary feels this helps the players hone their interview skills, and it's great for the fans. I think the people who see the show appreciate Gary as more than just a basketball coach. It isn't just X's, O's, and highlights. They see the sparkle in his eye and the more human side of the coach.

Senior night—the seniors' last game at their school—can be emotional for any coach, and Gary's no exception. He really loves his players. There have been postgame shows after some big wins where he's been on the verge of tears, but he catches himself. One particularly emotional moment came during a Friends of Gary dinner.

The Friends of Gary Williams (F.O.G.) are a group of heavy hitters like Bob Mitchell, Marv Perry, John Brown, John Rymer, Charley Castle, Jack Heise, Bob Bodell, Ed Downey, Irv Raffle, and many others who support the basketball program and stand behind what Gary does both personally and financially. The F.O.G. honored the coach at a reception a few years back in the Congressional Country Club. His daughter Kristin surprised Gary by bringing his new infant grandson David to the affair. I had the honor of reading the following tribute letter, which F.O.G. addressed to the baby. When I read the letter, I saw Gary cover his eyes with a napkin. He was either hiding his tears, or there were heavy onions in the salad.

May 31, 2000

Dear David,

Tonight at Congressional Country Club in Bethesda, Maryland, your grandfather, Gary Williams, is being honored for his career coaching achievements. Specifically, we are celebrating his 400th anniversary. It was on November 17, 1999, in Cole Field House, that the University of Maryland defeated the University of San Francisco. It was sensational.

Actually, the entire season was quite sensational! It was supposed to have been a rebuilding year for your grandfather since he lost four of his five starters from the year before. His starting five now consisted of only one junior, three sophomores, and a freshman point guard. This lack of experience in the Atlantic Coast Conference was considered a recipe for disaster. Not so for your grandfather. He ended this so-called "rebuilding season" with an ACC record of 11-5 and a spectacular overall record of 22-7 and his seventh consecutive invitation to the postseason NCAA tournament.

On this special occasion celebrating your grandfather's spectacular number of victories and his remarkable season, his friends wish to honor him by establishing an educational trust fund in your name.

David, by the time you are old enough to read and understand this letter and gift, you will already be aware of the many, many triumphs of your grandfather. You will know and have read all about his records and accomplishments. He is, without a doubt, one of the top coaches in the country. At this stage of his career, his achievements are legendary even though there are still many more to come. However, your grandfather's achievements at the University are even more than basketball victories. And what you cannot read and understand through his record victories is what kind of a person he really is.

This group tonight are your grandfather's close personal friends. We know him as our friend Gary. We love him on and off the basketball court.

We see the big grin on his face when he talks about "his little David" and we saw the immense pride on his face when your mother introduced him upon his induction into the Maryland Sports Hall of Fame. He had tears in his eyes.

We also see your grandfather choke up over anything the least bit sentimental directed towards him. He likes to evoke the New Jersey tough guy image, but to those of us that know better, this is not your grandfather. Your grandfather is a warm, giving, generous, and caring individual.

We see his sincerity in the inordinate amount of time and energy he spends on charities such as Coaches for Cancer, the Cystic Fibrosis Foundation, and his annual golf tournament.

We see his devotion to the Terrapin Club through his constant attendance at functions throughout the nation. We see his willingness to be first in line to represent the university in meeting with prospective donors.

My sister Charlene, father "JC," mother Dorothy, and yours truly in 1947. We were "America's Average Family," according to the *Miami News*. I hoped this wasn't true.

On our wedding day. Note Mary Clare's spit curls and my perfectly coifed pompadour.

My first promotional DJ photo. (WVRN, Rochester, NY, August 1957)

All photos courtesy of the personal collection of Johnny Holliday except where noted.

Meeting the Monkees with fellow KYA jock Chris Edwards. I'd later tour with them and Tommy Boyce and Bobby Hart. Mike Nesmith was my favorite.

The Oakland Athletics elected Sal Bando captain because he stood up for all the things they needed. He wasn't afraid of agitating management. I'm proud to call Sal a close friend.

The 1967 KYA-Radio Oneders, (front row, l to r) Sean O'Callaghan, Tom Sgro, Bud O'Shea, me, Ed Hider, Don Delbon; (back row) Owen Kashveroff, Jim Myers, Norman Goldsmith, Rick Barry, Don Novitsky, Phill Prusky, and Mike Orlich (John Madden's high school coach). Our record was 59 and 1. Rick Barry missed one game. Which one do you think it was?

It's A Holliday Every Morning

With Johnny Holliday And Friends

Mon.-Sat.　WWDC　6-10 a.m.
101 FM 1260 AM

1972 WWDC promo, (l to r) Guido, Billy Biceps, the real me, Howard C, and the Eastern Union Singing Telegraph Company.

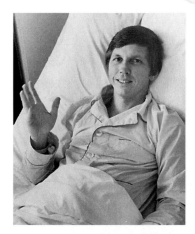

People who were aware of the conditions that night, and who saw the smashed plane, later told me that they didn't see how we survived the crash. Here I am on the road to recovery at Sibley hospital.

Sr. Marie Louise. She proved she could call football games better than Dan Rather, Maureen Bunyan, Sugar Ray Leonard, William Shatner, Pee-Wee Herman, the Temptations, and Sonny Jurgensen.

With Hall of Famer Joe DiMaggio, the Yankee Clipper.

Clowning around with fellow Radio Oneder and Redskins quarterback Joe Theismann. He's wearing my glasses.

Talking Maryland football with Ralph Friedgen on our Orange Bowl preview coaches' TV show.

I could have written this entire book on what Coach Gary Williams has done for Maryland basketball—his wins, his presence, his leadership—and how he has so favorably represented the University.

Pregame interview with Redskin coach Joe Gibbs. I did the pregame show on WMAL radio for 12 years.

Introducing Howard Cosell at an NFL Players association MDA benefit. I was always blown away when Howard would do the ABC Olympic reports without a note in front of him. "That's the way you do a show," he'd tell me.

Glenn Brenner was the best TV sportscaster in D.C. history. (l to r) Bob Ferry, former NBA player and Washington Bullets GM, Glenn Brenner, and Mitch Kupchak, former Bullet player and now L.A. Lakers GM, on a 1979 telethon.

From *Company*, (l to r) Larry Shue, Susie Bigelow, Dick Bigelow, yours truly, Carroll Sturgis, and Michelle Mundell.

Interviewing baseball's Iron Man, Cal Ripken, for SportTalk 980, WTEM, Washington, D.C.

With cohost Carole Lehan on *Catholic Radio Weekly*, a new show nationally syndicated by the U.S. Conference of Catholic Bishops to address the major issues facing the nation and the Church.

My family. (l to r) Kellie Smaldore, Steve Smaldore, me, Moira, Chris Rolle, Tracie Rolle, and Mary Clare at Moira's graduation from St. Joseph's University.

Yes, David, he loves to yell at referees and he cannot stand to lose. Yes, David, he pushes his players to achieve more just as he pushes himself to achieve more. Yes, David, everyone around him accomplishes more because of your grandfather. And this is evident in our basketball program, which has reached a higher level because of your grandfather. Requests for entrance into the university is at an all-time high. Our athletic department is solvent mainly because of the income generated by the basketball program. Student morale and pride in your grandfather and the university have never been higher. Alumni enthusiasm and fundraising are also at an all-time high.

David, this is the year Maryland starts to build its new basketball arena. It is going to be called the Comcast Center, but it should be called the Gary Williams Center, because this arena would not even be under consideration if not for your grandfather's hard work and dedication. He is personally responsible for the dream of a new arena becoming a reality.

Yes, David, you really have a true giant as a grandfather. He is quite a guy. You are a very lucky person. I hope you will always remember how much he loves you and I hope you can see and appreciate that this trust is being set up because of the love and appreciation that the people here tonight have for your grandfather. We love and admire him.

Very truly yours,
F.O.G.

Two of my own own grandsons, JT Smaldore, 12, and Chris Rolle, 9, are Maryland ball boys. Gary tells them that they can't be at the games unless they have good grades. This gets their attention really quick. Those remarks from a coach got through to JT and Chris more than anything their mom or dad could tell them about the importance of working hard in school.

Gary also runs a first-rate basketball camp for kids in the summer, always full, with a waiting list. One time I read about a small boy who had lost his mother and called the coach to try to get the boy and his friend into the camp. Gary said "absolutely" and took care of the arrangements and expenses. This is an example of the little things behind the scenes that most people don't hear about.

When I began broadcasting Maryland Terp games in 1979, Lefty Driesell was just starting the 11th of his 17 seasons as head coach. Only four had preceded Lefty in Maryland history: H. Burton Shipley (1923-24 to 1946-47), Flucie Stewart (1947-48 to 1949-50), Bud Millikin (1950-51 to 1966-67), who is now retired in Atlanta, Georgia but he never misses a game when the Terps play in Georgia, and Frank Fellows (1967-68 to 1968-69). Frank was a frequent visitor to Cole Field House practices. I expect to see him at the new Comcast Arena.

Three of my favorite teams are the Greg Manning, Albert King, Buck Williams '80-'81 unit, the '99 team led by Steve Francis, and the 2001-02 National Champions with Juan, Lonny, Byron, Steve, and Chris.

In my first year with the Terps, Albert King was named All-ACC, and All-American in 1981, just two years later. Albert called me "Mr. Datsun" since I was the national radio and TV spokesman for the car maker then. Albert was a good guy, a great player, and ranks number three in all-time scoring for the Terps at 2,058 points. Only fellow Terps Juan Dixon and Len Bias beat his record.

Albert went on to nine seasons in the NBA with the Nets, Philadelphia, San Antonio Spurs, and the Washington Bullets. When Maryland lost the '79 ACC tournament, Albert disappeared immediately after the game. They finally found him crying in the locker room, sitting on a stool hidden from view inside the running shower. Albert reluctantly came forward to accept his MVP award. When he did, a standing ovation from both the North Carolina and Maryland fans followed.

Also on the team was Charles "Buck" Williams, another All-American who went on to 18 seasons in the NBA. Buck was on the 1980 U.S. Olympic Team that did *not* compete in the Moscow games because of the U.S. boycott protesting the Russian invasion of Afghanistan.

Buck's 61.5 percent field goal shooting average is still a school record. He was drafted in his junior year by the New Jersey Nets and finished 18 seasons in the NBA. Today, Buck is back in D.C. He's still the same old Buck—only a little richer than he was in his student days.

Another talented Terp was Greg Manning, a standout guard who could run the floor with the best of them. Greg was an All-ACC for three straight years. In 1986, Greg became my color analyst while I was still at WMAL and Greg was with Roadway Express. Maryland athletic director Andy Geiger hired us both to work for the school in 1991.

Greg had been working his way up the ladder with Roadway Express, a long haul trucking company. I had just bailed from WMAL. We both felt that the time was right to leave our jobs and join one of the nation's finest universities. Greg and I became the closest of friends, and I couldn't have asked for a better partner. They don't come any finer than Greg. Our professional relationship would go for 14 seasons.

I was apprehensive about Greg joining our broadcast team because he hardly said a word during his playing days. It was soon apparent that he wasn't the kind of guy who was interested in self-gratification or selfish goals. He was a complete team player and brought this approach to our broadcasts while improving his analyst skills each season.

When he left his Maryland position as the athletic department's director of major gifts for his current post as Georgia State athletic director, he was one of the best color analysts in the country.

Greg, with his wife Cathy and son Greg Jr., an outstanding high school player in Alpharetta, and his daughter, Courtney, are happily settled in Atlanta these days. Can you believe it? Greg is Lefty Driesell's boss at Georgia State. It seems like a nice fit.

It's regrettable that Greg wasn't broadcasting with us in the 2001 season. He would have gone from playing on the team in 1978 to getting to a Final Four. I miss him. I really do.

Greg Manning: "After Bob Wade, and when Gary Williams came in, I don't think people realize how difficult the situation was with the basketball program. Debbie Yow was really instrumental in the success at Maryland. Debbie was patient with the football program, as well, and then brought Ralph Friedgen back, so I'd say it starts at the top, and Debbie has much to do with the athletic achievement at the school.

"Ernest Graham, Albert King, and I came in together at Maryland. Ernest was a great player out of Baltimore. Dutch Morley was my closest buddy on the team, and my Maryland roommate was Jeff Hathaway. Jeff was our team manager and trainer, and he is now athletic director at Colorado State.

"I didn't know squat about radio when I started broadcasting with Johnny. I'm the first to admit that. I never enjoyed talking to radio guys when I was a player. It was a pain in the neck for me and just came with the territory. I didn't know if I'd enjoy getting into radio broadcasting.

"John was someone who could have been like my father, but we became more like brothers. Through our close friendship I began to take notice of his professionalism, his preparation, how seriously he approached his work.

"It was challenging working with John. I've never met any other broadcaster who could pull off interviews like he did. He'd have nothing written down. He'd never shuffle or search for things to say. We'd do halftime interviews with guest like Tim Russert, Bob Novak, or assorted actors and actresses, and John would just conduct the interviews flawlessly, as if he'd been preparing for six months. It's amazing. Sometimes he expected me to be the same way.

"John would also get a little testy with the engineer if we came back late from a break or if the format wasn't up to spec. He'd get perturbed. He wants things damn near perfect on the engineering side. He wants things done the right way. That's what makes him so good.

"After working with John, I had absolutely no desire to leave Maryland. Professionally, I wanted to be an athletic director, but I wasn't out looking. I was very comfortable here at my alma mater. Georgia State contacted me, and it was a difficult decision to make. But I really miss the four months each year I was Johnny's broadcast partner.

"It's an added bonus that Coach Lefty Driesell is also here. It was a little uncomfortable for both Coach and me when Georgia State played Maryland in the ACC conference. I would have rather not played that particular game.

"It also sounds strange, but I didn't know that Coach Lefty was at Georgia State when I took the job. I'm not a huge sports spectator. I don't watch many sports, and I haven't been to an NBA game in ten years. I'd rather go out and run five miles.

"I did enjoy golfing with Johnny. He'd tell everyone what a great basketball player he was, but I can say that his golf game is bad. Maybe it's because he's always doing a thousand things, and he doesn't get a chance to practice. I'm not sure that excuse is going to fly, though.

"Speaking of flying, John and I would travel to the games in an old four-seater, piloted by Joe Drach. We called it the Drach-mobile. Joe had played in the service under Bear Bryant and is quite a character. In the Drach-mobile, we could fly right into the small airports near the college towns. Often, in the winter, John and I would be scraping ice off the wings with credit cards and combs. John would be the copilot, even though he knew nothing about flying.

"Once we were in a heavy fog, and Joe Drach asked John if he could see the runway. John replied, 'What difference does it make if I can see the runway? You're the one flying the plane.'

"On another occasion, we lost an engine coming out of Clemson. We had to make an emergency landing in a crop duster's field. Joe radioed ahead, and the farmer moved his cows out of the way just in time. These Drach-mobile adventures were years after John's near-fatal plane crash in 1975. When I asked him about any fear of flying, he told me he wasn't worried because that lightning wouldn't strike him twice."

Manning's move to Georgia State left a very big pair of shoes to fill for the color analyst job. Chris Knoche got the opportunity.

Chris was the very first recruit to play for Gary Williams at American University. He moved up to assistant coach under Gary and eventually to head coach at AU. Chris was always a very good interview, so I knew he'd do well in the broadcast booth.

Indeed, Chris was successful in transitioning to broadcasting following his coaching years. With a package of CBS radio shows under his belt, including some NCAA tournaments, he was a strong candidate. His long-term relationship with Gary Williams made him the natural.

To be honest, Chris and I had a few difficulties getting in sync during our first two seasons together. We were kind of up and down getting acclimated to each other's styles.

Now I can truthfully say it has worked out in our third year together. I think the Holliday-Knoche combination is right up there with the best in the country.

Chris Knoche: "When Gary called me about the color analyst job opening up, I first called Johnny. I knew that Johnny had this very winning personal and professional relationship with Greg Manning. Greg had the luxury of John's mentorship, and I think John helped mold Greg into the very successful broadcaster he became. And on top of that, Greg was a Maryland alum, and I'm not. He worked at the university and could get in some interviews with the players during the day.

"I live in Virginia and work for Axa, a brokerage firm in Falls Church. I was a bit of an outsider since I never wore the Terp uniform. I'd have the long commute to the games as one obstacle. I wanted to make sure that Johnny didn't have some other analyst in mind for the job. I wanted him to give me his blessing.

"John said, 'I think it will work. Good luck with your negotiations.' He was cordial and to the point.

"One of the first things I noticed working with Johnny is that he has this amazing ability to present every game as if it were the most important game in the history of Maryland. That's not easy to do since there are so many peaks and valleys in the season.

"As I sit next to him with the headphones on, he always sounds as if he really loves what he does. There's always real joy in his voice. That's terrific, and the way it ought to be.

"Johnny also has no ego. He's there to make everyone else look good. With all his accomplishments, he just comes across as a regular guy.

"Most people in Johnny's position don't hesitate in telling you what to do or letting you know how things are supposed to work. And they certainly don't hesitate in evaluating you right away.

"John didn't. He was patient with me and allowed us to find our rhythm. He didn't have to do that. It's a special quality he has, especially considering all the major success he's had in sports and music radio. I will always respect that.

"I grew up in the D.C. area, so I listened to Johnny's radio shows in my formative years. My dad, Hank, was a huge fan of both Johnny and Harden and Weaver. Part of Johnny's appeal for me was the opportunity to share this with my father.

"Here's some good trivia. My dad was the first number-one draft pick in NBAA history, for the Pittsburgh Iron Men. This was 1947. He ended his career as the deputy director of the CIA under George Bush and is now retired with my mom in Denver.

"Maryland basketball was always the biggest thing for me. I watched Lefty pace up and down the sidelines every Saturday. As head coach at AU I made it a point to schedule games with the Terps. I would have played them in the street.

"As Gary's first recruit, I can now say that Coach Williams is clearly recruiting better these days. Our first AU team was a ragamuffin group of mainly transfer students. Two years later we were winning games. Gary's coaching made it happen.

"Gary is much the same guy as when I first knew him, but I think the Final Four trip changed him in that he's able to enjoy things a little more these days. Yet, there is that same sense of urgency in the way that he coaches the practices and games, and in his meticulous organization.

"Johnny's so easy to work with. He tries to set you up to look good, he can take as good as he gives, and he never stops having a good time."

Another reason to "fear the turtle" is Athletic Director Dr. Debbie Yow. She's led the athletic charge for eight years at College Park. She gave Coach Gary Williams a long-term deal that will keep him at Maryland for the rest of his coaching career, if that's what he wants to do. I expect he will. And she hired Ralph Friedgen to return to his alma mater as head football coach.

Debbie recently concluded her tenure as president of the National Association of Collegiate Directors of Athletics, an organization with over 6,100 athletic administrators representing about 1,600 colleges and universities.

Dr. Debbie Yow: "As a broadcaster, the combination of Johnny's voice and personality set him apart from others in his industry. He exudes passion for his work, which is recognized and appreciated by Terrapin fans everywhere.

"I have heard it said that 'A professional is someone who can do his best work when he doesn't feel like it!' That pretty much sums up Johnny's broadcast duties for Maryland. The quality of his work is consistently excellent, no matter what the day has brought. That type of consistency is to be valued."

Debbie inherited me when she came to Maryland. I've been impressed with her determination to make the program succeed. Now, with balanced budgets and winning teams, she's proved herself. And she's done so with able executives by her side. Among them are Rob Mullens, Curt Callahan, Joe Hull, Kathy Worthington, and Michael Lipitz.

But before Gary, there was Lefty.

Charles Grice "Lefty" Driesell was the first Maryland coach to really make Cole Field House the place to be. Lefty shot the Terrapins back into the national ranks and finished in the top 20 for eight of his 17 seasons. His final record was 348-159.

I'll never forget the night of February 20, 1986, when Len Bias poured in 35 points for the Terps against North Carolina, winning 77-72. It was the first loss for the Tar Heels in the Smith Center. Lenny had also scored 41 points against Duke a month earlier, and that remains the third best individual effort in the Maryland record book.

Lefty called Lenny the "best shot blocker to ever play in the ACC" and thought that many of his goal-tending calls were due to his near-perfect timing. The officials couldn't believe they were legitimate blocks.

In 1998, Lefty celebrated his 700th career win. His statement was humble and gracious. "I haven't won any games," he told reporters after Georgia State rallied to beat North Florida 84-74. "I never scored a point, got a rebound or made an assist. I've had a lot of support from all the assistant coaches, players and administrators I've worked with."

When we first started working together, Lefty would go ahead to the road games a day early. His staff told me that he would insist that my pregame shows be done around his schedule—*the day before the game.*

"Are you kidding?" I asked the staff. "You mean I have to go out of my way to accommodate him?" This would be an enormous pain for me because I'd lose a day to travel. So I went to Lefty seeking a compromise. He listened and then agreed to do the pregame shows just before the game. Although Lefty was intimidating to others, I eventually found if you worked with him he'd come over to your way of thinking.

When my daughter, Kellie, once asked me what Lefty was like, I said, "I'm not going to say anything. Judge him for yourself when you meet him."

Her chance came when she joined me at a game in Atlanta. After my pregame interview, Lefty went on about how a particular player, Herman Veal, was like a son to him. Lefty told Kellie about some of the other players that he loved. When we finished, Kellie said that she thought Lefty was one of the most sensitive people she had ever met. He completely won her over.

The 1982 double-overtime victory against UCLA at Cole, and knocking off then No. 1 South Carolina in the famous 1971 stall-ball game, 31-30, in overtime, are two career highlights that Lefty recently cited to *Washington Post* writer Ken Denlinger in an article toasting the history of Cole Field House. The last Terp game held at Cole, before moving to the new Comcast center, was held on March 3, 2002. Maryland beat the Virginia Cavaliers, 112-92.

The closest I came to any disagreement with Lefty was in 1985, when he questioned some of my calls. He wanted no criticism. Basically, he wanted me to cover up if the team was playing badly.

So I went to my WMAL boss, Andy Ocherhausen, and said, "Look, Andy. If the Terps are playing badly, they're playing badly. Lefty is questioning my integrity as a broadcaster if he expects me to gloss over the team's mistakes. I can only call the game one way." Andy agreed and told me to continue doing my job my way.

I knew Lefty's wife was listening to the games. I guessed she might be feeding some of these negative reports about my broadcasting. Finally, I confronted Lefty and told him, "Coach, I don't broadcast for your wife. I don't even broadcast for College Park. We are a Maryland station, and we want you to win. But I've got to tell the truth. We can't be like other teams in the city, where every ball should make the basket when a player shoots, or if there is a foul against their players, then it is a bad call. You can't be like this. The fans will know it when Maryland is playing well. When the team is off, you have to report that. Otherwise, you lose all credibility."

Lefty boomed, "Somebody said that you said we blew the game against Notre Dame." I shot back, "Yep, sure did. The player took the rebound all the way down the side, uncontested, for a lay-up, and made the shot. Coach, you blew a lead."

"But you know we played our hearts out for that game. You could have said we played hard. You could've said we played tough. You could have put it in a different way."

This was about the closest we ever came to an argument during our years of working together. After listening to my explanation, he agreed with me.

Sometimes I would travel on the road with Jack Zane, longtime sports information director (SID), and now executive director of Maryland's "Walk of Fame" sports archives. Jack Zane is really "Mr. Maryland." He came to Maryland on the navy G.I. Bill in 1953 and worked in the sports information office at Maryland while he studied. A 1960 graduate, Jack returned to the athletic program in 1969 and has been full-time ever since. He lives with wife Judy in Cheverly, Maryland.

Without people like Jack Zane and other SIDs that I've worked with, like Joe Blair, Herb Hartnett, and current director of media relations, Dave Haglund, my job would be impossible to do. Eveything you hear me talk about during our broadcast is directly attributable to these fine gentlemen and their staff.

Haglund has some top-flight folks working in his department. Greg Creese works with Dave on football. Kevin Messinger handles basketball. Greg and Kevin are key components in our broadcasts with constant updates of information, along with setting up interviews with the student athletes throughout the season.

Thanks also goes to Mark Fratto, Stephanie Mociun, Jason Yellin, Jason Baum, and Meredith Traber for their help in the media relations office.

Once during an away game, I was intently reading in our hotel room when Jack asked me what I was doing. I told him I had a dress rehearsal at the Harlequin dinner theatre the next night and I hadn't looked at the script yet. Jack thought this was funny and tells this story to show how I juggle my acts.

I also have a problem with migraine headaches. One time in Winston-Salem I discovered I had left my migraine medicine at home. Jack helped me phone local drug stores to see if they carried my prescription. The only store that had it was Bobbitt's Pharmacy. I walked in and asked the druggist what his name was. Sure enough, it was Sam.

"You're not my grandfather, are you?' I asked. "Because his name is Sam, and he owns a Bobbitt's pharmacy, too."

Jack was also instrumental in helping us get a publishing deal for this book. Call us grateful. We now hope he writes his own book about Maryland sports, because he's devoted a lifetime to his alma mater.

On Lefty, he's the expert.

Jack Zane: "Lefty was tough with the media. No more than once a week did we have to smooth things over. He was a coach that recruited 365 days a year, so whenever the young Lefty saw or heard a negative comment he felt it was a detriment to his recruiting. But he wasn't one to hold a grudge. Most of the fellows that he had a conflict with could come around the next week and he'd work with them.

"John could get things out of Lefty that others couldn't. Johnny got to know him and could call him at all hours at his home. The best way to get cooperation out of Lefty was to lead him to believe that the thing is his idea. Johnny did his homework and got to really know Lefty. And Johnny could never be intimidated. You could never accuse Holliday as being shill for Maryland athletics. He's a professional."

On the road, I remember seeing Lefty sprawled on his bed in his hotel room reading the Bible. He was very religious. I also remember going over to Lefty's house the day he was let go at Maryland. He was absolutely destroyed. He felt he was held accountable for the cocaine drug overdose of his star player, Len Bias. Jack Zane remembers that darkest day for Maryland in this way:

Jack Zane: "Len had been in Boston the night before, had signed a million-dollar contract with Adidas, and Lenny, his dad, and his agent had just left College Park that evening. I walked into the office in the morning and every button on the phone was lit up. I took the first call, and it was about Len Bias. I received calls from all over the country.

"After the news broke, Leslie Visser, *Boston Globe* reporter (and also Dick Stockton's wife) called to ask directions to College Park. She arrived that afternoon and asked me, "Where does your wife do her shopping? I need to buy clothes for a week." *The Baltimore Sun* sent a reporter that spent 31 days on the story. Every TV station sent crews in.

"You'll never convince me that Len Bias was a drug user. I believe in my heart that this was his first time he tried coke. Lenny was a super kid. Congenial. Cooperative. The player of the year in America. Lenny did everything I ever asked him to. Lenny had spent considerable time traveling with the NBA. The Celtics took him as number one in the draft. Larry Bird announced that the players would join Lenny at rookie camp. Bias was the key to the dynasty. With Lenny's death, they lost the number-one draft choice and the Celtics went downhill.

"And, in my opinion, I thought it unfair that Lefty lost his job."

Lefty took the heat for Lenny's death. There were some messy allegations that Lefty had sent some folks over to Lenny's dorm room to "clean it up" after the tragedy. On a dreary day in October 1986, Lefty gave his farewell statement:

> *"I want to announce that I am stepping down as the head basketball coach at Maryland. I make this announcement with mixed emotions because I have loved every one of my 17 years as head coach at Maryland. But it is obvious that the administration wants to make a coaching change and I do not want to coach if I am not wanted. I am proud of all that the basketball program has accomplished during the last 17 years, both on and off the court. I am very proud of our success in winning basketball games. But I am even prouder of the fine men that have been a part of the Maryland basketball program. As a group, the university could not have better representatives than these student athletes. Finally, I want to thank all the friends of the basketball program, the students, and our many loyal fans for their heartwarming support the last 17 years."*

After all these years I think he's still deeply hurt by his firing. Still, the left-hander agreed to guest on my pregame show when the Terps played Georgia State at the 2001 ACC tournament in Atlanta. It was right for Lefty to do the interview with me and great for Terps fans to hear the legendary coach again.

And speaking of fans, one of the biggest supporters of Maryland athletics is syndicated columnist and television host, Robert Novak. Bob Novak is a man I admire and I'm pleased to call him a friend.

Robert Novak: "I was hooked in 1970 when the mediocre Maryland team inherited by Lefty Driesell in his first year as head coach upset nationally ranked Duke on a last-second long shot. I was there, and I wanted to partake of more such excitement. When I purchased season tickets for the next year, I was talked into joining the Terrapin Club—thereby starting a wild ride of following the Terps from coast to coast (and beyond Hawaii) that has gone more than three decades and still counting.

"When Lefty talked about making Maryland the UCLA of the East, I didn't really anticipate national championships. So the 2001-

2002 season was a remote dream come true. And there was a special twist. For the first time in all those seasons of following the Terps, I decided to make effort to attend every game, at home and away. I did it, all 36 games culminating in the golden moment at the Georgia Dome when Maryland and coach Gary Williams won their first national championship.

"And, of course, Johnny Holliday was there for those games. Johnny is a Renaissance man: disc jockey, rock 'n' roll expert, basketball player, musical comedy actor and singer, sports commentator and play-by-play announcer. Mostly, however, he is known as the Voice of Terrapin Sports. He's also become my good friend and companion on the sometimes hazardous trail of following the Terps.

"I well remember 1981, when after watching Maryland lose to eventual national champion Indiana in the NCAA regional at Dayton, Ohio, our flight back to Washington was cancelled. Johnny and I, along with a few other fans, caught a plane we naively thought was going to Charles Town, WV, a relatively short drive back home to the Washington area. In fact, we landed in Charleston, WV, which required a very long drive indeed. I remember Johnny doing yeoman's work at the wheel through the night, while I mostly snoozed.

"Johnny has been kind enough to put me on the air occasionally at halftime and even kinder to mention me. After I boycotted Terp home games for much of one season after the dismissal of Lefty Driesell, I returned to my seat, and Johnny noted over the radio, 'Novak's back!' Maybe nobody else cared, but Johnny did.

"Then, there was the time that I was listening to a Maryland-North Carolina game in bed in Washington's Sibley Hospital, following surgery on a broken hip sustained on the ice leaving a Maryland game. Johnny, on the air, said he was thinking of me, and recalled being at Sibley while recuperating from injuries from the crash of a chartered plane.

"Yes, it sometimes takes true grit to follow the Terps, but that's the quality that Johnny Holiday has."

Other notable players during Lefty's era include Ernest Graham, who holds the scoring record with 44 points against North Carolina State on December 20, 1978. Derrick Lewis was one of Maryland's all-time best shot blockers. Dutch Morely, Herman Veal, and Ben Coleman come to mind as impressive players.

Before my time at College Park, the roster of All-American players began with Louis "Bosey" Berger in the 1931-32 season. Len Elmore ('74) later performed for ten seasons in the NBA and ABA. Tom McMillan ('74) played in the NBA for 11 seasons and was a member of the '72 United States

Olympic team, earning a silver medal in the controversial game against the Soviets. John Lucas from Durham, NC was a two-sport athlete. He'd play basketball one night, and two days later, he'd be number-one singles on the tennis team. Now head coach of the Cleveland Cavaliers, Lucas completed 14 seasons in the NBA and was also a two-time ACC singles tennis champion. Gene Shue became a two-time All-Pro and later NBA head coach with Washington, Philadelphia, San Diego, and Los Angeles teams.

Bob Wade was named head coach when Lefty departed after the '86 season. Wade had been a pillar in the coaching ranks at Baltimore's Dunbar High School, but in three seasons at Maryland, Wade's teams won just 36 games and only a disappointing seven in the Atlantic Coast Conference. Bob took a lot of heat from the alumni for this pathetic record. Perhaps the move from high school to college coaching was too high a stretch for Bob. Most fans generally regard the Wade era as a "disaster."

Although I personally had no problems with Coach Wade, other members of the media did. Often, Greg Manning, Mike McKay (our engineer), and I would try to convince Wade that not all members of the media were evil. Sure there are bad apples, just like in any other business. Still, we advised Bob to try to weed out the bad from the good. I doubt we were very successful, as Wade's opinion of reporters never seemed to improve. The feelings were mutual as his win-loss record wasn't exactly the stuff the media could applaud. Coach Wade is now back in Baltimore with the recreation department. I suspect he's just as popular there as ever.

Despite the rap against him, Wade had some outstanding players. Adrian Branch, Derrick Lewis, Steve Hood, John Johnson, Keith Gatlin, and Jeff Baxter were standouts during Wade's time. I also fondly remember Tony Massenburgh, who is still playing in the NBA and was one of the truly nicest student athletes I've known.

In February 2000, my favorite sports writer, John Feinstein, spent some time with me before a game. He published a profile in the *Washington Post* Sunday magazine. Here's an excerpt.

> It is about two hours before game time at Cole Field House, and broadcaster Johnny Holliday is sitting in a corner of the press room doing what he does best: storytelling. He is describing the terrifying day in January 1975 when he and his daughter Tracie were involved in a plane crash. "The last thing I remember is turning around to tighten Tracie's seat belt," he says, then pauses because Chuck Walsh, the University of Maryland's basketball publicist, is standing over him, a concerned look on his face.
>
> "Coach is ready," Walsh says.
>
> Walsh is speaking in code. At Maryland, especially on game night, the words "Coach is ready" mean: "Let's get moving." No one on staff wants to

chance incurring the wrath of a keyed-up Gary Williams.

Holliday smiles, knowing that Walsh is wishing that Holliday was already inside the locker room with the coach. He has no desire to make Walsh uncomfortable. But he is finishing a story. "Tell him I'll be right in," he says. As Walsh sprints away, Holliday wraps up the story. "The last thing I heard was Tracie's voice saying, 'Daddy, Daddy' . . ." And then he is off to the Maryland locker room.

Williams became a grandfather for the first time earlier in the week at age 54. He has told friends he is thrilled, but some wonder if that's how he really feels about it. Another Maryland staffer whispered to Holliday earlier in the evening that he might want to tread lightly around that topic during the pregame show he always conducts with the coach.

Holliday sits down with Williams, who looks like he's in a 60-60 game with five seconds left and the other team inbounding the ball under the basket. He starts his tape recorder and introduces the show. Then, treading as lightly as you might expect a man with five of his own grandchildren to tread, he looks at Williams and says, "So, Gramps, what do you think we should look for tonight?" Gary Williams cracks up. Johnny Holliday has that effect on people.

. . . (Johnny) never seems bored on a broadcast, regardless of the score. He has worked with more partners than Fred Astaire and sounds as if he is best friends with every one of them—even when that isn't the case. He has gone through a decade of awful football at Maryland without complaining. "I feel bad for the kids who work so hard and for the fans," he says. "But I've never stopped enjoying it."

That awful decade of football–the final record was 37-73–abruptly ended when the new football coach moved to College Park in 2001. Nobody was quite prepared for the Ralph Friedgen experience. His success even surprised me, and I'm one of the guys who kept saying we'd get football back on top.

Chapter 11

Play-By-Play

It was a fantastic storybook first year for Maryland football. We accomplished everything we set out to do, and more. It was nice having Johnny be a part of it. He's been an institution at Maryland and done a fabulous job for so many years. Johnny makes my life a lot easier when I'm doing the radio and TV shows. I'd been on TV before but there's a difference when you are the TV show. Johnny's style is very easy and it's his experience that I feed off of. The shows turn out better on TV than I think they're going to. He makes it comfortable. It's been real good.
Coach Ralph Friedgen, *February 8, 2002*

My very last West Coast game before coming to Washington was the 1969 Stanford-Cal showdown. This was called "the Big Game" in San Francisco. Jim Plunket was the Stanford quarterback. I literally took the flight to D.C. a few hours later.

Today, my typical play-by-play work for Maryland football starts by putting in a couple of hours at home filling in the chart for the game. If kickoff is at one o'clock, I'll normally get to Byrd Stadium no later than 10 a.m. A press guide is distributed at the start of the season with over 180 pages of information on the players, coaching staff, their schools, etc. This helps me immensely. You can't just walk in and do this job. You need to prepare.

For away basketball games I travel on the team's charter plane, a 40-seat Delta jet. I need to be there regardless of illness or anything else that gets in my way.

One schedule had me going from a men's basketball game on Saturday to women's games on Sunday afternoon and Monday evening, and on to an ACC conference game on Tuesday night, followed by an early morning taping of Gary Williams's TV show on Wednesday morning. That was College Park, Atlanta, Raleigh, Winston-Salem, and back to College Park in five days.

On more than one occasion I've had a football game in the afternoon and a basketball game at night in two different cities.

One of my favorite moments of broadcasting Maryland football came on November 10, 1984 in Miami covering the Orange Bowl, Maryland's football game against the University of Miami, one of the nation's top teams at the time. Jack Scarbath, the greatest quarterback in Maryland history, and former Washington Redskin Pete Wysocki were broadcasting with me. At halftime, the Hurricanes were crushing the Terrapins, 31- 0. My hometown friends were razzing me mercilessly. Every time Miami would score, they were giving me the biggest grief. Maryland Chancellor John Slaughter visited our announcers' booth and told us not to worry because he thought the team would come back. Sure enough, as sports writer Shirley Povich once wrote, "The million-to-one shot came in, and hell froze over." Trailing 31-0 at the half, Maryland came back to win at the Orange Bowl, 41-38. It was the greatest comeback in Division I college football history. But hell didn't freeze over in the announcers' booth. It broke loose. Jack, Pete, and I were going crazy, absolutely crazy. It was incredible!

Quarterback Frank Reich led the victory, and he'd do the same thing again with the Buffalo Bills eight years later in the NFL. Trailing 35-3 early in the second half, Reich led the Bills to a 41-38 overtime victory over the Houston Oilers.

Ralph Friedgen was the offensive coordinator for the Maryland team in that Miami game:

> **Coach Friedgen:** "Not many people have asked me about that game, but I can tell you that we couldn't really do much right in the first half. We went into halftime 31-0 behind and Miami players started trash-talking us as we walked off the field. They were a very competitive bunch of players, but their crap started getting our guys pretty upset. A lot of our players were saying 'we can get it back' and this and that in the locker room. Coach Ross told everybody to be quiet. He told them if they didn't play any better the second half they'd be scrimmaging as soon as we got back to College Park. He asked me what we needed to do on offense to get better, and I said 'Everything's really there; we're just not doing it.' So all he did was change quarterbacks. He put Frank Reich in as opposed to Stan Gelbaugh and we went out and scored 42 consecutive points against a defending national champion. It was an amazing game of momentum.
>
> "There's a funny story about Tony Edwards, an offensive tackle with us in that game. He hurt his knee in the first half and we told him he couldn't play the second half. He went to the locker room to shower up but someone locked the door on him, and he couldn't get out. He wasn't that worried because he figured the rest of the game wasn't going to be very pretty to look at, so he tuned in on his radio.

"We scored three touchdowns in the third quarter, so then the game was getting pretty close. Tony decided he had to get out of the locker room, but he still couldn't. By the fourth quarter we were still scoring points and took the lead. Tony finally escaped and made it back to the field with one minute to go."

I doubt if anyone dreamed that Fridge would turn the Maryland football program around so fast. In one season, he took the Terps to their first bowl game in 18 years.

I first met Coach in 1982. What I most remember about Ralph as assistant coach is what a motivator he was. When Ralph was an assistant I did several pieces on the air about his philosophy and strategies about upcoming games. What struck me about those early interviews was how much he was really into football. There wasn't a lot of snappy patter and one-liners. Ralph was serious. Later, I would make a point of saying hello during Terps games when he moved on as assistant coach at Georgia Tech in '87. I know that Ralph was ticked off that he was passed over and never got a shot at returning to Maryland when Coaches Mark Duffner and Ron Vanderlinden got tapped in the '90s.

After 32 years as an assistant, Ralph finally got the head coaching job at age 54. How many guys have done that?

As soon as Ralph landed back in College Park, I went to his office to offer my congratulations. He looked up at me and said, "Well, things have changed a bit since I've left," referring to the rather dismal Terps football record of the past decade plus.

"Sure has," I agreed.

"We'll change that. We'll get it back on track."

People now ask me, "What's Ralph Friedgen like?" I answer, "It's a cliché, but what you see is what you get." He's a jolly, jovial fellow. He's unpretentious and straightforward—some people say maybe a little too straightforward sometimes. I've never worked with a coach as blunt and honest as Ralph. Honestly, there's nobody I've ever known that reminds me of Ralph.

Coach Friedgen: "When Johnny says he's never known any one quite like me, I'm not sure if that's a compliment, or not. What's he saying? That I'm unique? One thing is that I don't have any hidden agendas. I think players know where they stand with me. That's very important. That's how I would want to be treated. It's not telling them what they want to hear, but rather being honest with them.

"You have to build up trust with people. Any relationship you have in your life is based on trust. For a coach, they'll never play their fullest unless they trust you and you trust them. I never lie or mislead the players. I really don't lie to hardly anyone."

My Maryland football play-by-play began in '79 under Coach Jerry Claiborne—three years before Bobby Ross took over. Jerry was named National Coach of the Year by *The Sporting News* in 1974 and coached 13 All-Americans before his retirement.

Bobby Ross really brought the Terps to prominence with back-to-back-to-back bowl games and ACC championships (1983-85). Ross had a very strong coaching staff which included Joe Krivack, a genius quarterback coach, and Ralph Friedgen, a '69 Maryland alum and former Terps quarterback and guard who served as Ross's offensive coordinator and offensive line coach. That both Krivak and Friedgen would go on to become head coaches at Maryland shows what kind of people Bobby Ross looked for in his staff to help him become successful.

Coach Friedgen: "I've learned a little bit from everyone I've worked with. I still talk with Coach Ross, and I've heard from Coach Krivack. I've spent time with Coach Ward, who coached me as a player. From Coach Ross, I learned perseverance and competitiveness. From George O'Leary (head coach, Georgia Tech), I learned organization. He did a great job of that.

"From Frank Beamer, I learned how to handle different people. I had a guy who was with me on another staff and then came with me to Murray State. In the first situation, the guy wasn't a very good coach, and, with Frank, he was a very good coach. It was just a matter of how Frank worked with him.

"You can make players better players and make coaches better coaches just by the way you handle them. Everyone needs to be handled just a little differently to get the optimum out of them, and I think I learned this from Frank."

Coach Ross was personable, accessible, and the players loved him. He produced some outstanding talent, like Boomer Esiason who could simply do it all. Boomer went on to star in the NFL with the Cincinnati Bengals, Arizona Cardinals, and NY Jets and is today one of the best color analysts around.

One time, I needed to rearrange my schedule because my mother was having an operation. Coach Ross agreed to tape our TV show at 7:00 a.m. so I could catch an early flight to Miami and still make it back to do the game broadcast. When I arrived at the hospital, there was a big bouquet of flowers inscribed, "To Mrs. Bobbitt, Our thoughts and prayers are with you, Bobby Ross and the Maryland football team."

When Ross moved on, Joe Krivak was elevated to head coach. It was Krivak who was responsible for producing more quarterbacks for the NFL than anyone else in college football. The seven he coached during his career who have played or are still active in the NFL include Boomer Esiason, Frank Reich, Stan Gelbaugh, Neil O'Donnell, Scott Zolak, Scott Milanovich, and Aaron Brooks (Virginia). Krivak had been an assistant at the Naval Academy before returning to Maryland for the second time. His five-year tenure ('87-'91) was impressive, and he was the last coach before Ralph's 2002 Orange Bowl to take a Maryland squad to a bowl game, a 34-34 tie with Louisiana Tech.

He retired two years ago as assistant coach at Virginia. He and his wife, Jeanne, are close friends. He still takes my money on the golf course.

Joe Krivak: "I came to Maryland with Jerry Claiborne. I then went to Navy and returned to Maryland under Bobby Ross. Following Bobby's departure, I was given the opportunity to become the head coach. Most assistant coaches don't get this opportunity, so I am grateful to Maryland and the success that we had.

"The most important thing for me was to provide stability for our three sons. My wife, Jeanne, and I bought a house in Bowie, Maryland in '73 when realtors told us that we couldn't live in the D.C. area on my salary of $15,000. We've been there ever since. While working at Navy and Maryland I just steered my car in a different direction for the daily commute.

"Johnny and I got along well both socially and professionally. We try to play golf as often as we can. There is nothing pretentious about Johnny. I've seen more people run things by him for his advice and I've done the same over the years. He is always objective and forthcoming about the advice he gives. With football, you are in an ego business, but I've never seen a time when his ego got in the way. He just accepts what life presents.

"As we are talking here, I see that Coach Friedgen may be looking at the NFL. Professional football is certainly more lucrative, but you have to deal with a different set of problems. When you stay on the collegiate level you can impact peoples' lives. Most of your players are amateurs who will have to go out in the work force. You can really impact them on a personal level and make a difference in their lives. Financially, salaries in both the professional and collegiate level have accelerated tremendously, and the question you have to ask yourself is how much money do you really need to live? The truth is that you can't spend it all."

Mark Duffner was hired away from Holy Cross to coach the Terps in '92. Like Krivack and Ross, Mark would stay for five years. Unfortunately Mark's teams would never win more than six games in any one season. I probably spent more time with Mark, both professionally and socially, than any of the Maryland coaches I've worked with. Mark and I had so many laughs together on the road. I know he's happy these days coaching the line for the Cincinnati Bengals.

Mark Duffner: "My Maryland days were a good experience. We were 6-5 and 5-6 in the last two seasons, and that was the best record since 1986, so I think we advanced the program. We drew well in the '95 season, and Johnny was a big plus in helping us.

"I'm flattered to be asked to offer some thoughts about Johnny for his autobiography. I always looked forward to working with him. I once mentioned to John that I had lost my St. Christopher medal. The next day Johnny bought me a new one. He's a consummate professional, with great morals and ideals, and tremendous talents. I really just love the guy."

During their combined 10 years, Krivak and Duffner coached some strong student athletes including Barry Johnson, Russ Weaver, Eric Hicks, Scott Zolak, Neil O'Donnell, Jermaine Lewis, Scott Milanovich, John Kaleo, Frank Wycheck, Greg Hill, Geroy Simon, Marcus Badgett, Ratcliff Thomas, Dan Plocki, Eric Ogbogu, and Ziz Abdur-R'oof.

Ziz was my color analyst for a short time. He was good, but English wasn't his first language. Once on the air I was offering condolences to an alum's wife whose husband had passed away. Ziz added his "compliments" to the widow.

After Coach Duffner came Ron Vanderlinden. Vandy coached through the 2000 season, and now he's an assistant at Penn State under the legendary Joe Paterno. Vandy's standout players include Eric Barton, Delbert Cowsette, Jamie Wu, Al Wallace, Lewis Sanders, Brian Kopka, Peter Timmins, Matt Kalapinski, Melvin Fowler, Shawn Forte, E.J. Henderson, Kris Jenkins, and Lamont Jordan Fowler, the Terrapins' all-time leading rusher.

Jordan was a big fan of Gary's basketball team, and he'd hang around after Greg Manning and I finished our broadcast just to chat. I still think he has a big future in the NFL and I'm looking forward to seeing him play.

A few nights after it was announced that Ralph would lead the Maryland program, he visited with us at a basketball game at Cole Field House. He was sitting in the front row getting rather loudly involved in the game. An official came over to me and asked, "Who's the heavyset guy sitting courtside?"

I told him it was the new Maryland football coach.

"He'd better zip it before I throw him out of the arena," said the official.

Early in the 2001 season I asked Ralph what he planned to do about his kicking game, because he couldn't find a field goal kicker.

Ralph answered, "I don't know. But this kid, Novak, has got a lot of possibilities, but he told me at practice, 'Hey, coach, watch this. I can hit the uprights with this kick.' I said, 'I know you can, I've seen you do it in the game. Try and go *between* the uprights.'"

At the Tuesday practice before the amazing comeback win at North Carolina State, Ralph asked me which broadcast I was planning to do that weekend, since the Terps also had a basketball game and I couldn't do both.

"I'm doing the football game, Coach," I answered.

"What's Gary Williams think about that?" Ralph asked.

"He'd like me to do the basketball game, but in the past we've never had a decision to make because football was always in the tank."

Later, in all the celebration in the locker room—with people screaming, singing, and pounding Ralph on his back—he called up to me in the announcers' booth as the postgame show was ending. I was just starting to go to commercial.

"Hey, Johnny. You still there?"

"Yeah, Coach."

"I guess this beats doing the basketball game, huh?"

When reminded of this exchange later, the Coach adds, "I always like to kid Johnny, plus I knew this would irritate Gary, whom I like to kid too. We have to keep our sense of humor."

For the next season, Coach Fiedgen is trying to improve the facilities. He'd like to put an academic center in the team house, an auditorium, a dining hall, and a new entranceway. "It's a never-ending process, I can tell you that," he says.

The Coach is also trying to get any players who lettered to come back and get involved in the program. "This is one of the things that Maryland hasn't done in the past, and Johnny's been a help in doing that," Coach says. "Being here for so long, he has a good feel for the alumni and lettermen. He knows where they are now and can recall many of their same experiences they went through."

One player who is already very involved in the program is Jack Scarbath. Jack was All-American, a runner-up for the Heisman trophy, and first-round pick for the Washington Redskins. He finished his career with the Steelers. The first touchdown in Byrd Stadium belongs to Jack: a 28-yard run in the first game of the 1950 season.

Jack Scarbath: "We'd taken the ball and marched from our own 20-yard line. Our offense was the triple option, the split T. On that final play, Navy chose to allow me to carry the ball, probably because I was the slowest guy on the team.

"At the '84 Orange Bowl game I recall that we were broadcasting right next to the Miami VIP box. It was packed. But as the game grew for Maryland in the second half, the Miami people started leaving one by one. John's voice got louder as Maryland kept scoring, and when the game ended I looked over to see that the only two people left next door were the president of Miami University and his wife."

"You know, as a Maryland alum, you die with each down that doesn't succeed. During the nineties I kept hoping for a Bobby Ross or a Ralph Friedgen to come to Maryland, and thankfully, Ralph got here. I've watched him in his first year hire a very dependable, knowledgeable group of assistant coaches, so I know his success in the first season won't be a fluke. I just see good things for Maryland football in the future.

"As for Johnny, he's terrific and has a grasp of football and basketball that listeners can really follow. Whoever they put in the box with him, he carries them.

When Jack was with me on the radio, he could dissect X's and O's with the best of them. He has always been involved in Maryland athletics, from the Terrapin Club to the Maryland Educational Foundation, which he currently serves as chairman. Like Jack Zane, Jack is clearly suited to be called "Mr. Maryland." Mary Clare and I consider Jack and his wife, Lynn, to be among our closest friends. If you are ever traveling through Easton, Maryland, please stop off at Fred Frederick's Chrysler dealership. There you'll see beautifully wood-carved geese coming in for a landing. This is some of Jack's best work that he now does in retirement.

My biggest influence in getting into play-by-play was Frank Gleiber. Frank was the announcer for the Dallas Cowboys when I was in Cleveland. I spotted for him when the Browns played Dallas. Overall I spotted for five of the greatest broadcasters: the legendary Ray Scott, the Green Bay Packers' announcer; Chris Schenkel and Marty Glickman, both with the New York Giants; Jack Whittaker, with CBS; and Frank Gleiber.

But Gleiber was my favorite. A consummate pro. He would always take time with me before the games to ask how I was doing and ask me how things were going at WHK.

Gleiber was the featured performer. I was the lowly spotter. But he took an interest in me as a person. This left a lasting impression on me. I liked Frank's style, how nice and how smooth he was. In the back of my mind I thought if I ever got the chance to do play-by-play, I'd do it exactly like Frank.

Luckily, I would hone the skills I acquired as "every teen queen's dream" rock and roll disc jockey and improve upon them over the years for my play-by-play career. Whatever timing, rapid-fire delivery, spontaneity, clarity of speech, and creativity I can muster for play-by-play comes directly from my DJ days.

Are there any play-by-play professionals that I do not admire? I'd have to say no. I know how tough it can be sometimes. Anyone who is doing this —either nationally or on the local level—has their own style, and they have to be good in order to get the job done. I'm sure there are some people who don't like the way Holliday does it. You just don't know. You sometimes get feedback from fans, or the players, when you are doing play-by-play. I figure that if the phones don't ring after a game, then I've done a good job.

You call the game. If the other team makes a good play, you've got to say it was a good play. If Maryland is not playing good defense, you've got to say it. Do I want Maryland to win? Sure, but I can't let that get in the way of being a professional and being fair. People will probably know who's winning by the inflection of my voice.

But as a broadcaster, I'd lose any kind of credibility with my audience if it were all one-sided. I work for the University of Maryland these days. I never hammer the kids. I'll never second-guess Gary Williams or Ralph Friedgen. That's up to the color analyst.

Doing play-by-play is a symphonic experience. I wish everyone could see what goes on in a broadcast booth. They'd understand that it's not all me behind the microphone. It starts with a quartet made up of the play-by-play announcer, the color analyst, the spotter, and the statistician.

When I am complimented on being a "great" play-by-play announcer, I often reply, "It's not rocket science." In sportscasting, especially on radio, you're painting a picture. The highest praise I can have is for someone to tell me they've really enjoyed listening to my play-by-play because it made them feel like they were there in the arena. The key is to keep it fresh. Add the human interest statistics on each player. Keep your energy high.

The spotter picks out who carries the ball, who makes a key block, who catches the pass, etc. We have a large checkerboard chart in front of us which lists all the players from both teams, along with their numbers and position, their stat highlights, and, in my case, often a personal note about the players' parents or some other human interest annotation. The charts come blank and I write in all the information.

Our spotter, Steve Rear, is to my right, and our statistician, Brett Bessell, is to my left. The analyst, Jonathan Claiborne, is to the statistician's left. Our engineer, Tom Marchitto or Steve Stefany, sits behind us. I take the offense and call the plays. The spotter takes the defense.

Let's say Georgia Tech has the ball during a Terps football game. The ball is snapped and I'll see one guy go one way and another go left. I'll say, "John Myers flanks to the left and Kelly Campbell wideouts to the right. Godsee with a give to Burns, cracks up behind his center, David Schmidgall, and right guard Britt Key, and picks up four yards in the play."

The spotter points—boom, boom, boom—to three players from the defense boxes on our chart. I'll rapidly add, "And here's the defensives: He's hit by Michael Whaley, the rush end, with help from E. J. Henderson, and Marlon Moyer Moore." The spotter then points to a third player, and I immediately say, "And he got a good block from Kelly Campbell to spring him loose."

God bless Steve, our spotter. Without him, I'd be dead in the water.

Throughout the game, Brett is writing down and holding up numbers. I translate one of his shorthand numbers—6/55—to say, "Joe Burns for the afternoon has carried six times for 55 yards." While I'm calling the play, Steve is pointing, Brett is holding up numbers, and the engineer, Tom or Steve, is frantically vying for my attention for either a commercial drop-in or to go to station break.

Meanwhile, Jonathan is watching, ready to come in and explain *why* the player didn't gain more yardage. The analyst has the harder job, in my opinion. He has to understand and report *why* the players are, or are not, doing certain things. Whereas the play-by-play guy has to simply report who's to the right, to the left, who is carrying the ball, who passed, and who caught it. I've done both color and play-by-play, and I was totally out of my element doing the color.

I know I struggled through the color analysis for the Washington Bullets games with Tony Roberts.

Back when I worked with Tony, we were always hassling the Bullets' coach, K. C. Jones to sing on the air for us. K. C. is the Hall of Famer who thrived with the Boston Celtics and so impressed the fans that one sportswriter suggested that the "C" in his name stood for "Championship." This made sense. When K. C. played for the Celtics, they took the championship in the first eight seasons of K. C.'s nine-season career.

Anyway, Tony and I tried to get K. C. to croon for us because he was always humming, always singing whenever we were around him. He never took us up on our offer. K. C. was unassuming and not one to show off but always a delight to work with. And he was a pretty good coach. Those were great days and nights working with K. C. and Tony even if I was mostly not very good as the color guy. One note: Tony always hated his own voice.

On the basketball side, one of the great contests of the 2000-01 season came when Maryland played the Georgetown Hoyas for the "Bragging Rights of the Beltway." This battle was held in California, some 3,000 miles from the neighboring Maryland and Georgetown campuses. After 23 years of coaching solid college basketball, this win gave Gary Williams his first trip to the ACC Final Eight. This win meant a lot to Gary.

Former Georgetown coach John Thompson attended the game, as did former Boston Celtics star Bill Russell and Pro Football Hall of Famer Jim Brown.

Here's an edited excerpt of the last minutes of my play-by-play for that game broadcast from the Anaheim arena:

Terps to inbound. Holden looks to Blake. Fires it down the right side. Mouton leaps on the sideline to bring it in. And he steps out of bounds right in front of Gary Williams. Now we have a time-out on the floor with 2:03 left. The ball belongs to Georgetown with Maryland leading by seven. But 2:03 is a long, long time with Georgetown's dangerous long-range shooting. One of these teams will be back here Saturday and the other will go home on a charter back to the Washington-Baltimore area. Scruggs will get it right off to the left of Gary Williams. Blake back and away while Scruggs inbounds to Kevin Braswell. Here's Braswell as he penetrates. He has contact with Miller. If they call it. They're going to call it on Danny Miller. Wow.

Clock stopped at a buck forty-eight. Braswell's going to get a chance to close this to five. Braswell hits the free-throw attempt. 14 for Kevin Braswell. 11 for Juan Dixon. Two buddies who grew up together in Baltimore. Braswell gets set to fire a left hand. Misses that and Baxter with a rebound. And a big one. Terps up by six with 1:42 to go.

Here's Blake. Here comes the double team. Jump pass to Holden. He had Miller there for a moment. Tahj wisely gives it back to Dixon. "Bragging rights for the beltway" on the line tonight. With a minute 23, to Blake to Miller. Dixon leads to get the pass and then brings it back out. Runs some time off the clock. Wide open mid-left side. Blake just inside midcourt. Baxter on the baseline.

Craig Esherick says, "Go get 'em." Doesn't take the shot. Miller right. 13 on the shot clock. 56 seconds to play in the ball game. Here's Juan Dixon as he starts to make a move. He throws it to Miller. Fouled with five seconds on the shot clock. Miller at the Maryland line. Boomshe-Boomshe hit with the foul. That's the fourth on the senior from Cameroon. 49:09 seconds to go with Danny Miller at the Maryland line. Maryland about to get to the elite Final Eight for the first time in 26 years. Miller's free-throw attempt. You could see that was off the mark as soon as it left his hand. Danny Miller's come off the bench tonight as he's done all season long, but especially for the final five, six games of the season really to spark Maryland with key rebounds and great defensive plays.

Second attempt for Miller. He got it. Miller now with seven points and the Terps now up by nine. 72-63. Final 48 seconds here at Anaheim. Braswell with a long-range three-pointer that's off the mark and it's last touched by Maryland out of bounds. It will belong to Georgetown with 40 seconds to go in the ball game.

Braswell's pass knocked away by Miller then picked up by Perry. Left sideline drive jumper. No good. Dixon fights for the loose ball. Back to Braswell. He resets behind the arc and hits the three-pointer. And a timeout called by Georgetown, 72-66, with 31.4 seconds to play, but that's the Hoyas' final timeout of the ballgame.

… It's hard to believe, but things are very calm on that Maryland bench. A smile from Nicholas, a smile from Mouton. And a smile from Tahj as he knocks home his second one to give the Terps a 74-66 lead with 28 seconds remaining. Braswell has had a good night tonight. Here's Perry the jump pass outside to Hunter. Braswell from long range. The three-point

attempt is no good. They reset. Braswell again from long range. Misses that one and they get a third opportunity. Scruggs will throw it up from long range. That's an air ball, and Dixon's got it. He's fouled at the backcourt with six seconds to play by Hunter, and the Terps are going to win this ball game.

Gary Williams with a handshake and a hug for Byron Mouton, and now a hug for Nicholas and he's working his way down the bench and a chest bump with Lonnie Baxter (laughs). Dixon's free-throw attempt is good. 75-66 and Maryland by nine again.

… Dixon hits another one. Terps by ten with 6.1 seconds to play. And Maryland will advance to the game against the winner of Stanford -Cincinnati and it's all over. Terrapins finally get to the Elite Eight of the NCAA tournament, defeating Georgetown by ten. 76 to 66 and hugs all around of the far side with the players and the coaches.

The NCAA tournament continued with the Terps against the second-ranked team in the nation, the Stanford Cardinal. It was a game the Terps would win, and it earned them their first trip to the Final Four in the school's history. Here's how Chris Knoche and I called it.

JH: One minute, six seconds separate Maryland and Minneapolis-St. Paul. Holden, today, hit two big ones with a minute fifty-three to go. Three Cardinals on the line and things are mighty quiet on that Stanford bench. Holden's free-throw attempt is good. 13 for Holden, 85-73 Maryland.

CK: What a performance by this Maryland team. Thirty-nine minutes of fury and discipline and heart. It was meant to be from the start.

JH: [Assistant Coach] Jimmy Patsos quickly putting Lonnie Baxter on the floor. Taj Holden reloads at the foul line. Holden with 13 points, shooting for his 14th. Got it! 86-73 Terrapins about to upset the number-one seed and the nation's number-two team. One minute six seconds to go in Anaheim. Jason Collins inbounds to MacDonald across the timeline. A minute to go. McDonald long-range jumper. That's no good. Morris with a rebound and gets rid of it to Dixon in the corner. The Maryland fans on their feet. Less than a minute to play. To Miller down the right sidelines. Stanford's gotta foul. Pass to Morris. Back to Miller. Back to Dixon. With 44 seconds left to play. MacDonald reaching around and finally fouls Juan Dixon. That's number five for McDonald and the Terrapin fans are celebrating with 41 seconds to play in the game. They're up by 13.

CK: You know, Johnny, I think that Maryland has won over an awful lot of these fans in here. They came in and might have been Stanford fans

but you look around right now and you see everybody in here up and cheer-
ing. They might be cheering for both teams. But what a performance. You've
got to give a lot of credit to Gary Williams. The trials and tribulations this
year. He played right through it all.

JH: Dixon misses the free-throw attempt. That doesn't happen
very often. Juan has got 16 for the day. 86 percent at the line for Dixon.
Second attempt by Dixon is good. 87-73, and you know they'll be
some tears of joy shed for Gary Williams. Mendez outside the arc throws
up a three-pointer. That's no good. Tip, no good. Morris flies through
the air to get the rebound. Looks down the floor. He's got Nicholas. 27
seconds to go. Nicholas will hold the ball. And look at the smiles on the
Terrapin players. Dixon celebrating. The Terrapin coaches, Dave
Dickerson, Jimmy Patsos, and Billy Hahn are hugging Gary Williams
with 12 seconds to go, and Nicholas will kneel down and dribble out
the clock. The Stanford players are congratulating the Maryland players. Four seconds, three seconds, two seconds, and Maryland for the
first time in school history going to the Final Four in Minneapolis. A
bear hug for Gary Williams and a big lift in the air from Laron Cephas,
and Maryland has upset Stanford 87-73.

Juan Dixon, Steve Blake, Tahj Holden, Byron Mouton, Lonnie Baxter,
Chris Wilcox, and the rest of the team were among my favorites of all the
years that I've covered Maryland. They're personable, funny, accommodating, accessible, and a great bunch of kids.

They proved how great again on February 17, 2002, in their upset
victory against archrival Duke. It would be the last game between Duke and
the Terps at Cole Field House. Maryland led from start to finish and won by
87-73. It was one of the most exciting games I ever called at Cole.

Another of my football color analysts was Gib Romaine, who had
started on Coach Claiborne's staff and stayed on when Bobby Ross took over.
Gib's claim to fame is that he was Randy White's position coach. Randy
went from All-American at Maryland to All-Pro with the Dallas Cowboys.

Gib knew the game well and was a great partner, with only one serious
shortcoming. Anytime the Terps got behind or were about to lose, he'd become very quiet. He took it very personally.

Once when the Terps were having a particularly rough afternoon against
Vanderbilt's Commodores in Nashville, Romaine became less and less talk-
ative as the score mounted. This is not good for the listener. It began to
sound like I was doing the broadcast alone.

Finally, I said on the air, "Gib, don't die on me now. I need you."

I understood how he felt, but it's radio, folks. You have to put your
loyalties aside and get on with the job. Gib bounced back and he was a de-

light to sit alongside of for the years we worked together. Today Gib is doing fine as assistant athletic director at Mt. St. Mary's in Emmetsburg, Maryland, the home of the legendary hall of fame basketball coach Jim Phelan.

At Maryland I've worked with ten football analysts so far. Tim Brant was my first partner. A local boy, Tim played football at St. John's College high school, and then at Maryland for Coach Claiborne. Tim landed a sports job at WMAL after graduation and moved up the ladder rather quickly to sports anchor on WMAL TV.

Everyone liked Tim. He knew his football and was a welcome sidekick my first year. He moved on to CBS, and then to ABC, where you can catch him on college football. Tim and his partner, Andy Parks, did the WMAL radio morning show for many years.

The Terps played a road game at Clemson my first year. Tim and Gib had gone out for a late dinner, but I declined. I hit the sack early, around 10:30, after catching up on my game prep.

In came Brant and Romaine around 1:00 a.m. The two proceeded to wrap me up in my mattress and then tried to carry me out of the hotel room. To where, I had no idea. It was a superb effort on my part to convince them to unwrap me and put me down.

So don't let that choirboy look fool you the next time you see Brant on ABC-TV football.

Sometimes when I was driving my car tuned to the Tim and Andy show, I would think that had I not chosen Maryland broadcasts over WMAL employment, it would probably be me doing the WMAL morning show today. And I know I made the right choice.

Jerry Sandusky was one of my favorite analysts. His father, John, had been line coach for the Miami Dolphins under Don Shula. The magic we had together was much like what I shared with Greg Manning on the basketball side. *Baltimore Sun* columnist Milton Kent once reviewed us as "an unbeatable radio combination," or something close to that. Jerry and I'd spend countless hours on the road just telling stories, talking about family, with me generally laughing at everything he said. If there's one person who can always break me up, it's Jerry.

Jerry had to give up his job as my sidekick because of his son's illness. I was really sorry to see him leave, but it was family first for Jerry despite how much I wished he would stay on. But that's the kind of person he is.

Today, Jerry is the sports director with Baltimore's WBAL Channel 11, and I'm thankful to report that his son fully recovered. Deep down, I wish Jerry would return to radio. He was that good.

Ken Broo came to D.C. as sports director for WUSA Channel 9, the station that had rights to cover ACC games. It seemed like a good idea to have Ken work with me, taking over for Jerry in 1997. Ken reminded me when we first met that he once sat in the bleachers watching me play his New

Jersey high school faculty with the WINS-WINNERS in 1965. Way to go in making me feel both good and old at the same time.

Being on television with Ken was nice because he could get his pre-game interviews for radio and at the same time tell the players they'd be on his tube highlights that night. No question Ken took his shots from the media, and unfortunately his days in D.C. were numbered. After three years at WUSA, Broo returned to Cincinnati where he is still a TV sports director.

Jonathan Claiborne is now starting his third year as my color analyst for Terps football, and he's been getting good reviews for his work.

> **Jonathan Claiborne:** "We're in the press box three floors up from the 30-yard line. Like most radio booths, the place is small, but it is constantly filled with people coming to say hello to Johnny, athletic directors, celebrities, players, and others. I get introduced because I'm sitting there, but even when he's pressed for time and under pressure to run the broadcast, Johnny always does a great job of welcoming people.
>
> "John controls the rythym of the show. We have great engineering folks, but John is very mechanically talented and leads the broadcast. He determines when to break or go to Tim Strachan and me with a question. He does it so smoothly and seamlessly. And always with energy and excitement.
>
> "I'm a trial lawyer with the firm Whiteford, Taylor, and Pleston. When I introduce myself to new people there's a hint of recognition. Then I mention I work with Johnny Holliday and invariably people say, 'Oh, yeah, Johnny Holliday...' He knows everybody and is well respected by them all."

Being the son of legendary coach Jerry Claiborne, Jonathan knows football. Maryland football. Not only from the players' perspective but also from a coach's son's perspective.

Jonathan came to Maryland University after a successful high school career at Northwestern High, just up the street from the College Park campus. He was Academic All-Conference in the ACC and went on to law school. Today he's a practicing attorney in Baltimore.

Sadly, he lost both his mom and dad during the 2000-01 season, but he was still able to perform under very trying circumstances.

During Mark Duffner's tenure as head football coach, we added Tim Strachan as our sideline reporter. Tim had been one of three top quarterbacks in the nation during his All-Met high school career at DeMatha under coach Bill McGregor.

With scholarship offers from both Penn State and Maryland, Tim was enjoying his vacation a few weeks before the Maryland season opened. Tragically, he suffered a near fatal accident diving into the waters of Bethany Beach, Delaware. A broken neck left him paralyzed and confined to a wheelchair.

After the accident, Coach Duffner brought Tim on to help him coach the quarterbacks. I suggested that if Tim wasn't busy during the games, we could use him as our sideline reporter, which would also help Tim in his pursuit of a communications degree. Mark said, "You got it. I'll make sure that Tim isn't busy." And that's how it came about. Tim is now a law student at Georgetown.

But don't tell Tim he's 'confined' to anything. He makes his way around pretty good in his motorized wheelchair or in his specially outfitted van. His mom, Mary, says he's so busy these days he needs a secretary.

I've known Tim for most of his life. He grew up not far from my house, and my daughter, Tracie, used to baby-sit Tim and his brothers. When he joined our broadcast team, I gave him a headset but offered zero advice on how to do the sideline reports. I wanted him to just be Tim, because I knew he'd click with the players and the audience. He has great insight as to trends and strategy. He gives us injury updates because he's right there. During a 1996 Virginia game, for example, when Brian Cummings got hurt, I looked down on the field and Tim was right next to him, chatting away.

We go to Tim when the players come out of the locker room, because he's been in there with them. He'll tell us the mood, their attitude. We never ask him to tell tales out of school, but he's added a depth to the broadcast that we never had before. He knows when to get in and out.

Tim is just damn good, and I've heard from people like Roger Gardner, Jim Buckle, and Keith Sampson (from Learfield, our former rights holder) to the folks at Maryland like Debbie Yow and the coaches on the enormous positive impact Tim gives to our broadcasts.

Tim offers a quote he picked up from his dad: "The past is history, the future is a mystery and right now is a gift. That's why they call it the present."

Tim Strachan: "When Johnny asked me to be his sidelines guy, I had no idea what I'd be getting into. But he didn't prepare me at all. And I'm glad he didn't. By not making such a big deal out of it, he made it easy for me to adjust to the role. He made it comfortable for me, and that's one of the things that makes Johnny so good.

"I was so lucky at the age of 21 to get this opportunity to work with Johnny and Maryland. Johnny brought me along and over time started giving me suggestions on how I could improve my reports. He does it in a great way, just in conversation, by dropping hints on what he expects from me. To be ready to add to or anticipate what may happen in the game. It has really helped me.

"I like to kid him about his age. He's got the Dick Clark disease. And he likes the give and take. He'll be talking about some team from 1973, and I remind him on air that I wasn't born then.

"Another thing I like to kid him about is the weather. They're in the announcers' box and I'm on the field. They talk about the weather constantly, but they're not really affected by it at all. Once I was doing a game against Wake Forest, and it was bitterly cold. Maryland had the ball on their 2-yard line with 30 seconds left in the half. Johnny called down, 'Hey, Tim, what do you think they're trying to do?' and I said, 'I don't care. I'm going inside. I'm freezing.'

"I also try to stump him. We were talking about how useful the walk-on interviews were, what a guest adds to the broadcasts. I told Johnny that I thought I might be the first 'roll-on' interview because of my wheelchair. Johnny said, 'I'm not touching that one.'

"As for Ralph Friedgen, I just want to hug him. It's unfortunate that it has taken so long for us to get someone like the coach."

"Tim's a wonderful person," agrees Coach Friedgen, who knows how sports affect your life experiences.

Coach Friedgen: "Football is part of the students' education. There our things you learn on the football field that you don't necessarily learn in the classroom. You learn how to be a competitor, and you learn how to deal with stress. You learn the meaning of teamwork and how to work with people. You learn how to be productive on days you may not be 100%. You learn how to work through your ups and downs. I can go on and on and on. I believe that when you can take what you've learned on the football field and parlay it with what you've learned in the classroom, then you have a tremendous chance to be successful in life."

When asked about the many Coach of the Year awards he earned his first season out, Ralph explains:

"When I look at all the awards, I really think they're program awards. It's not just Ralph Friedgen who got those awards. It is our whole staff. It is our players, our coaches, our administration, and our academic support. Everybody has a part in that. What those awards tell me is that our program is recognized nationally, which is a tremendous honor. That's something I am very proud of because I represent our program. But I don't see them as my awards, and that's why I keep them here in the office. They're indicative of the hard work of a lot of people."

And some of the hard-working people on the football side are: Offensive Coordinator Marlie Taafe, Defensive Coordinator Gary Blackney, Offensive Line Coach Tom Brattan, Wide Receivers Coach James Franklin, Running Backs Coach Mike Locksley, Special Teams Coordinator Ray Rychleski,

Outside Linebackers Coach Al Seamonson, Inside Linebackers Coach Rod Sharpless, Defensive Line Coach Dave Sollazzo, Director of Football Operations Tom Deahn, Head Trainer Sandy Worth, Strength Coach Dwight Galt, and Equipment Manager Ron Ohringer.

Chapter 12

Kensington Home Base

Throughout my career people have always asked me, "Where do you find the time to do all your projects?" My answer is simple. If I didn't have the time in the first place, I wouldn't be doing them.

But to build my career also meant to know when and how to relax. My relaxation comes with doing things with my family. Nothing fancy, just real domestic-type stuff. I played golf with Mary Clare. We both participated in the girls' school activities, and I took the girls with me to many of my public appearances.

I often say that Mary Clare was responsible for raising the girls. Sometimes I joke that the marriage worked because my schedule kept me out of the house. Broadcasting's a hazardous business to be in since so many marriages go left and right. People in the public eye are subject to many temptations. And the opportunities to stray can prove dangerous if the marriage isn't strong.

Truthfully, I probably spend more time at home than the average guy does. I'd like to think that despite my many projects and frequent travel, I always show up, present and attentive.

Going into my marriage I knew that it takes a deeply shared commitment between a wife and husband to keep a marriage tight and to raise happy, successful kids. Our primary goal was to keep it a real home. And Clare always knows how to keep everything real.

Once we were having dinner with "Capt. Dan" Rosenson, the helicopter traffic reporter at WWDC, and his date, Leslie Stahl. Leslie was an aspiring correspondent at the time, mostly interested in discussing her career strategy. The dinner conversation became monotonously centered on how Leslie could quickly climb the success ladder. During the rare pause in this one-sided dialogue, Leslie turned to my wife and asked, "What do you do?"

After a moment, Clare deadpanned, "Well, I clean toilets. I push vacuums, and I dust once in awhile."

"How nice," Leslie responded, although we were all sure that Clare's answer hadn't registered. The moment passed. Leslie returned to her escargot and her own agenda.

Years later, I had Leslie on my radio show promoting a book. She was a very successful reporter and author by then. Leslie was great that day, but I doubt she had any recollection of the satirical humility behind Clare's dinner commentary.

Mary Clare Holliday: "It was fashionable to marry young when John proposed to me in 1957. I was just 18 when we married a year later, and we had very little except each other. There was certainly no money for a honeymoon, or new furniture, or any of the other nuptial items that newlyweds expect these days. Our lack of possessions was equally matched by my total inexperience in the kitchen. Love was a great distraction from these minor problems.

"As John became successful in radio there were adjustment issues. I was sometimes jealous of his work time versus the time he spent at home. There were groupies, although we didn't call them that back then, and I'll admit that sometimes I felt as though I were number two on the hit parade, with his career topping the chart.

"Fortunately, we learned very early to trust one another and work out our problems. With no family within 1,500 miles to take refuge, we had to solve our troubles on our own. Besides, I knew I'd get no sympathy calling my mom to complain. Her philosophy was 'Once you're married, you are on your own.'

"Although John and I are both Irish (I'm one-fourth German, too), his family background differed from mine. It was lucky for us that the commonality of our parents' generation and values led John to reject the alcoholic trap of the Bobbitt household and choose a very different, positive foundation for the Holliday marriage.

"He's watched others in his business become full of themselves and excessively egotistical. Because he was so humbled by his upbringing, I believe he honestly feels he's no more special than anyone else. When he is asked to speak at prestigious events, I'm more accustomed seeing him spend time talking with the servers, or to the folks who help organize the events who aren't credited in the program. I love him deeply for this quality.

"These recent years have been the best for me. I was the traditional wife, and John was the big star for most of our marriage. As I've pursued my painting and sculpture career, I found that John would be very supportive of this for me. We've found time to listen to each other more fully, continue to enjoy each other's company, and share a happiness that is even greater than our early years of marriage. He'll tell you that I laugh at his sense of humor 1,000 times more today than years ago.

"I think we've both decided to stick together."

Clare and I share a down-to-earth attitude that has served the family well in the home and in our community. I have always consciously tried to keep to the same level of people I've worked with in the industry despite my professional stature at any given time. I don't pull rank or think I'm better or more special than the engineers, account reps, secretaries, etc. that I work with. I'm not cut out to play the self-absorbed SOB role. I doubt that I could pull it off even if I tried.

However, I felt I needed to be a strict father at home. I think kids require that. In doing so, I felt that my kids would always know I'm there for them.

As in performance, timing is important when you set out to instill values or discipline in your children's lives. There were times when the daughters disregarded the Holliday House Rules like coming in way late from a dance or throwing a wild party when the parents were away. Rather than respond in the anger of the moment, I sometimes waited for a calmer time to discuss and then dole out the punishment. A good night's sleep will often put some perspective on issues.

When one of the girls got into trouble, Mary Clare would always remind me of why *we* were there. "She's a *kid*, John."

My eldest daughter, **Kellie (Holliday) Smaldore, D.O.:** "My Dad always made time for our family. He attended our games and school events and was the life of the party. My girlfriends loved him, and, without fail, he would make us laugh. That is not to say he didn't humiliate me when I was growing up.

"When I'd come home from a date, he would spy on me from behind the curtains or switch the lights off and on to beacon me in. He loved to talk about our personal life on the air. The town of Kensington always knew when I missed my curfew (which was frequent) and was grounded for a week or two.

"Dad was always supportive and motivating. He gave me the courage and confidence to do whatever I wanted to do. I had to work hard for my grades from high school through medical school. There were times when I was ready to throw in the towel and quit.

"When I would call home to complain, my dad would tell me he knew I could do it. If I decided not to do it, he let me know I could always move home and be a checker at the grocery store or work at the library. He never put pressure on me. I knew he was a self-made man with only a high school education. He got where he did through hard work and persistence.

"My Dad was forever doing fundraisers, whether it was a benefit basketball game for a needy school, a telethon, or taking in a foster kid for the weekend. There is no better example a parent can set for their child than to show generosity and kindness to others.

"I couldn't ask for a more wonderful father. I married a man with many of the same qualities as my dad, and I can only hope that my two boys will grow up to be as terrific a father as their father and grandfather."

My middle daughter, **Tracie (Holliday) Rolle:** "As a young child, I remember looking forward to the times Dad took me to work with him at WWDC. He'd wake me at 5 a.m., and we'd grab a donut and head for the studio. There, I'd sit and watch him broadcast from 6-10 a.m., and occasionally he'd put me on the air. Sometimes, if he was lucky, I would actually speak.

"Of course, I have many memories of doing commercials with Dad and my sisters. He was always so full of encouragement and praise, even though we were probably pretty awful.

"As Ms. 'Little Jock,' I watched from the stands when he'd play in the Oneder games, hoping I could be as good an athlete when I grew up. I'd also get upset when people would criticize him from the bleachers. They mostly poked fun at how small he was, but the same people would be standing in line after the game for his autograph. I guess size doesn't matter all that much, does it?

"I'll never forget Dad's head resting in my lap in the back seat of our 1969 Ford Mustang. It was after our 1975 plane crash, and my dad's friend, Nick Howey, and my Mom were frantically driving him to Sibley hospital for treatment. Drifting in and out of consciousness, he kept asking me, 'Are you OK, Baby-doll?' We didn't know at the time how seriously injured he was.

"For many years afterward, I would call him on the anniversary of the crash to celebrate another year that we were alive and well, because God gave us a second chance that night."

My youngest, **Moira Holliday:** "Dad and I have always had a special bond. I am his baby, and was forced by him to promise at a very young age that I would never grow up, never get married, and most important of all, never leave my daddy.

"He's always made sure that my sisters and I had everything that he didn't have when he was growing up. But I think his generosity can best be understood by what he does for others, even complete strangers.

"He once read a story in the *Washington Post* about a bus driver who had lost his wife in an accident and couldn't afford to buy a headstone for her grave. Dad called the man and offered to buy it for him. Dad invited the father and his son and daughter to be his guests at an Orioles baseball game and arranged tickets for them.

"For some reason, they never showed up. But Dad didn't appear angry or resentful that he had gone out of his way to help, with no sign of appreciation in return. He doesn't expect anything when he does something nice for someone; he just genuinely wants to help.

"His sense of humor is another thing that I love about him. No one has the power to make me laugh until my sides hurt like he does. And sometimes it's not because he's telling jokes, but rather the little quirks my sisters and I call 'Dad-isms.'

"First, he is offensively predictable. It's decaf coffee with every meal. From spaghetti and tacos at home, to Caesar salad with chicken at the Columbia Country Club, he always orders decaf coffee.

"And he'll bombard every waitress and waiter with a series of kidding questions, always beginning with: 'Where'd you go to school?' If the answer is the University of Maryland, they'll be sure to get a nice tip.

"Dad's always the last one out of the house as he shouts down to the end of the driveway, 'Clare? Have you got the keys?' It is impossible for him to shut the door without asking that question. It makes my Mom and me laugh so hard. Why would we have the keys when he's driving?

"But what a comfort it is to hear that question every time we leave home. It means that everything is right."

I'm as proud of my daughters as a father can be. I'm also satisfied that my two oldest daughters picked the best possible fellows to marry. Chris Rolle and Dr. Steve Smaldore are more than exceptional, and we share close bonds, particularly on the golf course.

In fact the only time we've ever found it hard to communicate was at the Marsh Hawk course of the Ford's Colony Country Club in Williamsburg, Va. I used a six-iron on the 17th hole to drive the ball 157 yards to the pin. My only hole in one was witnessed by Chris and Steve. When we saw what had happened, we didn't know how to respond or what to say to each other.

Our Kensington house (once described by the *Washington Post* as a "split-level, vaguely California-mission home") is perched on a hill in the shadow of the enormous Mormon Temple. The temple sits illuminated like Oz in our neighborhood. The county is forever painting over the "Surrender Dorothy" graffiti that some unknown pranksters repeatedly spray-paint on a nearby bridge.

I've read that the township of Kensington started as an old railroad community in Montgomery County dating back to the 1790s. It was then known as Knowles Station. As with many Washington, D.C. suburbs of those early days, Kensington was first a "getaway" from the city's swampy summer heat. The earliest residents could hop a train or trolley and get to work downtown and retire at night under the shade trees of Rock Creek. Eventually, people moved in year-round, and the character of Kensington became established.

My office is on the first floor of my house. It's there I keep the video and tape library of my professional work. Guests may be surprised that I don't display much of my professional life inside the home. There are few photos, awards, or other indications that I am in "show" business.

The truth is that I once had almost every piece of memorabilia prominently exhibited throughout the house until Clare and my daughters decided the "Johnny Holliday" museum was becoming too much. They packed everything in boxes and shoved the whole lot in the attic. I came home to find that my "shrine" had vanished.

But that's OK with me. Photos of my kids and grandkids are more heartening.

Clare keeps her art studio in our basement. Many of her best works dress up the rooms of our home. Clare is a gifted artist. The University of Maryland recently commissioned her to do a painting, which they turned into a poster, "Terrapin Traditions," that shows the school's athletic buildings over the years. From the 1923 Gymnasium to the new 2002 Comcast Center, this one's a beauty. I would like to give my wife a shameless plug here by encouraging every Terrapin fan to purchase this collector's item. On the web it's http://store.fansonly.com/md/store.

I always become the invisible man when I escort Clare to her gallery showings. Clare's artist friends are interested in her work, not my music and sports stories.

Kensington isn't the ritziest D.C. suburb by any means. You'd have to go to Potomac, Maryland or McLean, Virginia to see the true mansions surrounding the nation's capital. Kensington is simply a fine American neighborhood. Unpretentious. Comfortable. Great neighbors.

Our family has attended Holy Redeemer Catholic Church for the past 30 years. Recently I got front row tickets to see the Golden Boys: Frankie Avalon, Fabian, and Bobby Rydell, at Dover Downs in Dover Delaware. Three of my closest buddies, Dr. Tony Natoli, Mike Kinnahan, and Bob Silk, made the trek with me. We went without the wives.

Backstage, I introduced my pals to the stars. They all had hit records when I was in Cleveland.

"So that was you four in the front row?" Bobby Rydell asked, adding, "We thought your group may have been with a gay convention."

Last year, Kensington made national headlines when someone in the local government decided to ban Santa Claus from what was supposed to be a nonsectarian "Christmas" pageant. Dozens of my neighbors showed up in Santa suits to protest. I would have joined them in my own Santa outfit, but I was covering the Terps in the BB&T Classic tournament at the MCI Center that day

The guy I always call the "Czar of Cedarbrook" or "Kensington Fats" is my good friend, Bob Silk. For me he's kind of an unofficial mayor of Kensington. Another friend with mayoral ties is Kevin Plank. Kevin came from St. John's High School to the Maryland football squad under Coach Vanderlinden, where he was a linebacker and special teams captain from 1992-95. His mother, Jane, once served as the town's elected mayor.

Kevin came up with an idea for a new sports undershirt that would help players deal with perspiration. Today his Under Armour company in Baltimore ships undershirts to just about every college and NFL team. His web site at http://www.underarmour.com explains how the shirts work.

One of my favorite neighborhood characters is Mr. Heoung (it rhymes with "sing") who runs the Kensington Market. This Asian gentleman nailed me with an unusual greeting one day:

"*Good morning, Sir!* How am I doing?"

I said, "I'm pretty good, how are *you?*"

"No, no!" cried Mr. Heoung, "I didn't ask you how *you* were doing. I asked you how *I* am doing? You see? You're not listening. People don't listen to each other."

I had to agree that he caught me on that one, but then again, Mr. Heoung has always surprised me. For years he always greeted me with "*Good morning, Sir.* "It didn't matter whether it was after lunch, or late in the evening, it was always—and only—"*Good morning, Sir.* "

I thought, "This poor guy knows nothing but '*Good morning, Sir.*' He doesn't even know *what time of day it is.* "

One day I walked in as he was talking fluently with six Hispanic workers, their coffees and lunches piled on the counter. I asked, "Mr. Heoung, you know Spanish?"

He replied, "Si. I know five languages—German, French, Vietnamese, English, and Italian. *Good morning, Sir.* "

It turned out that Mr. Heoung was educated at the International School in Paris.

The Southland Corporation fired him after a robbery occurred while he was the manager on duty. The company blamed him unjustly, and his abrupt disappearance didn't sit well with his former customers.

So we started a successful petition drive to bring Mr. Heoung back. When Southland rehired him, we had a homecoming celebration complete with flowers. Mr. Heoung was so touched that he asked me for an autographed photo for the store bulletin board, which I happily inscribed.

A few days later, former President Clinton's press secretary, Michael McCurry, walked into the store, pointed to my picture, and joked, "Why is Holliday up there and not me?" The next day, Mr. Heoung cut a small photo of McCurry from a newspaper and stuck it up on the board beside my bigger, glossier one.

And speaking of glossy photos, a few words about my aunt, the movie star.

None of us knows for sure exactly how my Aunt Marjorie left Miami to become an actress in Hollywood. Nor do we understand how she came to marry an actor named Michael St. Angel, an Illinois native born in 1916.

The well known columnist Walter Winchell was Uncle Michael's best man at their wedding, and Winchell noted the event in one of his columns, "An Angel Takes a Holliday."

I do remember Uncle Michael would send me things from Hollywood when I was a kid in Miami. My favorite gift was a pair of great loafers. Although a few sizes too big, I stuffed newspaper in them and they fit fine.

Aunt Marjorie was my mom's older sister. Both were beautiful, and my sister and I agree that Mom was every bit as talented as my aunt. Mom simply chose to have a family. Aunt Margie sought the professional spotlight and appeared to have modestly succeeded, with a role as a powder puff girl in *The Dolly Sisters* as her standout credit.

According to what I think I know, Marjorie hit Hollywood after first working as a model in New York and being discovered by a talent scout. She was under contract to Fox Studios, and her mail was always getting mixed up with actress Judy Holliday.

In summary, I love my family, Kensington is a wonderful neighborhood full of dear friends, I'm not as bad a golfer as my cronies claim, and my Aunt Margie was a powder puff girl.

Who could ask for anything more?

Chapter 13

A Few Good Jocks

"Johnny Holliday is not only a talented broadcaster, actor, and athlete, but an outstanding coach. I know because he was my coach in both baseball and basketball. Of course he organized both teams and made himself the coach."
— **Sal Bando**, *World Champion Oakland Athletics*

In 1984, my boss at ABC, Shelby Whitfield, assigned me to do the USFL Saturday Night Game of the Week on ABC Radio. I did the play-by-play, Barry Tompkins hosted the pregame show, and Paul Hornung was my color analyst.

Paul Hornung was a number-one draft pick straight out of a Heisman Trophy college career at Notre Dame. He was quarterback, fullback, half-back, and a kicker, to boot. "The Golden Boy from Notre Dame" was what they called him. A Hall of Famer, Paul was terrific to work with. Always well prepared, Paul would really speak out and give his opinion on what he was seeing on the football field. Sometimes he'd ruffle players' feathers with his honest observations.

If you want to know which defensive player hit the hardest in pro football, just ask Paul. He'd tell you it was Dick Butkus by far. "He'd almost twist your head off," Paul used to say.

Our first meeting took place at a Tampa, Florida, hotel. I was sitting by the pool when I sensed a figure hovering above me. I looked up to see Hornung in a Hawaiian shirt, sunglasses, and puffing a cigar about the size of Chicago.

"You Holliday?" he asked.

"Yep," I answered.

"Golden Boy here."

My comeback was, "If you're going to talk to me then you'd better take that basketball out from underneath your shirt." He started laughing and from that point on I knew we were going to click.

The red carpet was always laid out for us when we'd travel together. I was with Mr. All-American, a world champion running back with the Packers. Everybody knew Paul Hornung. (But who was that little guy he was with?) We'd get first-class treatment everywhere we went.

I also remember that after the ball games and a bite to eat together at the hotel, we'd call it a night. Paul had a reputation as a playboy in his prime, but we'd never go raise hell on the town like he did as a player. Oh, sure, he'd still have a drink with you, but no, we did not bet on any games.

I still keep in touch with him. It was a real pleasure to work with a Hall of Famer.

Although my career has connected me with many accomplished athletes, it's easy to name the most skilled player I've known for the longest time. This is Sal Bando, All-Star third baseman and captain of the world champion Oakland Athletics. Sal retired as general manager of the Milwaukee Brewers in 1999 and today serves as special assistant to the president of the team.

In Cleveland, my apartment was just behind the high school, and I'd play ball with the kids in the afternoon. One young boy who really stood out was Sal.

I once saw him play a high school football game where he broke his toe early in the game but went on score five touchdowns. Sal was a stocky 6'1", 190-pound quarterback. He also starred on the basketball and baseball teams in Warrensville Heights.

As a professional player, he became a great role model and example for the fans. Like Cal Ripken, Sal would sign autographs for hours. The team elected him captain because he stood up for all the things they needed. He wasn't afraid of agitating management. He'd speak his mind and represent the players' interests. He worked as hard as anyone I've seen on the field. I'm very proud to call Sal a close friend.

Sal recalls how we hooked up.

Sal Bando: "Johnny always loved baseball, and one day he was playing ball behind my high school in Warrensville Heights. I was out there also looking to play ball. The next thing you know, he and I were playing catch. Then I joined him with some other guys in a home run hitting game. I was 16, and Johnny looked like he could be in high school, too. I found out he was the disc jockey on WHK, and I began to listen to him on the radio. But we began as friends on the ball field.

"Johnny was very popular in the city. Most definitely. But his popularity wasn't just related to being a disc jockey; it was all the other things that he did. Basketball, baseball, commercials. He was out there and people really came to know him. He was much more than just a voice on the radio.

"Also, in those days, what Johnny was doing on WHK was so new. You either loved that Top 40 stuff or you hated it. I loved it, and I had great parents that let me grow in the ways I needed to grow.

"Our next association was when I started my professional career in Oakland with the Athletics, and Johnny was on KYA in San Francisco. We immediately got together. Rick Barry sat out of the NBA in '67, and he was with the Oneders then. When Rick returned to professional basketball the next year, I took his place on Johnny's team. My claim to fame is that during the year Rick Barry played, the Oneders lost only two games. When I played, we lost just one. We had our own refs, but that's beside the point.

"The Oneders always wanted to win. That one game we lost got very physical. The faculty was trying to show their students how tough they were, and it got a little out of hand. But in that game, and for all the ones I remember, Johnny was always the peacemaker. We would sometimes let our egos and machismo get the best of us, but Johnny remained the cool person during it all.

"I loved playing with the Oneders. We had our own bus and uniforms. It was classy. We played twice a week. Johnny did his thing, and the experience brought me back to feeling like I was in high school. I was a pretty good basketball player—not as good as Rick Barry, obviously—but I had played in school.

"Johnny handled everything. He organized the games, made them competitive, and it was great publicity for his radio show. It let the audience personalize the team and know who we were.

"In the off season I ended up doing a sports segment at KYA that would air in the mornings and in drive time and this was mainly due to my friendship with Johnny. In my own career we started right there in Oakland in '68, and that was the makings of the Athletics dynasty. We became world champions in 1972 and again in '73. My most exciting professional moment came when the Athletics won the first World Series. When you win that first one, you have reached the pinnacle of what you've always dreamed about.

"What really helped me in '68 when I first arrived was knowing Johnny. I was by myself—single—and, for me, having Johnny, as a friend that I knew back in Cleveland was a big stabilizing factor. Johnny and Mary Clare introduced me to their friends. They became my extended family. I really looked forward to the evenings we played with Johnny's club. Then I married my wife, Sandy, the next year and it all played a big role in my success with the Athletics.

"Johnny is the kind of person who just seems to be out for helping other people. I don't think I realized this as much when I was younger, but as I got older and watched him, and saw his giving nature, I came to appreciate what he stood for. Our relationship since the San Francisco days has been such that we don't have to try to keep in contact to stay friends. In fact, I just got together with Johnny recently when the Maryland Terps came into Wisconsin. It was like we'd never been separated, although it had been several years since we had talked.

"But when I was in San Francisco that first year I can tell you that my whole life was the Athletics and Johnny's Radio Oneders."

The last two years that the Washington Senators played in D.C. gave me a chance to know Ted Williams, the "Splendid Splinter" and Hall of Fame legend. Ted managed the Senators when I'd interview him on my WWDC pregame Senators show. Ted was bigger than life. Having grown up a serious fan when he hit 521 home runs with the Boston Red Sox, it was somewhat intimidating to go face to face with him before every game. Fortunately, he made it so easy for me.

The first time I interviewed Ted was a near disaster. Halfway through the interview, my engineer, Tom Hammersky, looked down and noticed that the tape recorder wasn't working. I asked if we could start all over again, and Ted said, "No problem. Let's go." Some managers would have exploded.

Ted even gave me some hitting tips one day in the dugout. I had confessed that I was always pulling the bat when I played in high school. Ted handed me a bat and showed me what I had been doing wrong. Too bad this lesson from a HOF batter couldn't have happened when I was playing for North Miami High School.

Washington Redskins shows are always a hit in D.C. Bobby Beathard was the first general manager to team with me on Washington TV. Always casual, colorful, and decked out in his trademark shorts and jogging shoes, Bobby was fun to work with. Bobby went on to be general manager for the San Diego Chargers. Bobby retired last year, and there had been some talk of him returning to work for Dan Snyder and the Redskins. I, for one, am sorry that it didn't work out.

My WMAL radio Redskins preshows gave me the chance to work with Sonny Jurgenson and Sam Huff. As a quarterback, no one could do it as well as Sonny. Both Sam and Sonny were always a delight to be around. They'd come on air with their thoughts on the upcoming game. Our give and take ad-lib sessions were always fun.

When Bobby Beathard moved on, Charley Casserly took over general manager duties, and my HTS coaches' show with Charley were quite enjoyable. They called Charley one of the bright young professional managers. He was respected for his draft choices. It was a terrible mistake for the current Redskins regime to get rid of Charley.

Charley Casserly: "I understood when the Redskins team was sold that there'd be a good chance I'd be leaving Washington. I had been with the Cooke family for 23 years and was very close to John and his son. It was clear that whoever came in [as owner] might want their own person there. I offered Dan my resignation, and after a period of time, he accepted it. I understood that's how it works. I got on with my life.

"It would have been very difficult to stay with the Redskins under the circumstances that existed, with all the people who were getting fired that I had worked with for so many years. It would have been hard to stay.

"But I'm happy where I'm at now with the Houston Texans. I was the first hired, so I've been here as general manager for two years. We've got a great owner in Bob McNair and a great organization with the people we've brought on. It's a tremendous challenge to build a team from scratch, but at some point here I'm sure we'll have a winner.

"I've known Johnny close to 20 years. I loved working with him. He's the consummate professional. Here's a guy who is in the Rock and Roll Hall of Fame but can also handle play-by-play for all sports on any level. He has a clear sense of how to handle an interview. We did Redskins TV and radio shows on local stations and for Home Team Sports starting in 1989. I've seen him act and heard him sing.

"I had no experience when I first did the shows with John. I had to ask him for advice, but he's so smooth the way he adapts to your style and then just brings you along. Before I knew it we were rolling.

"He's a great friend. I can't say enough good about him."

Although Charley and his wife, Bev, are in Texas, Mary Clare and I still try to stay close. Redskins owner Dan Snyder publicly admitted that he made a mistake in letting Charley go.

Joe Theismann owns the Redskins' records for passing yardage (25,206), completions (2,044), and attempts (3,602), and his 12 years in the NFL were stellar. Joe led the Washington Redskins to a 27-17 win over the Miami Dolphins in Super Bowl XVII. Who can forget that awful play in '85 when Joe broke his leg? That unlucky break ended his career.

However, Joe was running back punts and holding for extra points before he became the first-string quarterback for the Skins. He got more playing time with our charity basketball team than he did with the Skins when he first arrived.

I knew Joe would be a great addition to the Radio Oneders. To entice Joe to play with the team, I invited him, along with teammate Ken Stone, to the Harlequin for a dinner and show. He liked the show (it was *Finian's Rainbow*), and they both agreed to play with us.

Joe took as many shots with the Oneders as he is now taking for his color commentary on ESPN. He also scored 71 points against a high school faculty during one game. Nobody, including Rick Barry, ever scored that many points. When it came time to write a check for his expenses, he always had us send his share to Children's Hospital. He never took a dime.

You can love Joe or you can hate him, but I know that when he did interviews at Redskins Park, he would treat the local reporters with the same respect and cooperation as he would the national heavyweights. He'd treat the reporter from Salisbury, Maryland just the same as he'd treat the reporter from the *New York Times*. I can appreciate and relate to that because it has always been the way I have tried to operate.

Brig Owens was drafted by the Dallas Cowboys in '65 and traded to the Redskins the next year to begin his 12-year career as a Skins defensive back. His Skins record of 36 intercepted passes still stands. Brig played on our WWDC Radio Oneders teams during the off season. He was a tremendous asset and one of the all-time best players in our group.

At the collegiate level Brig had played football at the University of Cincinnati, and you could see he was also one heck of a basketball player. One of the most personable of all the Redskins and a real family man, I'd be hard pressed to name a nicer person than Brig.

Here's another athlete who was easily accessible to fans wherever the Oneders played. I could see then why Brig would eventually go on to become a terrific players' agent. Today, he counsels athletes through his sports management firm of Bennett and Owens. A graduate from Antioch Law School, he and Mark Murphy, now the athletic director at Colgate University, are the only former Redskins I know to be lawyers. (There's a good opportunity for a lawyer joke here, so drop me a line if you think of one, and I'll include it in this book's second edition.)

Don't ever play golf with Pete Wysocki. It's even money that his club might hit you. This former linebacker for the Redskins and onetime player in the Canadian football league is also one of the funniest fellows I have ever met. He liked to do dialects, especially the old vaudevillian Georgie Jessel. Pete was the captain of the Skins' special teams, and he was very outgoing and much in demand as a public speaker for charities. He was extremely good at that.

Pete was a member of the WMAL sales staff and he did color commentary work with me on the side. "Sock" could analyze with the best of them. With his quick one-liners he maintained a rapport with players and coaches alike.

Today he is facing the biggest challenge of his life—leukemia—which, thankfully, is in remission. I last saw Pete at a fundraiser where he spoke eloquently about the will to live and the challenges of chemotherapy. There was nothing funny that night. He moved many in the audience to tears.

Redskins kicker Mark Mosley and I worked together on a Channel 20 show, and my Home Team Sports shows included stints with general manager Bobby Mitchell, former head coach Jack Pardee, and Dexter Manley.

Dexter was the vocal leader of the Redskins. He has that engaging smile coupled with an All-Pro football body. He led the team in sacking the quarterback, and when I first met him in the locker room following a particularly successful game, Dexter took a look at me and said, "You don't dress bad for a white guy." This was a case of the pot calling the kettle black, because Dexter often showed up off the field in jeans with holes in the knee.

Dexter was always a challenge when he and I shared a mic. I never knew what he would say next, or if he was even going to show up for the program. Sometimes he didn't.

Sadly, Dexter got involved with drugs and served time. I'll never forget a late-night call I received from Dexter when he was in the John Lucas rehab program for substance abuse. He was phoning from Texas asking my advice on what approach he should take with owner Jack Kent Cooke regarding his return to the team from jail and rehab. I tried to explain to him how important a figure he was to the team, but he wasn't buying it that night.

On a later occasion, popular Fox TV host James Brown joined Dexter and me on one of our Redskins shows. James and I were both amazed at Dexter's disagreement when we tried to convince him that he'd be "Mr. Redskin" if only he would stay on the straight and narrow.

Charley Casserly reminded me of the time he and I were doing a Friday taped broadcast and we had heard that Dexter might be suspended the next day. The problem was that our show was scheduled to air on Sunday, and we couldn't be sure that the suspension announcement was actually going to take place.

"So we ended up taping two shows," Charley recalls. "One where we talked about the suspension, and a second one where we talked about how happy we were that the Redskins had changed their mind. I told the producers, "Just be sure you air the right show." (They did. Dexter was suspended.)

Dexter lives in Houston these days. I hope he eventually turns his life around, as I really liked him when we were working together.

The most troubled player I've known is Denny McLain, an attention-grabbing pitcher who came to the Washington Senators from the Detroit

Lions ball club. There he had won two back-to-back Cy Young awards (1968-69). Denny played one game on our WWDC Radio Oneders softball team at the same time he was on the Washington Senators' disabled list. It was the staff of Walter Reed Medical Center against an all-star Oneders team. We won, of course.

He insisted he play despite not being able to pitch for the Senators because of a bad shoulder. Go figure. The late *Washington Star* writer, Morrie Siegel, got wind of this and put it in one of his columns.

The truth about Denny's arm is that he first hurt it in '66 and continued to abuse it because he never gave it a chance to heal. Eventually, he was in great pain. He was trying to throw the ball from different positions, different levels, and that wasn't working either. He relied on cortisone shots to keep going, so his arm wasn't much good when he got to Washington. This is what he told me.

He also told me how much he hated working for the Senators under Ted Williams.

"Teddy was tough to play for and talk with. He had the idea that pitchers were stupid people. My bottom line is that I never saw a hitter reach 1000. But I've seen pitchers go through a season without losing a ball game. Teddy had a real negative attitude toward pitchers, and I resented it from the get-go," he said.

Denny was personable with a great sense of humor and could charm the pants off anyone he met. A talented guy, he did a musical stint on the organ for a while at the Shoreham Hotel, the same place that political satirist Mark Russell played for nearly a thousand years. Morrie Siegel, doing a stand-up comedy routine, joined Denny on stage. ("Mo Siegel was as bad a comedian as he was a writer," joked Denny.) When Denny later came on our WWDC pregame show, I never knew where the ad-libbing would lead.

Unfortunately, Denny was convicted of drug possession, extortion, and racketeering in 1985 and sent to the Atlanta Federal Pen. It was hard for me to believe he was found guilty. I visited him in the big house, but it was not something I looked forward to—especially since my first attempt to see him failed when his family showed up the same day and Denny had to choose between his family or me. This, after I went through all the hassle of being frisked and waiting to make my way through the different lock-ups. I called my ABC boss, Shelby Whitfield, and told him the trip had not been a successful one. Shelby said to head back home and reschedule another visit.

When I returned, I was startled to see that he had gained a tremendous amount of weight, but he was the same Denny I had known, and anxious to talk about the good ole days in D.C. He sent his regards to Bill Sanders, our WWDC general manager, to Capt. Dan, and to "the good-looking broad," which I couldn't identify immediately, but think it may have been Bill Sanders' secretary.

Denny continued to claim he was innocent during our visit. I truly felt sorry for what had happened to him, especially when he later lost his daughter in an automobile accident. During our visit, Denny opened up and shared his feelings about being "rehabilitated" in prison. This was taped for a broadcast interview for ABC:

> **Denny McLain:** "It's awesome to see the walls when you walk into prison. They're 30 feet high and, supposedly, 30 feet into the ground. It's right out of a Jimmy Cagny movie.
>
> "Rehabilitation is a tough term when you are indicted on hearsay, convicted on hearsay evidence, sent to a county jail with manacles on your feet. You have to perform bodily functions in front of other people. You're led to a shower in handcuffs behind your back. You have a family visitor, and then they check every orifice in your body to determine that you're not carrying contraband back to your jail cell. They read your mail. They listen to your phone conversations. If this is rehabilitation, then we're all in trouble.
>
> "The judge herself said my case was too close to call when the jury was out, and then she came back and gave me 23 years in this prison. This has been eating away at me, but I'm going to fight like hell for my appeal. You know, the big thing for professional players was alcohol when I was coming up. I remember being shocked when I saw two Washington Senators smoking marijuana because I didn't think this sort of thing went on. But lawyers and judges single out professional players for their drug experiences because they have the name. I don't think baseball, football, or basketball players should be singled out any more than anyone else.
>
> "For the most part since I came to prison I've heard from the front office and the media, but it's been disappointing that I haven't heard from any of the players. I could sure use some support, because this is the pit here inside prison. The nice thing that has happened is that I've received tons of mail from people that I don't know. They may not know everything about my case, but they do have compassion for my family and me."

During our prison interview I asked Denny point blank if he ever bet on games or assaulted anyone. He responded:

> "As a matter of fact, I never bet on any games that I participated in. The only baseball bet I ever made was with a [network radio] producer on the World Series and he wrote me a check for $500. I have bet on football games, but other than that one World Series, I've never bet on a baseball game. My trial got so ridiculous that the prosecutor said I assaulted two sports writers. The alleged assault was dumping two buckets

of water—not the buckets, just the water—and how they got an assault charge out of this is beyond me. But that's how ridiculous my trial became. Any little stupid thing I had done in my life became a criminal act. Despite the fact that the courts are not supposed to bring up anything from 15, 20 years ago.

"My basic problem was a physical problem. When my arm went, I followed. You meet people in this business, and you don't know what their background is. I've always been open, and never declined to meet people. Looking back, I probably would have met less people and did more checking beforehand. This is what I would have done differently.

"In all candor, I have a very bad tendency to trust everybody. I've heard of deals here in prison that I would have bought into. But they only let me spend $95 a month as a prisoner, although I don't know where they came up with that figure. I get paid 11 cents an hour for working as a prison cook. God forbid, I can't find some humor in all this."

I don't know who taught Sugar Ray Leonard his interview skills. It could have been Mike Trainer, his attorney, or Charlie Brotman, his publicist. Whoever it was, they did one heck of a job. Ray was, and still is, a terrific interview, and he always has that twinkle in his eye. Trainer once said Sugar Ray is the kind of guy who's always looking at the edge of the cliff, fascinated as to how close he can get to it.

Being in Washington gave me the chance to really follow Ray's career. He never forgot his humble beginnings in Palmer Park, Maryland, south-east of the District, and was always a charismatic yet very down-to-earth kind of guy when I saw him. I covered his rise to the Olympics (he was the light welterweight Olympic champ in 1976) on through his work as a professional boxer. (Ray won the world welterweight title in 1979, and four more titles with a career record of 36-2-1.)

The first Leonard fight I covered was at the Capitol Center arena when he went up against David "Boy" Green. I broadcast his classic fights with Roberto Duran in Montreal and Thomas Hearns in Vegas.

Almost every time I interviewed Ray, he would try to work in how he'd someday like to be a spokesperson for Nissan, as I was for a time. This was our inside joke.

One of the Leonard fights I covered was on June 25, 1981 when he went up against Ayub Kalule:

"We are down to the final 15 seconds as a right and a left finds its mark by Sugar Ray. Again connecting to Kalule who looks like he's about to go down. Another right and there goes Kalule. He's down. He's gone down for the first time, but it looks like the bell is going to save him in number nine.

"The count is on the far side of the ring. There's the bell. But wait a minute. Is the referee going to stop the fight? Yes, the fight is stopped. He's knocked down and knocked out. Ray Leonard has beat Kalule. Ray Leonard does a somersault in the center of the ring. The bell almost saved Kalule. He's knocked down for the first time and almost knocked out of the ring and defeated by Sugar Ray Leonard.

"Ray's arms are being raised in the center of the ring as Juanita gives her husband a kiss, joined by Little Ray. A tougher fight than anyone thought but now it's on to the hit man, Tommy Hearnes, for Leonard who tonight becomes the junior middleweight champion of the world."

And now a few words with the Scotti brothers from halftime at the Orange Bowl, 2002:

JH: A couple of halftime guests with us tonight. Let me get their headsets on for a couple of guys you'll remember well from their days as Maryland football players in the late '50s. We'll let Tony Scotti sit down first, and the former pride and joy of the Philadelphia Eagles, Ben Scotti, sit down next. The Scotti Brothers are with us. Welcome Tony and welcome Ben.

Ben: *Johnny, it's good to see you, and it's great to be in the Orange Bowl. We may not be winning, but we're here.*

JH: Tony, you played for the Terps in '58 and '59, and you, Ben, played in '56, '57, and '58. In the lobby of the hotel today it was like a reunion old-home week with former players like Dick Scarbath, Jack's brother, and others you played with. It's nice to see those guys.

Tony: *Right. You know they're so excited. It seems like Ralph Friedgen is bringing all the great ball players back to Maryland to support the program. We have a lot of confidence in the coach, and Dr. Mote, and Deborah Yow. We believe that this is the first of many trips to the bowl games.*

We go back to my days in Cleveland. They began producing records (Survivor's "Eye of the Tiger" is one of their big hits) and now run one of the most successful syndication businesses ever. The TV show *Baywatch* is their baby. At one point they owned nearly 50 percent of all the games shows, like *Price is Right* and *Family Feud*, running in 33 countries. They point out now that they learned a lot at Maryland.

I emceed the Maryland New Year's Eve party last year in Miami the night before the Orange Bowl. Debbie Yow, Ralph Friedgen, and Dr. Dan Mote were celebrating when Tony Scotti called me over to meet his wife, legendary French singer Sylvie Vartan.

"Look, Sylvie. It's Johnny Holliday *and not your first husband!*" said Tony.

I learned that Sylvie had been married to French rock and roll singer Johnny Hallyday. Ironically, I used to play an introduction of one of Hallyday's live concert recordings, with the kids screaming "Johnny! Johnny!" right before my old radio broadcasts. The University of Maryland is proud of the accomplishments of the Scotti brothers.

Nobody has ever said an unkind word about Coach Morgan Wooten, the most successful high school basketball coach in history. He's been at DeMatha High School in Hyattsville, MD since 1956 and received the ultimate honor from the basketball fraternity with his election to the Basketball Hall of Fame in the summer or 2000. I've known him for 30 years.

Morgan's record is an amazing 1,200 wins and only 183 losses. No other high school coach even comes close.

Just look at the players he has produced who have gone on to such great college or NBA careers. Adrian Dantley, Danny Ferry, Perry Clark, Jerrod Mustaf, Kenny Carr, Eddie Fogler, Sidney Lowe and a list of about a hundred others that he's sent to the pros. His players have earned over 250 college scholarships. Years back, he was once offered some big bucks (and free college tuition for his five children I heard) to coach North Carolina State. He turned it down. If any of my grandsons attend DeMatha, I hope they can play for the coach.

Add to his great career the drama of near death when his liver failed. Coach Wooten got a liver transplant, and he was soon back in business coaching his team.

Morgan and I were honored to take part in a historic event a few years ago. Cardinal James Hickey celebrated Mass on Oct. 8, 2000 at D.C.'s MCI Center to close the first ever archdiocesan Eucharistic Congress. It was the largest Catholic Mass celebrated in the metropolitan area since the visit by Pope John Paul II in1979.

By now I'm pretty much known in the Catholic community as an "easy touch." If there's an event where a speaker or host is required, my fellow Catholics frequently call on me because they know I'll say yes, and I'll do it for free. I have a hard time saying no to almost everybody, but I'm really useless when the request comes from a priest or a nun, and even more so when it comes from a cardinal.

Just before the Mass, I hosted a family celebration program that included a one-on-one interview with Morgan up near the altar. The coach shared his recipe for success during our pre-Mass interview. As far as I'm concerned, Morgan stands for everything right and good in athletics.

Morgan Wooten: "To do well in life, you have to have your priorities in the proper order. God must be first in your life. Family second. For my players I tell them that school and studies should be next. And then comes athletics, singing, or whatever your hobbies are. As long as you keep your priorities in good order, then you have a pretty good chance to have a good life with God's help. If you step back and think about why things are not going right in your life, it is probably because you've allowed your priorities to get out of whack. Things aren't going well at home? Well, maybe you've let your family slip down to fifth place. Often, your problems that seem so insurmountable at the time can be resolved if you reset your priorities."

Chapter 14

Baseball Legends

Joe, the players today are different than the guys you played with, aren't they?
Joe Garagiola: Yes, Johnny. They are richer.

I'd have to agree with umpire Jim Honochick that Joe DiMaggio and Ted Williams were the all-time best baseball players. I never saw either of them play in person, but as a kid listening to the radio, I was thrilled by their home runs. And later on to have the chance to interview DiMaggio, when he came to Washington for the Cracker Jack Old-timers Baseball Classics, or Manager Ted Williams for two entire baseball seasons during my Senators pre-game show were major joys in my life.

This is not to say, however, that we're not seeing players of great caliber now. Today's youngsters have their own heroes. I think first of baseball's "Iron Man," Cal Ripken, Jr. It would not disappoint me if any of my grandsons grew up to be just like Cal.

"The best way to sum up Cal Ripken," says Fred Manfra, the Voice of the Orioles, "is what you see is what you get. If you watched Cal before a game you'd see him autograph for the fans. He enjoyed the interaction. He put out 100 percent on the field. You couldn't ask for more from a baseball player, or from any athlete, or from a person in any other business. I think Cal Ripken saved baseball, especially following the last labor situation."

Fred Manfra and I worked together at ABC for many years. His wife Marlene and his family are my daughter's patients. When asked to share some thoughts on our relationship, Fred contributed the following:

Fred Manfra: "First of all John is one the best and most versatile broadcasters in our business. You give him an assignment—whether it be dog-sled racing, boxing, tiddly-winks, Maryland football and basketball, or Orioles baseball—and he'll do an outstanding job. Also, he's one of the most professional people I've been around. No matter what the situation is. No matter how much pressure is on, he always keeps things light and does a tremendous job.

"I've always been amazed at the energy Johnny brings not only to his work, but also to his life. His personality is one where there's always a laugh around the corner. I enjoy working with people who keep things light. It relieves pressure in a pressure-packed business. You need that laughter when you are covering a major event and a lot is happening. You need somebody there like John to give you the latest impression of a celebrity—as John does since he can do so many voices. Especially his impression of Angel Cordero.

"I enjoy listening to John on Maryland football and basketball very much. When John's behind the mic, I follow the Terps quite a bit. It's a pleasure to listen to him. John is very important to the Maryland sports program because people identify that voice with the teams. When they hear Johnny's voice they immediately think of the Terrapins. It is a great association and a big selling point for a university program.

"We were at ABC together, but I was in New York and he was based in Washington. We'd telecommunicate and always share a laugh as we discussed what was going on. The only times we really got together is when we were on assignment covering the Olympics or something like that of a major nature.

"Once we were in Seoul and John got a call from Rick Barry inviting him to a basketball game there. When John arrived at the arena and sat down, Rick asked him for money to cover the tickets. That was funny.

"I appreciate John's work, and what is even more important, he's a good person. In our business you can often find outstanding broadcasters who aren't outstanding people. Johnny fits the bill for both."

The Cracker Jack Old-timers Baseball Classic games came to Washington D.C.'s RFK Stadium in 1984. For the next three years I was in seventh heaven to be able to do the pregame shows and on-the-field interviews. What an exciting opportunity this was to meet some of the legendary baseball players of our time.

Jack Brickhouse, veteran of 33 years with the Chicago Cubs, along with Hall of Famer Chuck Thompson and the "old redhead" Red Barber did play-by-play. Red was best known as the Voice of the Dodgers and Yankees. He's credited with the first words ever spoken during a major-league game on national TV.

The following are some excerpts from my pregame broadcasts, which were carried coast-to-coast on ABC radio.

Hank Aaron and Joe DiMaggio

JH: No baseball classic would be complete without an appearance by Hank Aaron and Joe DiMaggio. It's so nice to have you gentleman back again. Hank, I know this must bring back a lot of thrills and memories for you to have a chance to see guys you've played with and against.

Aaron: It's always great to play in the Cracker Jack classics and it's always a thrill to be back in Washington. And to see some of these fans. Some of them weren't even born when I was playing.

JH: What pitch was it that Al Downing threw you?

Aaron: Believe it or not, it was a fastball on the outside part of the plate. I had not had great luck with Al Downing. He always had been tough on me. But for some reason I decided that I was going to move up on the plate that night, and he didn't get the ball that far away from me.

JH: He had a good curve ball, didn't he?

Aaron: He had a little bit of everything, but the thing I remember is that when Al first joined the Yankees, he could throw very hard. He had that tremendous control. But then he hurt his arm somewhere along the way and came up with that screwball which was very good for him and kept him around for another nine years with the Dodgers.

JH: Didn't Curt Simmons give you a lot of problems?

Aaron: He certainly did. Curt was one of the pitchers that I regretted seeing each time I went to the plate.

JH: And Joe, I know that the fans all over America listening to this broadcast tonight are happy to hear your voice again and also to see you in action.

DiMaggio: I always look forward to coming to the Cracker Jack games. You know I've been doing something like this at Yankee stadium for almost 35 years and I haven't failed to do that. Of course I no longer play in the games, but I like to come out and visit with the fellows and the fans and have a good time. That's what these games are all about.

JH: Joe, who is the toughest pitcher you ever faced?

DiMaggio: Mel Holler. The Cleveland Indians. When he threw the curve ball or the sinker, he moved the ball around, and the sinker ball was very difficult to hit.

JH: And during the 56-game hitting streak? The guy who you got that base hit off of. The last one. Who was that?

DiMaggio: (pause and laugh)

JH: I shouldn't put you on the spot.

DiMaggio: I don't remember his name, but he was a left-hander for Cleveland. And the next day I was stopped.

JH: And Hank, of all the home runs you've hit—755—nobody is going to catch you, believe me. Who are the toughest pitchers, left-handed and right-handed, that you've faced?

Aaron: Most of the home runs I hit were off of Don Drysdale, but believe it or not he was the toughest. No question about it. He was so intimidating. You know, well over six feet and threw the ball very hard and he could be very mean at times. You never knew what he was going to do. I'd have to say that he was the best right-hander I faced. Of the left-handers, you always have to put Koufax on the list. One of the other left-handers is a fellow you probably wouldn't think of. Curt Simmons. He gave me an awful lot of trouble because he threw so much speed stuff. Koufax and Simmons gave me a lot of trouble.

JH: Joe, of all your years, and it seems like it was more than the 13 years you spent with the Yankees, which year stands out in your memory as one you'll never forget?

DiMaggio: I'd have to say that there are many outstanding years. 1936, for instance, playing in the World Series. But I'd have to say my personal one is 1937 when I hit 46 home runs and drove in 167 runs. The only reason I know that is I just read it in a book so I thought I'd get that off as an accomplishment (laughs).

JH: Hank, was the '57 year with the Braves the most memorable one for you?

Aaron: It certainly was. I got voted the league's most valuable player that year—the only time I was ever voted MVP. We defeated the Yankees in seven games and, well, it was a fitting year for me.

JH: Does it seem just like yesterday when you came up in the big leagues?

Aaron: Yes, until I put on the uniform and then my hands start hurting (laughs).

JH: Joe, I was thinking back of all the magnificent records you had with the Yankees. I want you to reflect, if you can, about the catch of a shot you hit, I guess to straightaway center field. Al Gionfriddo went back and robbed you.

DiMaggio: No, that was left center field. The strange thing about that particular play is that Eddie Mixus, who was playing outfield, had just messed up a couple of plays, a couple of base hits. And I was getting to bat; there was a yell from the bench, "Time!" It was Shotten, who then sent out Gionfriddo to play left field. On the very next pitch I hit a ball, which appeared to be a home run, but unfortunately it didn't carry as far as I thought it would. Gionfriddo got back to the fence so he could make that one phenomenal catch. And he was in just for that one play. He was playing me for just that one position. That was the only time I think I was ever angry on the field. I almost kicked second base, and fortunately I did not.

JH: I've seen pictures of that.

DiMaggio: Yes, you have, and fortunately I wasn't close enough to the bag or I would have.

JH: Those games were classics.

DiMaggio: Yes, they were. There was always good pitching against each other. There was never one of these things where games were decided in one inning.

JH: Let's talk more about the 1941 hitting streak. I believe the pressure on you was probably more away from the ballpark than it was on the field.

DiMaggio: You are absolutely right about that. You know I was able to stand the pressure out in the coast league when I hit in 61 consecutive games, so 1941 was a throwback to that. But you're right about the pressure being off the field. It was a good thing that I roomed with Gomez that time because he was really able to fend off all of the people who wanted something or other from me. Autographs at three o'clock in the morning. People coming and knocking on your door or asking me to make breakfast appearances. So the best thing for me to do was to get to the ballpark at about 11 in the morning just to get away from the hustle and bustle.

JH: I doubt if that record will ever be broken. Do you, Joe?

DiMaggio: Oh yes, someone will come along. You know I see where Boggs went to 25 games and was stopped, but he's such a young player with great hitting power. He can hit to all fields and is the type of hitter who is certainly a threat. Mattingly is another one. But someday, someone is going to come along and do it.

JH: Hank, it's great to talk with you, and Joe, we thank you for helping us to open our broadcast. It's so good to see you again.

DiMaggio: Thank you. It's good to see you again, too, John.

JH: How better to continue this warmup show than with four Hall of Famers and four of the most popular men who ever played the sport: Brooks Robinson, Sandy Koufax, Ernie Banks, and Bob Feller. Memories? I'm sure you've got many, Brooks.

Brooks Robinson

Robinson: I sure have, John. You play almost 23 years professionally and you have a lot of great memories.

JH: Do Gold Glove awards mean more than home runs and RBIs to you?

Robinson: Well, I think that when people think of Brooks Robinson they probably think of defense more than anything else. But I'm happy that I was able to win 16 Gold Gloves in a row, which signifies that you're the best fielder in that position. Hands down, I have the best fielding average, but that award is what the players and managers feel is the best in that position.

JH: Defensively it's super, but look at your 268 home runs.

Robinson: The big question mark when I first came to the big leagues was would I be able to hit big-league pitching? It took me awhile to get the hang of it. Eventually things turned around and I became a pretty decent hitter.

JH: Your .429 in the World Series in 1970 had to be a highlight, too.

Robinson: It sure was. I tell people that in my 23 seasons I never had five games in a row like that, so that was a once-in-a-lifetime episode and it happened to be in a World Series.

JH: Now you have to realize that your broadcast partner, Chuck Thompson, is upstairs tonight broadcasting this game, so you have to watch what you do on the field.

Robinson: (laughs) I owe him $20, so if he says anything bad about me he's not going to get it.

JH: Good luck tonight, Brooks.

Robinson: Thanks, John.

Sandy Koufax

JH: Sandy Koufax has some tremendous memories, I know, in your years in the league. Hall of Fame member in 1971, and you won 25 or more games three times. Any particular year stand out, Sandy? What's the most memorable for you?

Koufax: I don't think so, John. You know having a good year, and if you win the pennant, then that's a fun year.

JH: Which Dodger team will you always remember best?

Koufax: The 1963 club is one of my favorites. And probably the '55 club is a favorite because that was my first year. But I hold a special spot for the '66 club, which wasn't supposed to win. There were problems, supposedly, and we managed to win. We didn't do so well in the World Series but at least we won the pennant, which was our major ambition in those days.

JH: How do you approach a game like tonight? You are one of the younger guys on the field.

Koufax: I don't really think a whole hell of a lot about it, to be honest. I'm here to have a good time. I haven't approached it in any way.

JH: Any one particular batter when you were throwing that you recall having some tough times with?

Koufax: All of them. All good hitters give you tough times. The idea is to try and limit your damage. You lose a few battles in a war but I tried to pitch the good hitters with nobody on base. Hank Aaron is going to give you trouble. Billy Williams is going to give you trouble. Hell, the whole lineup tonight is going to give you trouble. And the guys who aren't here tonight a pitcher still has to get out.

JH: We wish you good luck tonight. Thanks, Sandy.

Koufax: Thank you, John.

Ernie Banks

JH: When you talk about memorable moments in baseball you have to think of Ernie Banks.

Banks: (laughs) I can't remember any memorable moments. Seriously, I can remember starting out with the Cubs in 1953. Or hitting my 500th home run in 1970. I remember being elected to the Hall of Fame in '77, and 13 All-Star games. Basically that's what baseball is. Fond memories, and I'm just so happy to be part of a great game like baseball.

JH: What a tremendous feeling you must have and the rest of your team here this evening when you step out on the field and hear that tremendous ovation.

Banks: It is a marvelous feeling that is a big part of baseball. When people come out and cheer you on and support you, it gives you that extra incentive to go on and perform well. It proves you have a rapport with people of all ages from around the world. You're a professional.

JH: Among the players here tonight, only Hank Aaron and Frank Robinson top your figures at RBIs. That has to be a magnificent accomplishment.

Banks: We all feel good about producing runs. That's what we call productivity. Driving in runs and scoring runs. I'm happy to be with so many fine players in the National and American leagues. Hank Aaron, Will McCovey, Frank Robinson, and all this is basically what the game is about. Players who have produced runs for their club and that's the important factor of a major-league player.

JH: Great to have you back and good luck tonight.

Banks: (laughs) You see I can't remember anything. I don't remember.

JH: (laughs) Thanks, Ernie.

Bob Feller

JH: Bob Feller. On this date in 1951 you pitched your third no-hitter. Does it seem like yesterday to you?

Feller: It doesn't seem too far back. I remember that Vic Wertz was the last batter and he hit a loud foul. I mean it was a home run that was about ten feet foul. I was a little worried, but the ball finally did curve in foul territory. It was too close for comfort.

And in the next pitch I threw him a ball that caught the outside corner and struck him out for the final out of the ball game.

J.H.: How did you keep your arm in such good shape over all those years?

Feller: I did a lot of running and some light exercise. I chopped wood and did a lot of manual labor. I did not use ice. No tricks like keeping my arm warm in hot showers or wearing a jacket to keep my arm warm on cool days. Of course, there wasn't near as much air conditioning back in those days. But I did pitch more complete games than any pitcher in history since the advent of the live ball.

JH: This game tonight brings back so many memories, and it's so great to have you back this evening. Thanks.

Feller: It's my pleasure.

JH: Starting on the mound tonight for the National League will be Hoyt Wilhelm with one of the Hall of Famers tonight hitting against him, Al Kaline. And for the American league, Whitey Ford. And one of the hitters who will try to take Whitey deep tonight is Ralph Kiner. Let's start with talking tonight with Ralph Kiner and Whitey Ford. How are you going to pitch to this guy, Whitey?

Whitey Ford and Ralph Kiner

Ford: Very carefully. You know when I was flying down here, I hear that Ralph was trying to hit 14 home runs in the month of June, and now its July 1st so I'm not too worried. Somebody just broke his record, but he's amazing. I only hit three home runs in 18 years.

JH: '46 through '55 were some amazing years for you, Ralph, with the Pittsburgh Pirates.

Kiner: I had some great days with the Pirates but later on I played with the Cubs and also with Cleveland, but I remember hitting against Whitey Ford. The first thing you did when hitting against Whitey Ford is have the ball inspected. You have to check out the ball and make sure there are no nicks on the ball. The other thing you need to do is look for the sharp breaking balls. He'll occasionally throw it close just to brush you back a little bit, so you have to be pretty careful with him.

JH: Is he insinuating that you might have have doctored up the ball a bit, Whitey?

Ford: Probably later in my career when Kiner was very old and I was getting old.

JH: Who's the toughest batter you've faced, Whitey?

Ford: The toughest batter for me was Nellie Fox. I struck him out once in 11 years. He really hit me well. He'd try to hit the ball through the box over third base, and he could pull it. He was the toughest of all the hitters.

JH: Besides you facing a guy like Kiner this evening, how do you plan to pitch to these other guys?

Ford: I want to pitch to them inside because I don't want them to hit towards the mound (laugh). Johnny Bench hit one off me last year and if it came back to me it would have killed me. I'd just as soon pitch slow and let them pull the ball.

Kiner: Listen, if Whitey pitches all of them inside, then whoever is playing third base is going to get killed.

Ford: Well, we have Brooks Robinson over there. He's young.

JH: Who is the toughest pitcher you've faced, Ralph?

Kiner: Hands down it's Ewell Blackwell, no question about it. Side arm, right-hander. You couldn't find the ball and I think any right-hand batter that had the misfortune of hitting against Blackwell would say the same thing.

Hoyt Wilhelm

JH: Let's turn now to Hoyt Wilhelm. Nine teams in the majors, Hoyt, including the Giants, Orioles, Dodgers. Will we see a few knuckle balls?

Wilhelm: I might try and dash a few out there. Of course, they ain't gonna do nothing probably.

JH: When did you first develop your knuckle ball? In the minor leagues? In high school?

Wilhelm: In high school really, and for some reason I kind of had the knack for throwing it. I worked at it and it developed.

JH: And that was the innovation, too, of the big mitt?

Wilhelm: When I came to Baltimore, right?

JH: When you were pitching in the majors, any one batter that you can recall that even though you had a great knuckler, you just couldn't get that guy out?

Wilhelm: Having pitched for ten years equally in both the American and National Leagues, I'm sure there were guys who hit off of me, but I can't put my finger on any one guy really.

JH: Interesting note that your first time up at bat in the majors you crack a home run, but from that time on it was tough sledding, home run-wise.

Wilhelm: Well, after that I started pitching. A pitcher isn't supposed to hit home runs.

Al Kaline

JH: Now, the MVP of the '83 "old-timers" ball game is back tonight.

Kaline: Hopefully, I'll do well enough tonight to repeat. To be the first player to repeat.

JH: Do you still get the thrill of these games when you play?

Kaline: I think tonight is one of the best games they've had. I enjoy playing these, although I don't really expect any results, but this one by far is the class of the old-timer games. I enjoy getting the chance to talk with these players. You do want to hit the ball very much but often the results just aren't there. Certainly, the people don't come out to see what we used to be able to do, but when we get in the batter's cage we'd like to hit the ball with a reasonable amount of authority. Not make a fool of ourselves.

Willie Mays

JH: One of the best ever to play the game, and you can hear them yelling for him just off to our right here, is the "Say Hey Kid," Willie Mays. You look like you're ready to play tonight, Willie.

Mays: I don't think I am, but I enjoy what is happening tonight. You can understand that the people that are here really love us, and what we did. It's a wonderful thing.

JH: I can't tell you how nice it is just to have you back in the game when you come up here and step to the plate.

Mays: The fans know I enjoy coming here and taking care of the guys. Just being with the guys. And the fans to me are what made me, not just because I played ball, but also because they feel that baseball is a part of me.

JH: In your baseball years, what is the best memory? Would it be the Hall of Fame? Or would it be one game that stands out? What's the best for you?

Mays: I think it would be the Hall of Fame, because when you first start out you have no idea you're going to reach the Hall of Fame. But I really didn't play for that. I played for the 24 guys that were on my team because I always felt that if we had a clubhouse that was happy then we'd have a happy ball club. Like the four home runs I hit in Milwaukee. If I hadn't hit those home runs and we lost the game, then we wouldn't have had a happy ball club. I think I played more for my teammates than I did for myself.

JH: I can still hear Russ Hodges as if it were yesterday. "The Giants win the pennant! The Giants win the pennant!"

Mays: Yes, I remember Russ very well. He's probably one of nicest guys I ever knew.

JH: Great to have you back, Willie. Now let's take a moment to visit with three more All-Stars, Enos "Country" Slaughter, Jim "Catfish" Hunter, and Bobby Doerr.

Enos "Country" Slaughter, Jim "Catfish" Hunter, and Bobby Doerr

(Note: Jim Hunter passed away on Sept. 9, 1999 of Lou Gehrig's disease)

JH: Enos, let's start with you. We're going to talk for a moment about some wonderful memories from your playing days from 1938 to what, 50 something?

Slaughter: 1959. Right. I'll tell you that the most exciting thing was just to be able to play and to put on that uniform every day.

JH: Jim, you played with some great Oakland A's teams in California and, of course, with the New York Yankees. You must have a stockpile of memories.

Hunter: I guess that main thing is that I played for two very colorful owners, Charlie Finley and Mr. Steinbrenner. Both of them kept everything going. And I owe a lot to Mr. Finley because he gave me the contract to start in Kansas City and, again, a release so I could go and play for New York Yankees. I couldn't have picked a better club than New York having played for Oakland, where anything could happen. But when I got to New York I didn't think anything else could happen, [but it turned out] I hadn't seen nothing until I got there. Mr. Steinbrenner was a little different than Mr. Finley but still very similar.

JH: Jim, this is your first time in this classic. Do you have any idea what to expect? You'll be surprised at the ovation you're going to receive from these fans tonight.

Hunter: I know one thing. This RFK Stadium is the hottest stadium I have ever pitched in. There's no wind that can get inside of this place. And it must be cold in the wintertime, too.

JH: You're still in baseball, though, because you are helping your youngster coaching down there back home.

Hunter: Yes, I help coach collegiate ball and I'm the groundskeeper for a Little League team, so I'm around baseball all of the time.

JH: Bobby Doerr, former great second baseman of the Boston Red Sox, you spent your entire career with one organization, the Red Sox. And to play every year in Fenway Park is something unusual.

Doerr: How lucky can you be as a right-handed hitter?

Hunter: (laughs) That's right!

JH: It still must give you a thrill, Bobby, when you put on the uniform and get the chance to visit with guys like "Catfish" and "Country" Slaughter.

Doerr: It is. Everybody is so enthusiastic about baseball and I guess that's why they were such great ballplayers. You love the game. One thing I think we take for granted—and I think so much about this—is that it is so fortunate we can live in a country that lets us choose a profession that we think so much of, and make a pretty good living out of it.

Boog Powell and Joe Garagiola

JH: Let's now go and recall some moments with Boog Powell and Joe Garagiola. Boog, you had some terrific seasons with the Minnesota Twins, but when you started with the Washington Senators, they were still playing in old Griffith Stadium, weren't they?

Powell: They sure were in the old ballpark. I have fond memories. It wasn't a very good ball club but we have good memories. I really got my feet wet with those days with the Senators. Probably my most memorable moment was opening day 1960. Walking out to the bullpen and the wind was blowing straight in. We were playing the Red Sox. Everybody was saying it was one of those days where nobody was going to hit one out. And Ted Williams hit one over that old 421 sign and into the tree beyond center field. It was one of my first days in the big leagues and that was impressive. I thought maybe I was in a little over my head.

JH: Was Williams the toughest batter you faced?

Powell: No, the toughest batter is here tonight and a teammate: Al Kaline. He's the toughest one I had to try and get out.

JH: And you are still involved with baseball doing some color commentary on TV?

Powell: Not as much as this fellow next to me, Garagiola.

JH: And Joe Garagiola has a whole headfull of memories from your days with the Cardinals and the Pirates.

Garagiola: Every day I walked on the field was a memorable day, John (laughs).

JH: What was the most interesting thing about handling the pitching staff with the Cardinals when you played?

Garagiola: I was a great handler of pitchers [in St. Louis], but when I left for Pittsburgh I became awfully dumb. The same strategy I used didn't work in Pittsburgh. When you have a good pitcher he can make the catcher look smart. When I hear that expression, "he's a great handler of pitchers," I usually see a guy who is hitting .210 and has a great pitching staff.

JH: Let's talk about your hitting. You had some clutch hits although you didn't hit that good of an average over the years.

Garagiola: Let me say, John, that every hit I got, and every hit that Boog Powell got, were clutch hits. There is no such thing as a "cheap single." I hear guys say it's a cheap single. There is no such thing. When you get a base hit, it is a big base hit.

JH: Joe, the players today are different than the guys you played with, aren't they?

Garagiola: They are richer.

JH: A lot richer.

Garagiola: A lot richer. They now hit .257 and get five-year guarantees, with a weight clause that gives them $50,000, and if they sleep on a waterbed they get an extra $10,000. They have so many clauses in their contract. That's the big difference.

JH: And if they do a commercial for some kind of beverage than they get a little more tossed at them, like this gentleman here, Boog Powell.

Powell: There's nothing wrong with doing those kinds of beverage commercials. I kind of enjoy doing them. I had a good time, and as some people say, "there is Lite after baseball."

JH: (laughs) You had to get that one in. So when you talk about your career with the Orioles, where do you start?

Powell: When you think back to the early '60s we were sort of a mediocre ball club. We had the talent there. We had a good pitching staff. We had the good defense. I guess the thing that turned the whole organization around was in '66 when we got Frank Robinson. Frank just came in and was not only an on-the-field leader, he was an off-the-field leader, too. Winning the triple crown didn't hurt either when he hit 49 home runs that drove in 130 runs. He just made a big difference in our organization; he was that "other guy" that we needed. We needed one more guy, and Frank was that guy.

Umpires Jim Honochick and Tom Gorman

JH: The crowd pleasers associated with baseball are, or were, the players, but the men in blue are remembered not only for their unbiased ability to call the game but also for their outstanding work on and off the field and the personalities they have. Two of the most colorful umpires are Tom Gorman and Jim Honochick. Jim, I want to ask you which has given you the most success and notoriety in your illustrious career: working behind the plate or doing television?

Honochick: Really, doing the Miller Lite commercials has made it for me. For 25 years before that nobody knew I existed. I'd work a ball game and walk off the field and nobody knew who the umpire was. But after I did one commercial for Miller Lite beer, everyone knew me. That really did it for me.

JH: In your day of working behind the plate and working the bases, you saw some tremendous ball players. What comes to mind looking back?

Honochick: I think of the great ball players in my day. The DiMaggios, the Garcias, the Newhousers, and the Lemons. You don't see many winners like that today. I wonder if we're seeing any players of that caliber coming up in the ranks now. I'm curious about that.

JH: Of course the gentleman standing next to you today is back again. He was with us last year and I'm speaking of Tom Gorman. From your '50 to '75 umpire career in the National League, this is always still a big thrill for you to come back isn't it, Tom?

Gorman: The biggest thing about these old-timers games that I can see is that when you see these boys get dressed, it puts them back 20 years. They're dying to get out on the field and play. And since they've retired they don't get a chance to see each other. All the boys are so nice, and they like seeing each other again since they've left the game.

JH: When you're working these games, like last year, don't you think back to when you were working the plate with these players?

Gorman: Oh yeah. It takes you right back when a Billy Williams or Ernie Banks stands at the plate. And you can see when they look at that ball they still have the same instincts.

JH: When you were working behind the plate, who do you think had the best eyes?

Gorman: The greatest hitter I ever saw was Ted Williams. Stan "The Man" Musial was another good hitter for me. The pitchers tried to out-smart them, but they looked for their pitch.

JH: How about you, Jim?

Honochick: Teddy Williams and Joe DiMaggio were my favorites and then Mickey Mantle came down the pike.

JH: Mantle was sensational.

Honochick: He sure was. But I still say Williams and DiMaggio were the best.

Chapter 15

ABC Radio
World View

The U.S. heads home from Sydney with 97 medals, the most of any nation. Thirty-nine are gold, and one belongs to the USA basketball team. The Americans struck gold today, beating France by 10. Ray Allen and Vince Carter each had 13.
In Sydney, Johnny Holliday with ABC Sports Radio

Once at the 1984 Los Angeles Olympic Games, I was preparing for the boxing competition with former champion Ken Norton, our ABC expert boxing analyst. Just then, Angel Bourdon, our ABC engineer in New York, called, asking me if I'd seen my fellow ABC reporter, Howard Cosell. At that precise moment Howard walked in, wearing his blue ABC blazer, surrounded by his entourage.

I said, "Howard, New York is on the line and they want to know if you can do your show right now."

"Can I use your headset, John?" he asked. I handed it over.

He said, "Angel. Are you rolling? Let's go. This is for national. Three, two, one. This is Howard Cosell at the Sports Arena in Los Angeles. The United States boxing team…"

Boom, boom, boom. He does the first segment.

"Back in a minute. Three, two, one. And so the Olympic team has the opportunity…"

Boom, boom, boom, he completes the report. "This is Howard Cosell, from the Sports Arena, speaking of sports." And then he did two more reports for WABC in New York.

Ken and I were absolutely blown away, because he had just done two shows without a note in front of him.

Howard took off his headset, looked at me, picked up his cigar, and said, "That's the way to do a show." And he walked away.

Cosell became famous for his ability to do his reports off the cuff. He had a unique knack for it. For example, he'd be in a bar, and his folks would ask the patrons to be quiet. He'd do his report and the crowd applauded. I'm told he'd also do his show from his house while he was in pajamas.

One of the reasons I know so much about Howard is that my boss, Shelby Whitfield, was not only Howard's boss at ABC, but also one of his closest friends. Shelby coauthored some books with Howard, his last being *What's Wrong with Sports* in 1991. That book didn't receive the kind of numbers it deserved because Howard died from cancer shortly after publication. He wasn't around to promote it.

Shelby's now working on a comprehensive biography, and it should be the authoritative account.

Shelby Whitfield: "Howard Cosell was a brilliant man. He was a chameleon. You either loved him or hated him, but he changed the face of broadcasting. No sports broadcaster had an opinion before Howard.

"He started out as a practicing attorney, representing Willie Mays, and he was also a lawyer for Little League baseball. That's how he got into sports. Part of his act was shtick, but I always loved him."

One of the best assignments I've had was covering the Olympics, which began with the 1984 Sarajevo games. I was amazed to receive the gear I was to wear in Sarajevo—complete outfits of jackets, pants, hats, gloves, boots, socks, and sunglasses—which arrived at my house in a gigantic brown ABC suitcase that was as big as I am. Each of the reporters and crew got a suitcase like this. And we needed those clothes. It was teeth-chattering cold in Sarajevo.

For my first assignment I joined the ABC crew at New York's JFK airport, taking off first to Frankfort, Germany. There, the German inspectors searched our 100 or so identical suitcases lined up on the tarmac, as we watched from the terminal. That done, we proceeded on to the then beautiful city of Sarajevo.

With a lump in my throat, I watched the carrying of the Olympic torch from right in front of our ABC studio. Carol Heise-Jenkins, gold medalist figure skater in the 1956 games, and I remember riding up to the top of the mountain for the downhill events through cloudy, soupy conditions. We couldn't see our hands in front of our faces, and then, abruptly, we were above the clouds in brilliant clear sunshine, with Carol as radiant in '84 as she was in '56.

I was impressed by how lovely the people were in Sarajevo, walking together arm in arm through the downtown streets. Men and women, and women and women, were always holding each other closely. We should bring back that kind of togetherness here in the States.

The one thing they could work on in Sarajevo, I thought at the time, was their smoking. Everybody smoked. That bothered me, especially at the restaurants. The gosh-darned smoke would come barreling out the door the moment you walked in.

In Sarajevo, I covered bobsled, luge, hockey, and figure skating. We stayed in brand-spanking-new apartments built for the event. I roomed with Barry Tompkins, now one of the top fight commentators for HBO. We had to leave our room keys with the security guard each day.

"What's going to keep you from going through my stuff?" I asked one of the guards.

"Nothing," he answered without cracking a smile.

On the last day at Sarajevo, I was eyeing the Canadian CCTV jacket and thought it might be nice to trade my ABC jacket for one of theirs. Many of us ended up trading our ABC stuff that day, and trading each other's coats and sweatshirts caught on.

All in all, track and field and boxing are my personal favorite Olympic events. Another memorable experience happened in Barcelona, where I got my first taste of the Mediterranean. Janet Spaulding, my producer, and Tom Marchitto, our engineer, had gone with me to the beach after our all-night shift, just to relax. We were soaking up some rays when Janice said, "Oh, my God. Don't look now." I immediately jumped up, said "What?" and saw we were surrounded by topless women. To fully appreciate this new experience required keen observation.

I covered all the summer and winter games from the opening ceremonies in Sarajevo, 1984, to the closing festivities in Sydney in 2001. The opening ceremonies were often difficult, because those were long-form radio formats. You're talking and describing things for hours. That's sometimes tough to do.

The man responsible for my Olympic work is Shelby. He and Tony Roberts had done Washington Senators play-by-play along with Ron Menschine on WWDC. Shelby authored a news-breaking book in 1973, *Kiss It Goodbye*, about the Washington Senators. This was one of first books about the tainted business of sports. Shelby's revelations about pressures placed on baseball club-employed announcers prompted a congressional investigation and led to an FCC regulation which required a disclaimer to be made about who hired and approved announcers.

Our association began back in 1970 when he did the first sports talk show on D.C. radio, originating from Fran O'Brien's downtown restaurant. In 1981, Shelby tapped me for work at ABC when he moved to his executive office there.

Shelby Whitfield: "I tracked Johnny down in Hawaii, where he was broadcasting the Aloha Bowl (Maryland vs. Washington), and offered him a job with ABC Radio. John replaced Lou Boda, who had been with ABC for 25 years. Lou was an old-line broadcaster, very opinionated, and he didn't really buy into my new ideas for the format. I remember getting some criticism from associates for hiring a disc jockey to do sports reports.

"But the switch worked, and Johnny was with me for 18 years until I retired. One of the secrets of his longevity is his noncontroversial approach. Although he's versatile, he always sounds the same, and it is a young, contemporary sound.

"ABC was the first network to develop multinetworks. In other words, ABC developed five radio networks that could appeal to different demographics. Johnny started out on the ABC Youth Network, and then I moved him and my other old friend, Fred Manfra, to the ABC Information Network.

"We were very aggressive. We were the first to get the exclusive broadcast rights to the Olympics, starting with the Los Angeles Games. Prior to that time, no networks had ever established exclusivity. We'd spend more money to cover events across the country and employ stringers in each town who could feed John reports. I also developed a strong system of actualities, or taped "sound bites," at ABC. We had a bigger staff, with more producers, which was very important in Johnny's case since he was based in Washington. The producers in New York helped him stay on top of events.

"Those were very memorable times with John at the towns we visited. Once in Sarajevo, we went to dinner at a restaurant run by prisoners on work release. All of the cooks, waiters, etc. were prisoners. That was interesting. At another restaurant they'd let you pick out your own goat, and they'd slaughter it for your meal. At Seoul we had a running joke between us about what kind of dog we were going to eat for dinner. We saw some whole different ways of life through those Games.

"Of all the great Games we covered, I'd say that Seoul, where our boxers got robbed, and the beauty of Lillehammer stand out. One of the things I should mention about our coverage is the time difference. We took great pride, and Johnny was a big part of this, in beating the TV reports with our real-time news. The TV crews had to do taped reports, but we were on the radio. TV producers complained that our coverage was costing them ratings points.

"In Atlanta, I was in my hotel room two blocks from the park when the bomb went off. It was scary. A commercial plane crashed at Long Island around that time, and we were all wondering what would happen next.

"John and I did all the Olympics together, Calgary, Barcelona, Albertville, etc. He was always working his tail off. You could count on him. He and Fred Manfra were my two key broadcasters wherever we went. I've known John for 33 years now, and without a doubt he's the hardest working, extremely talented, and one of the greatest people in the world that I've ever met."

In Atlanta, I was about ten minutes away from the park, sleeping in my apartment when the bomb exploded. I had no idea until ABC called me and said we had to go to the studio to cover it. It was frightening that night traveling to the studio to do our broadcasts.

ABC's Bruce Morton was also with us, reporting the events. Bruce remembers being awakened by his vibrating pager creeping across the nightstand.

"We walked up 10th Street back to the studio," Bruce recalls. "It was very eerie because Atlanta police helicopters were buzzing over head."

Rick Barry was with me at the summer Games in Barcelona when we watched the United States roll to another gold medal in basketball. This is where I first worked with Dick Vitale, whom Shelby had hired as our expert basketball analyst. Dick would go nonstop with his rapid-fire delivery. He was a charismatic performer, just like you see him today. He truly loves what he does.

In Calgary I covered the Jamaican bobsled team when they overturned. Everybody held their breath as the Jamaicans skidded all the way down the track on their heads, with nothing but helmets protecting them. When their bobsled came to rest and the rescue team reached the athletes, they stood up and raised their hands in a triumphant gesture. They were shaken up, but the helmets saved them. We all exhaled.

I had interviewed the Jamaicans just before the race and remember how accommodating they were. The Jamaicans were one of the big stories at Calgary. Speed skater Bonnie Blair was the other.

At the Albertville winter Games, we stayed at one of the most beautiful places in the world, Annecy, France. I took a side trip to visit the cloistered sisters of the Order of the Visitation convent there. This is where the order of nuns who taught my daughters originated from. Only two sisters out of 27 spoke English. One was Sister Pat, originally from Denver, Colorado, who asked me if I'd bring them back some milkshakes from McDonald's and a TV program from the Olympics so they could watch the Games. I asked Sister Pat "How do I get to the McDonald's?"

"You just go down the street," she said. "You'll see it because there's a big clown out in front." I still keep in touch with Sister Pat.

I rode the media shuttle together with ABC's Peter Jennings to and from the Games in Calgary. He was a very friendly, approachable, and down-to-earth guy. Calgary was the last Olympics that ABC had exclusive rights to cover.

In Seoul, South Korea, our drivers scared the hell out of us, and I wondered every night if I'd make it to my hotel room alive. The noise outside kept me up the whole time I was there. Plus, there was no air conditioning. Seoul did have a wonderful subway system. I took trips during the day to the antique district.

In Seoul, Skip Bertman was the coach of Team USA. Skip was head baseball coach at LSU. But I had pitched against Skip in high school when my North Miami High played his Miami Beach team. I wasn't sure if he'd remember me, so I took a clipping of the high school box scores from our early games with me in case I could get some time with him.

When I finally connected with Skip, I told him that I was holding our box score in my hand and North Miami had beat Miami Beach 6-1 when I was there, and he had gone 0-3 against me.

He said, "Oh, really? I remember playing against Licata, Geissinger, Grubbs, and Pent. What did you play?"

"I pitched against you guys."

"A small guy with glasses? Good curve ball? Sneaky fastball? And absolutely no control?"

I said, "That's me."

Skip said, "I don't remember you."

So much for my fame with Skip Bertman.

I normally bounce out of bed and throw on a sweatshirt, jeans, and baseball cap just before the alarm sounds at 4:20 a.m. I've been getting up this early for 21 years now to do sports for ABC Radio. Thirty minutes later I'm at Washington's ABC bureau studio on DeSales Street.

Once in the studio, I print out the ABC Sports Call, a listing of all the taped "sound bites"—or actualities, as we call them—in the system. General examples would be the quote of a player who had just won a championship, or the remarks of a coach, like Ralph Friedgen, who had just decided to turn down a more lucrative coaching offer.

Next I choose about five actualities for the morning broadcast and write the script, citing the cued "cuts" for the engineer working my show in our New York studio. This could be Beaumont Small, Jim Nedelka, Bill Mayo, Mark Rosenblatt, Angel Bourdon, Buddy Valenti, Steve Johnson, Harold Hodge, Don Bayley, Rod Hoffner, Steve Kalomeris, or John Calabro. Everything has to fit into two and a half minutes.

"From ABC Sports, I'm Johnny Holliday. Emmitt Smith became the first running back to gain a thousand yards in 11 consecutive seasons. But Dallas fell to the Lions 15-10."

Boom. The cue for my New York engineer is "Lions 15-10," and Smith's "sound bite" quote is aired ("Yea, I was well aware of how close I was...").

I continue along for one minute, and then say "This is ABC Sports." This gives the stations a chance to break away for a spot, or in some cases end the report, or tape the whole show for later airing.

I resume the broadcast. The ABC closing theme music starts when the clock hits 2 minutes 24 seconds. I sign off with, "I'm Johnny Holliday, ABC Sports." And I'm out.

These broadcasts are carried on the ABC satellite service and three of the ABC national radio networks, so I figure that more than a few folks are listening.

My boss, Mike Rizzo, took over in 1999 when Shelby retired. Mike is as detailed and organized as anyone I've worked with. Always welcoming new ideas, his goal is to keep ABC sports radio the front-runner in the field. With Rizzo as our leader, there's no doubt we'll continue to grow. (One thing I love about Rizzo: he's my direct line for getting those tickets to Disney World.)

While covering the NCAA Final Four in St. Petersburg, Mike was there to coordinate the broadcast. In Sydney, under Rizzo's leadership, ABC Sports Radio was first with breaking stories, updates, and interviews from the Summer Olympics. Our coverage was outstanding and recieved rave reviews from our 4,000 affiliates. Mike was responsible for gathering the finest group of broadcasters to represent ABC. Mike's wife Jennie made the trek to Sydney and helped make certain things ran smoothly.

I've also enjoyed working with operations director Cliff Bond for seven years. Cliff and I worked the same shift in the Atlanta and Sydney Games. Cliff's a devoted runner and eater. How Cliff can eat and eat and still stay so slim baffles all of us.

The first player I'd want if I still had the Radio Oneders would be Steve White, one of our ABC sports producers working out of NYC. Steve goes six feet seven and played collegiately at Fordham.

ABC also has the finest network anchors and reporters. Ann Compton, Lauren Rogers, Bettina Gregory, John Bascom, Andy Fields, Bill Greenwood, Vic Ratner, Pam Coulter, Barbara Britt, and Tom Gauger are among my favorites. In the corridors of ABC in Washington, I'm likely to run into Ted Koppel, Carol Simpson, John Martin, Claire Shipman, Chris Wallace, and even Charlie Gibson, from *Good Morning America*, when he's in D.C. Charlie got his start in Washington on Channel 7.

One of my coworkers, Doug Limmerick, is the first guy I see each morning. Doug is one of the most listened to morning anchors on radio, and we're lucky to have him on the ABC Information Network.

Doug was once one-half of Q-107's radio team, Doug and Dude (Walker). Limmerick keeps the newsroom on its toes, but he's also a Top 40 nut, always challenging my memory on some oldies songs.

Doug Limmerick: "Every morning Johnny walks into ABC at 5 a.m. with that bad hair covered up by a baseball cap. He's usually coming in from a Terps game somewhere so he's operating on one hour's sleep. He tries to throw me off with a Jonathan Winters impression or some wisecrack. I tell him, don't worry; sooner or later, he's going to make it as a play-by-play sports announcer. It's a trip working with 'the legend.'"

My friend Ira Mellman is a former sports director at WINS and CBS and ABC radio. Today he's news drector at WBIG in Washington D.C.

Ira Mellman: "The secret to being good on the radio is the ability to tell a good story. The first time I met Johnny was when I filled in for him on his ABC Radio morning sports reports. What I noticed was that my conversations with him went on and on ... and were filled with laughter. The reason ... Johnny Holliday tells a good story.

"He has told me many, and in every instance, it's been a good one.

"From the years as one of the nation's great rock jocks in Cleveland, New York and San Francisco to one of the most successful commercial voices in the nation's capital to the incomparable voice of University of Maryland sports, and to simply talking with him on the phone, Johnny Holliday has been able to tell me the story like no other."

One thing's for sure at ABC; Rusty Lutz, Andrew Cremedas, Jim Kane, Scott Anderson, Chad Murray, Rebecca Abraham, Patricia Carroll, Raja Helou and the rest of the folks who write for and run the news desk are essential. They coordinate the stories and handle the news assignments and feeds under the leadership of our dynamic news directors, Merrilee Cox, who runs the Washington bureau, and Chris Barry who oversees the entire ABC news operation in New York. If it weren't for the news desk crew and their DAs (Kristin McNary, Liz Turrell, and Zak Leibowitz) nobody would know what stories to work on.

Our Washington engineers, including Jim Donaldson, Art Gauthier, Tom Marchitto, Steve Stefany, Steve Densmore, and Dar Maxwell, make sure the lines are up and flowing to New York.

In February 1996, I was picked to take over for Charlie Hughes, who had handled the voice-over job for *This Week with David Brinkley* so admirably for many years before he retired to Florida. Robin Sproul, bureau chief of ABC News, asked me to try it, and Director Bob Golembeck told me exactly how he wanted the various openings and closings for the show done.

Like most network shows, the voice-over work is prerecorded. Most of the copy is ready by Saturday mornings, but I'm really at their beck and call when they need me. I've gone in at nights and early Sunday morning to record my parts. I'm usually at Mass when the show airs live. I catch the replay on local news Channel 8 at night. I'm sure that very few of the audience know it's me.

I had been working on *This Week with David Brinkley* for about two weeks before I actually met Mr. Brinkley. He and I were leaving the building together when I introduced myself.

"Well, hello Johnny, it's good to meet you," he said as only he could, with that classic clipped inflection. I told him that I'd seen him standing by the Magruder's grocery store on Chevy Chase Circle. I asked him if he lived near there.

He said, "Absolutely. Lived there many years. Do you live near there? I said, "Nearby in Kensington."

"Not too far away. Good to meet you. Gotta go. See you later."

He sounded just like me doing him years ago on my WWDC radio show.

When Brinkley retired, Sam and Cokie took over. Both, in my opinion, are the two top journalists in all of broadcasting, but you don't need me to tell you that. Sam has a style unequaled by anyone else in broadcasting, and Cokie always lends an elegant, authoritative approach to the news. Classy is my word for Cokie Roberts. And together they are dynamite.

My daughter, Moira, interned with Cokie during summer breaks from college, and Cokie accepted an invitation to speak at Moira's St. Joseph College graduation. When it came time to hand out diplomas, Cokie hugged Moira on the stage. That was a proud moment for the Hollidays.

Being an announcer for a network news show like ABC's *This Week With Sam Donaldson and Cokie Roberts* is tough to beat. I'm thankful to Sam and Cokie, to Robin Sproul who gave me the job, to Roger Goodman (vice president of news and special projects in New York), and Dorrance Smith, the executive producers when I started, and to Virgina Mosely, who succeeded Smith in that position. I'm fortunate to be able to follow their direction and come off sounding the way they want the announcing done. This is self-satisfying, and something I'm most proud of on my resume.

Cokie Roberts: "He's been one of the most familiar voices in radio for decades, as a disc jockey, sportscaster, and the 'voice-over' for commercials. I know him best as the 'voice of God' announcing TV shows, including my own. And Johnny Holliday has loved almost every minute of it. What a life!"

I especially enjoy my association with John O'Leary, Andrea Owen, and Avery Miller. I thank everyone I work with at ABC, including the people whom I get stuff from but never see.

In 1993, I began a first-rate association with Home Team Sports, including ACC baseball championships with Larry Conley and Terry Gannon, working with Phil Chenier on Washington Bullets telecasts when Mel Proctor would take some time off, and doing Orioles baseball with John Lowenstein.

HTS also gave me a chance to do play-by-play for ACC Women's basketball for seven years. If my Maryland schedule hadn't been so demanding I might still be doing women's hoops today. The coaches and players couldn't have been more cooperative. I was fortunate to have worked with many fine analysts as well.

Mimi Griffin, who later made her mark on CBS as a major analyst talent, was one of my first partners. Mimi was super, with a quick wit and beautiful personality.

Then came Henrietta Walls, a former standout at the University of North Carolina. Henrietta still holds some Tar Heel records. This was her first TV work, and she did more than fine. She also worked at Michael Jordan's summer camp when we partnered together.

Nora Lynch Finch, an assistant AD at North Carolina State, did a share of games with me. Talk about sparkling and upbeat. That was Nora. She knew basketball inside and out.

Christy Winters had played for Chris Weller at Maryland and been a key member of Coach Weller's teams in College Park. Christy was a natural in front of the camera. I always thought she could have had a modeling career if she wanted one. She was as beautiful on camera as she was a workaholic as a player on the court.

Many readers will immediately recognize the name of Val Ackerman. Val had played at the University of Virginia before she took a shot and slam-dunked a law degree. Today she's the commissioner of the WNBA. We spent only one season together, but I remind Val when I see her that I still have the videotape of the very first game we did from Florida State. She pleads with me not to let anyone see it. I tell her, "I'll think about it." (You were good, Val.)

Pam Ward also did games with me. Pam got her start at Washington's All Sports station, WTEM. I could tell it was just a matter of time before the networks grabbed her. Today she is one of ESPN's stellar talents.

Debbie Leonard coached at Duke before going into private business. But she stayed in touch with the game by working for HTS as an analyst with me. I thought Debbie had a special rapport that often takes years to perfect. She came prepared for the game as anyone I worked with.

I first met Bernadette McGlade while she was the assistant athletic director at Georgia Tech. Bernie was an outstanding player at North Carolina. With a former player's perspective it was no surprise that Bernie could relate so well to the court action. Now she's an associate commissioner for the ACC, along with Fred Barakat.

All in all, the thing I'm most proud of from my association with women's basketball is the ACC women's basketball officials' Distinguished Service award given to me following the 1998 season. It came as a complete surprise during halftime of the Georgia Tech-NC State game in Raleigh's Reynolds Coliseum. This award reminds me of how proud I am to have been in on the ground floor as women's hoops began to gain popularity and acceptance. The March 4, 1998 press release read:

Johnny Holliday, longtime radio voice of the Maryland Terrapins, has been honored with a Distinguished Service Award by the ACC women's basketball officials.

Holliday, who has served as the television play-by-play commentator of ACC women's basketball for the past seven years, was formally honored in pregame ceremonies at the UNC-North Carolina State women's game Feb. 22. The presentation was made by ACC commissioner John Swofford and ACC supervisor of women's basketball officials Bill Stokes.

"This is a wonderful honor and I deeply appreciate it, particularly with the emergence of women's basketball, which continues to grow in popularity," said Holliday.

Said Bernadette McGlade, ACC assistant commissioner for women's basketball: "Johnny has been the ultimate professional and adds a lot of excitement to all of our basketball broadcasts. He is greatly committed and dedicated to ACC women's basketball and is very deserving of this award."

I began with Home Team Sports in 1985. Bill Aber, the leader, and his management team of Jody Shapiro, Bill Brown, and Darryl Landrum were the driving force behind HTS and allowed me the chance to work with some other outstanding analysts. One of the best was Bob Rathburn, Voice of the Atlanta Hawks and long time play-by-play man for the ACC with JP Sports. I met Bob in the '80s when HTS had the CAA package. Come tournament time Bob did pre-, half-, and postgame shows, while Bob Tallent and I handled the floor action.

It was during a tourney at William and Mary that Bob and I discovered that our radio-TV careers had followed similar paths. Rathburn handles every assignment he's given with the same top-notch quality.

Kevin Grevey was loved by every Bullet fan in D.C., having been a standout member of that team. To this day I am amazed that some major network hasn't signed Kevin on. He's that good.

Bucky Waters, former Duke coach, is well known for his HTS telecasts. I wish I could have done more games with Bucky than I did. He has the total package, and his TV work is stupendous.

Bob Tallent's dry sense of humor made him an interesting analyst. He was a great player with GW University after beginning his collegiate career with the University of Kentucky under the legendary Adolph Rupp. He'd later become the head coach at GW. He brought a southern, down-home, friendly approach to our coverage.

Bob recently told me a personal story about Maryland coach Gary Williams. Bob (as GW Coach) and Gary (as AU coach) were attending a Washington Bullets outing at Crofton Country Club in the late 70s. As the sun set on the event, Bob's two-year-old son, Mathew, accidentally fell into the darkened 12-foot end of the club swimming pool. Luckily, Gary saw it.

Fully dressed, Gary instinctively and immediately dove in and pulled Mathew to rescue.

"In my house, Gary Williams is a saint," Bob says today.

"It was no big deal," said Gary when I reminded him of this incident.

Chapter 16

The Plane Crash

"We had not been told what kind of plane was involved in the acci-dent. As we pulled near the scene, we saw fire in the sky."
Dave Statter, WUSA-TV

Just before Christmas, 1974, the *Washington Post's* Ken Ringle wrote a story about terrible floods in Nelson County, Virginia. He profiled Dora Morris, a 90-year-old lady who lived in a log cabin perched on a mountaintop. The floodwaters came surging around her humble home, but she survived. Many of her neighbors were not so lucky.

Dora's isolated log cabin had no electricity even before the floods came. Ken reported that she had just received her first telephone, so I decided to call her up on the air.

Dora was one crusty old bird. At one time she had been a stringer for her local newspaper. I asked her whether she'd ever been to Washington, and she told me, "No, never been and never want to go." She had just received a birthday card from President Ford, and she wondered, "Why is *he* sending me a birthday card? I don't know him."

"Mrs. Morris, I'd like to fly down and visit with you and bring my daughters," I told her on my show. "Fine. Come on down," she answered.

Although Dora was fascinating, I also hoped to show my girls another side of life. This visit would provide an example for my daughters that not everyone had the material things that many of us take for granted.

It tuned out that Kellie had a school commitment and only Tracie, then 11 years old, could go. The next morning after the radio interview, I was surprised to see that listeners had dropped off about 350 lbs. of food and clothing for me to take on my trip. The pilot, John Steinberger, whom I had never met before, volunteered to fly us down in his Cessna 172.

On January 29, John notified me that we could fly, and we met at Hyde Field in Clinton, Maryland. I contacted the Red Cross in Lynchburg, Virginia, to meet us when we landed. The plan was to drive from Lynchburg to Dora's little log cabin in Lovingston.

Tracie told me that she wasn't sure she wanted to go because she was afraid the plane might crash. I told her not to worry.

I also called Ken Ringle before the trip, and he advised, "Dora's a very proud woman, so you'll need to watch your approach. Your daughter should warm her up because she loves children. Maybe as an afterthought, you could tell her that you'd like to drop off some gifts from your listeners."

Dora provided some down-home directions: "Go up Rt. 29, past an abandoned warehouse, and when you come to a fallen tree, turn right. Drive right over the creek and follow through the stop sign and keep on going to the top of the mountain. You'll run straight into my cabin."

I could hear Dora's dogs barking as our Red Cross truck pulled in. Here came this little lady, with a tiny knit cap on and a small apron around her waist. Dora stood about four feet nine inches tall, carrying a stick, and surrounded by cats and dogs. I felt as if I had landed in the 1800s.

Tracie signaled a bathroom visit as we arrived, and Mrs. Morris walked her around the back to the outhouse. When they returned, I started to engage in some small talk, but Dora was soon spouting on about folks down the road, a dog that had been run over, and a cornucopia of local events. She assumed that I knew everyone in Lovingston and had intimate knowledge of every detail she was describing.

I thought to myself, "I don't know what the hell she's talking about." As darkness fell, I finally said, "We've got to go, but we have some things to leave you from our listeners if you don't mind." She told us to bring them on in, and pulled out a flashlight as she escorted us into her little cabin.

Dora had a bed on the side, a small living area, and a pot-bellied stove square in the center. Something scurried across the floor as we entered, startling us.

"Don't worry about Freddie, he's OK," Dora reassured us. Freddie was her pet skunk.

We noticed boxes piled from floor to ceiling. Her entire hallway was packed. I realized that the *Post* story had gone national, because *everybody* had sent goodwill packages.

"I don't know what I will do with all of this stuff," Dora admitted hesitantly. "I don't really need any of it. I guess I can give it away."

We went through the motions of unloading our own modest packages onto Dora's impressive heap. We hugged her goodbye, rode down the mountain, and arrived at the Lynchburg airport. It was around 7:00 p.m. when we took off for home.

Tracie asked me if she could ride in the front seat on the way back, but I thought it would be safer for her in the back of the plane, where she could also sleep.

As we approached Hyde Field, pilot John began struggling with unexpected strong winds. Unfortunately, the airport had only one runway, so John had only one direction for landing. He tried one approach but aborted. We were pitching from side to side like mad. I remember John having the runway lined up, and I woke Tracie in the back seat so she could fasten her seat belt.

I remember the plane clearing some high-tension lines. John said "Hold on, we're taking it around again," but before he could, the wing on my side went up with a big booming thud. Way off in the distance I heard Tracie yelling, "Daddy! Daddy!"

The next thing I remember is waking up in an ambulance. A sudden gust of wind had forced the left wing of the plane to bash down on the runway. The plane spun around, narrowly missed a hangar, and smashed into the ground. My head went straight into the console when we crashed. I was unconscious for 20 minutes.

Washington TV newsman Dave Statter participated in my rescue. I didn't realize this until I began writing this chapter. I received the following e-mail from Dave, who reports for WUSA, Channel 9. The efforts of Dave and the rest of the Prince George's County fire and rescue team made my last 26 years on earth possible. I sincerely thank them.

Dave Statter: "Even though I've been in broadcasting for almost 30 years, my first contact with Johnny Holliday was not what you would expect.

"I was a volunteer firefighter in Oxon Hill, Maryland, from 1974-1980. I was, at the same time, working as a DJ in La Plata and Prince Frederick. I happened to be on the call when the plane crashed near Hyde Field in Clinton, Maryland.

"We had not been told what kind of plane was involved in the accident. As we pulled near the scene, we saw fire in the sky. At first, everyone thought this was the plane crash and figured by the size of the fire it might be a fairly large plane. All the responding fire trucks and ambulances went toward the fire. It turned out that the fire was just a large brush fire—fanned by the high winds—and had nothing to do with the plane crash. The crash site was across Steed Road and was found a few minutes later by the ambulance from the Clinton station [ambulance 259]. Some of the units were then rerouted from the fire to the crash site, and we assisted in helping the injured into the ambulances. It was only later that we realized that it was Johnny Holliday in the plane."

People who were aware of the conditions that night, and who saw the smashed plane, later told me that they didn't see how we survived. This really shook me up. Tracie's seat belt had snapped, but she became wedged in between the seats, which probably protected her and saved her life.

The ambulance drove us to Greater Southeast Community Hospital, which I later learned would be a near fatal mistake. An attendant was holding a compress on my nose when I awoke in the "meat wagon."

"Why does my nose feel like it's behind my left ear?" I asked in a voice one octave higher than normal.

The old schnozzle was completely smashed and cut wide open. Luckily, Tracie had only suffered a rope burn on her face. The pilot's "cross to bear" for getting us into this mess was a broken arm and assorted cuts and bruises. I think he also lost his license when the crash was determined to be caused by his error. In the face of the winds he should have opted on to National or Andrews Air Force Base where he would have had a choice of different runways. He also lacked sufficient night flying experience. Remember that this fellow volunteered to fly us down, and I didn't know him from Adam.

"You know," said Mary Clare reflecting on the accident, "Many folks have asked us why Johnny went with a pilot he didn't even know. It's because John and I are not suspicious people or worriers. We are both optimists and continue to think the best will happen, not the worst."

Other than my split nose and Tracie's rope burn, we had no other visible injuries. At the hospital, the emergency doctors examined us briefly and released us. "Your doctor can set your nose tomorrow," they said. *They were going to send us home.*

At the time of the accident, Mary Clare was having dinner with Dr. Nick Howey, owner of the Harlequin Dinner theatre. Tracie and I had planned to join them when we returned from Dora's mountaintop. I gave Dr. Howey's phone number to an aide, and the hospital contacted Mary Clare—who asked nervously how we were.

"We are not at liberty to give that information," the hospital operator replied.

"Listen," said Clare. "I'm not driving 40 miles to identify bodies. I want to know their condition."

The operator still wouldn't cooperate. Clare next called our friend Dr. Jerry Principato, and he, in turn, called the hospital to get the prognosis. Jerry immediately—and strongly—demanded our transfer to Sibley Hospital, in northwest D.C. Jerry met us there to set and suture my hurtin' nose. I finally nodded off to sleep around 1:00 a.m.

The next morning, another close family friend, Dr. John Judge, and our family pastor, Monsignor Leo Cody of Holy Redeemer church, came to visit. John was our statistician for the Maryland football games. While they were visiting, another doctor, James Boland, catapulted into the room and solemnly announced, "We have a problem."

"*We* have a problem—or just me?" I asked.

"Your blood count indicates there is a rupture to your spleen," Dr. Boland said. "We need to remove your spleen immediately."

"Do I have any options?"

"No," said Dr. Boland.

The funny thing is that I had no discomfort. I wasn't in any pain, but I might have gone into a mild shock after Dr. Boland's surgical newsflash. I woke up in intensive care after the surgery and ended up staying in Sibley Hospital for 29 days.

Had I gone home after the crash, Dr. Boland later explained, I would have quietly died in my sleep from internal bleeding. Again, the Holliday luck was still with me.

During my month of recuperation, Capt. Dan would do a low fly-by every morning in his helicopter to cheer me up. Clare blocked all listener visitors, and only close friends of the family came to call. I received many cards and letters during my recuperation. I tried to answer every one of them. I don't recall who took over my radio show, and to be honest, I didn't give much thought to my radio absence or what was happening at WWDC. I was too uncomfortable after the surgery. I had fears about not being able to do things, but that never happened.

My nose still shows signs of being rebuilt. That's OK. The original wasn't that great to begin with.

While recuperating I learned that the State of Maryland had passed House Resolution No. 67: "Resolved by the House of Delegates of Maryland, that every member of this body wishes a speedy recovery to Johnny Holliday and we hope that he will quickly return to his radio program." Del. Frank Shore was my backer on this one.

Three nurses took care of me, but I was a very bad patient. Two of them I could control, but the third, a tiny lady, was like a drill sergeant. She was my early shift nurse whom I first met when she opened my window blinds and said, "Mr. Holliday, it's time to get up."

"I can't get up," I protested.

"It's time to get up, Mr. Holliday," she repeated.

"I can't get up," I insisted.

"Move over," she yelled, and she actually *climbed into bed with me.*

"Here's how you get up," she told me, almost cheek to cheek—*on both ends.*

"You put one hand on the rail, you put another hand on the rail, and you pull yourself up. Now let's see if you can be a big boy and get out of bed."

"Oh great," I thought. This is just what I need.

A few days later she made me walk. I was like Tim Conway's "little old man," creeping along with my mobile IV unit.

"Mr. Holliday, you're doing very well," she said.

"Right, I am doing really well," I agreed sarcastically. The night before the crash, I had played 40 minutes in a basketball game, and now I could hardly walk.

The next day, she took me for a stroll in the hallway. I was creeping along, thankful she was by my side to hold me up. Suddenly, a code blue emergency alarmed. My nurse—and everybody else in sight—left me hanging on to the wall. I was there for 15 minutes before she returned for me.

About a week into my stay, I decided that the very nice adjustable bed I had in intensive care felt better than the ordinary one they had deposited me in for recovery. I could fine-tune the special bed and relieve some of my pain. I began to ask for an adjustable bed, but I couldn't get anyone to take me seriously.

"We have to keep the adjustable ones in intensive care," the hospital told me.

"Well, can't you just get me one of those beds from somewhere?" I pestered. I launched a chronic campaign for an adjustable bed. Bob, the hospital PR fellow, eventually caved in.

As I began to feel better, I'd ask Dr. Boland when he thought I could go home. He'd say, "You're looking better; let's talk about it tomorrow." This exchange went on every morning for 20 days. Tomorrow never seemed to come.

I wanted to be out of the hospital by February 16 for Clare's birthday, but we settled on celebrating in my hospital room. Dr. Boland walked in during the party with a black bag. Something's up, I thought, because he never carried a black bag. Out of the bag came a bottle of champagne.

One evening around 2:00 a.m., I had this deep desire for some cookies. I ambled out of bed with my IV attached and crept by the nursing station. I still couldn't see very well because my eyes were swollen. The nurse asked, "Where are you going?" and I told her I'm going to get some cookies from the vending machine. She said, "Okay, hurry back."

"Hurry back?" *Right.*

I took the elevator down a floor and heard a maintenance man buffing floors near the snack machines. As I leaned down to put my coins in the slot, this janitor stopped his buffer and asked in a thick Spanish accent, "Are you Johnny Holliday?"

"Yes, hello," I answered.

"What the hell happened to you?"

"I was in a plane crash."

"Jeez, you coulda been killed."

I agreed with him.

"What you doing now?" the janitor asked.

"I'm trying to get some cookies."

"Well, you're working the soda machine. The cookie machine is over there," pointing to the left. "Nice to meet you, Mr. Holliday."

"Same here," I smiled.

I was hurting, but I had to laugh. I've forgotten the details of many big events in my life, but I will never forget that chance encounter with the janitor and his "Jeez, you coulda been killed." Yeah, he was right.

Finally, I was released from Sibley. All the nurses and doctors came out to see me off. It was very emotional and I started to cry. Clare took me home and set me up in our big plush green chair facing my window. Again, I started to cry like a baby.

She said, "What are you crying for?"

I answered, "I'm just glad to be home."

During my hospital stay, Clare had been campaigning for president of Holy Redeemer School Association, where my kids went. The election fell a few days after I got back home from the hospital. Naturally, I wanted to go and vote. Clare said, "No, you can't. You're not up to it." But I insisted.

When I hobbled out of the car on election night, all the nuns and many families at the school—warmly greeted me. They actually told me their prayers had been answered that I was okay.

Clare won the election, beating some attorney.

I've kidded her over the years that had I not shown up, the vote would have gone the other way. I'm sure I delivered the "sympathy vote" for her.

Dr. Boland had recommended that I visit Florida for some R and R. In his words, "the warmth would help me heal twice as fast." We set off for Miami. At the airport, Tracie refused to get on the plane. "I'm not flying," she insisted. Who could blame her after already crashing once in her young life? The pilot helped us calm her down and gently persuaded her to board the plane. After the flight, the pilot announced over the intercom, "I hope everyone had a great flight, including Tracie." That was a nice touch.

I returned to WWDC in the middle of March. I was generally back in action immediately, and began rehearsal for *Carnival* at the Harlequin Dinner theatre. The part I played in the show was Paul the Puppeteer, a character who just happened to have a stiff leg. When I first came out on stage I could see some members of the audience point, and I heard their whispers, "See his leg. It's because of that plane crash."

Carnival opened on May 22. Richard Coe, the admired theatre critic for the *Washington Post*, reviewed my performance in these words, "Johnny Holliday, WWDC's radio waker-upper, almost ranks as a Harlequin regular for he has appeared there effectively in *How to Succeed in Business* and *Company*. Paul is not an ingratiating role, but Holliday sings well and easily in a controlled, commendable performance."

By May I had returned to the softball Radio Oneder games and picked up where I left off. I will say that the whole experience was a great weight loss program. I shed about 25 pounds.

Five years after my accident, *Washington Post* columnist Bob Levey asked to do a follow-up. I told him, "That the initial feeling after you come through something like this is that you'll never do anything wrong again. You'll kiss your wife and give to the poor. Your church attendance will go up 700 percent. You know, that kind of thing.

"But that wears off after a while. What remains is that a lot of things have been more important to me from that point on. My wife, my kids, my job, my friends...

"It's like, I used to be terrible around the studio. I'd see a guy goofing off, I'd get furious. I thought everybody ought to work as hard as I do. Now I don't feel that way any more. I guess you could say I found some peace from this."

Following the interview, I asked Bob if he'd ever considered doing radio. He said he'd never really thought about it. I told him he had a great set of pipes.

I think he took my advice, because Bob's been doing radio work now for many years.

Four years ago I was hospitalized for a week, undergoing some tests. I've kept it private because a close fiend of mine in radio had some heart problems years back, and the local media reported it. Although my friend fully recovered, I thought it might have hurt his radio career. I didn't want them to make this same assumption about me.

On the other hand, some broadcasters like Larry King turn their heart attacks into career enhancements. My own tests turned out to be a false alarm.

Anyway, the first call I got in the hospital came from Gary Williams. He told me, "You gotta get out of there. We don't want to lose you. You are too valuable to our program." I though that was pretty nice of him, although I joked at the time that Greg Manning might have paid him to call me.

Surviving the plane crash really opened my eyes. I realized how fragile life is. I became more aware of how much my family really meant to me. I also decided to be kinder to the people I worked with. The other thing that struck me was the thought that maybe there was a reason I survived. Maybe there was something else that God intended for me to do.

Looking back now I could say that one "something else" was my daughter, Moira, who was born four years later. Our physicians had told us then that the reason Clare and I weren't getting pregnant is because I was probably sterile from all the medication I had taken during my recovery.

Moira is now 23 years old, so the sterility theory wasn't borne out, pardon the pun. My desire to spend more time with Clare, Kellie, Tracie, Moira, and my grandkids was reinforced after the accident. It's a priority that I have tried to keep.

Chapter 17

John Joyce

I first became involved with Vietnam veterans when a listener sent me an anonymous poem, "Does Anyone Remember Me," which poignantly dealt with the POW issue. I added some background music and narrated the poem on my WWDC show. Listener response was strong.

Carmella LaSpada, the founder of No Greater Love, heard the poem on WWDC and asked me to emcee a benefit for the residents of the Old Soldiers home. No Greater Love is a national organization dedicated to providing programs of remembrance for survivors of those who lost their lives in service to their country or terrorism.

Carmella is a ball of fire, with more energy for public service than ten people combined. How could I refuse this honor?

At the event I met Max Cleland, then head of the Veterans Administration. Max's words to the Old Soldier's home residents were so uplifting and inspiring. He and I worked on several events in the succeeding years and became friends. I invited him to come see me at one of my dinner theatre shows, and he accepted. Today, he's the senior U.S. Senator from Georgia. A true American hero.

In 1997, Larry Mathews produced "They Served With Honor," a radio story about the opening of the Vietnam Veterans Memorial. Larry earned a Peabody Award for his effort profiling Jan Scruggs, the veteran responsible for getting "The Wall" built.

Scruggs had started fundraising for the Wall in 1979 with $2,800 of his own cash. It was finished and dedicated—completely financed through private contributions—in November 1982. By comparison, the Lincoln Memorial took 20 years and the Washington Monument 40 years to become realities. Jan Scruggs, who was raised in Bowie, Maryland, managed to get the city's *most visited* memorial completed in a thousand days.

At the celebration party following the airing of "They Served With Honor," I told Jan how my own brother-in-law, John Joyce, had been killed in Vietnam. Jan suggested that I think about coming to the next Memorial Day service on the Mall and talk about it. I kind of fluffed off the suggestion because I didn't really believe it would happen. It was party conversation, or so I thought.

Surprisingly, Jan called me a few months later to confirm my appearance. After some thought, I said, "Jan, I am not sure I can do this. This could be emotionally tough."

Jan said, "Just tell the story exactly as you told it to me. Remember that everyone at the memorial service will have been touched by the same kind of personal tragedy—the loss of a loved one in Vietnam—or they wouldn't be there."

So I thought about what happened to John. After I phoned my sister-in-law, Rosemary, to review some of the facts I may have forgotten, I wrote the script. On Memorial Day, May 26, 1997 I spoke to a group of several hundred at the Wall. I broke down a few times but managed to get through it.

When it was over, I told Mary Clare that this was one of the hardest things I had ever done. I include it here as a tribute to John and to all the men and women who have served our country.

> *Good afternoon, everybody, and welcome to the 15th anniversary of the Vietnam Veterans Memorial. There are 58,202 names inscribed on the wall, with seven more names to be added today. It is my distinct honor to join you today to tell you about one particular name on the wall: John H. Joyce of Dorchester, Massachusetts, and a proud member of the armor division of the United States Army. John Joyce was my brother-in-law, married to my wife's sister, Rosemary.*
>
> *Jack and Rosie were married in 1965. At that time I was working in the beautiful city of San Francisco, where Jack had spent three months in nearby Monterey learning Vietnamese, and he would soon go to Vietnam as a liaison, as a buffer between the American and South Vietnamese forces. Captain Jack Joyce believed in all his heart in what he was doing. It was his job; he was to carry it out to the best of his ability.*
>
> *In 1966, Jack received his orders and was preparing to leave for Vietnam. I can clearly recall today some 31 years later just how uncomfortable I was sitting at the kitchen table with Jack, Rosemary, and Clare as we talked about what would take place if Jack failed to return. I asked, "Why even discuss that? He will return safe and sound."*

However, Jack was very calm as he explained to us that as a career officer this discussion was something that had to be done. But not to worry. He assured us that he would be back.

So as not to make his departure any more emotional, and believe me it was emotional, Jack decided it would be best if Rosemary not go with him to Travis Air Force Base to see him off. So I drove him to the base to say goodbye, to say good luck, and tell him that we'd all be waiting for his safe return to the States. As fate would have it, I would be the last family member to see Jack Joyce alive.

That was July of 1966. On December 19 a meeting had been scheduled for Jack to listen to some concerns and complaints of the Vietnamese people. He was to attend that meeting by helicopter. But fog had rolled in and prevented the chopper from taking off. So Jack and his men took the road in a jeep convoy. En route they hit a land mine. And all were killed.

Jack and Rosemary's daughter, Mary Katharine, was a little over a year old at the time. Rosie was expecting her second child any moment. It was two days after Jack was killed on December 21st of 1966 that their son was born. The son that Jack would never see.

The officer who had to break the news to Rosemary had first gone to her parents' home in Miami Shores, but Rosemary was in the hospital. Her parents would not tell the officer which hospital it was. They simply did not want Rosemary to go through that kind of ordeal after just giving birth.

Rosemary was always amazed at how thoughtful Jack was. He never forgot a special day or anniversary. So Rosemary's first thought when the officer returned was that Jack had sent someone special to congratulate her on the arrival of Jack's first son. Eventually, she was told that he had died for his country.

Everyone he came in contact with respected Jack. And following his death at the age of 29 Rosemary received countless letters of praise from the men who had served under his command. The news of Jack's death hit our family hard. The same as many families here today who have experienced this tragedy.

We flew to Washington for the funeral. Rosemary and Jack's father had requested they be allowed to view Jack's body just to be certain it was he. At first, Rosemary said it's not my husband. She thought there had been a terrible mistake. Then his father saw behind Jack's ear a clearly visible and familiar scar. The two said their goodbyes. The casket was closed.

Jack Joyce was laid to rest across the river in Arlington National Cemetery, promoted posthumously to major. Had he lived, who knows how far Jack would have traveled up the armed forces ladder of success? I'm sure those of you with us today share the same feelings about the loved ones you lost in Vietnam.

We're here today for one purpose: to remember the men and women who served this country and in doing so, lost their lives.

*Those of you who may live in, or travel through Dorchester, Massachu-
setts might like to take a little drive and pause for a moment on the street
named in honor of John Joyce, killed in action in Vietnam.*

Chapter 18

Put Your Money On
Sr. Marie Louise

"Sister, are you going to pick the New Orleans Saints to win this week?
I think you should. It's a good career move."
Glenn Brenner, Channel 9 Sports

When Kellie reached her final year of junior high at Kensington's Holy
Redeemer School, Mary Clare and I began looking at potential high schools.
Many of Kellie's friends had applied at Holy Cross or Stone Ridge, both fine
private schools. Kellie decided that Georgetown Visitation Preparatory School,
or "Visi" as we call it, would be her choice.

Founded in 1799 adjacent to Georgetown University, Visitation is the
oldest girls' school in the United States. The Visitation Sisters, a cloistered
religious order founded by St. Francis De Sales, instruct the 400 girls that
Visi enrolls each year.

You know some of St. Francis's most famous sayings: *"You can catch*
more flies with a spoonful of honey than with a barrel of vinegar," or *"There is*
nothing so strong as gentleness and nothing so gentle as real strength." Among
Catholics, Francis De Sales is known as the "Saint of Common Sense." Sounds
good to me.

Kellie was thrilled when her letter of acceptance arrived and also enthusiastic when some of her friends were also accepted.

Four years later, Kellie's proud parents were in tears when she received
the Knights of Columbus honor for outstanding senior at the Visi awards
banquet.

Tracie also graduated from Visi and left her mark in athletic competition, playing on the basketball and field hockey teams. Like Kellie, Tracie excelled in the classroom and won the Benedicta Cup in her senior year as Visi's "Best All-Around Girl."

Moira would also add some nice trophies to her awards collection, receiving Visi's Rubacky 3-E award in both her junior and senior years, along with the Fine Arts certificate.

When they talk about the Visitation family, we know from firsthand experience that it is so. The Visitation sisters were wonderful role models for Kellie (class of '78), Tracie ('81), and Moira ('97).

I've become a shameless evangelist for Visitation. I once talked the Redskins' General Manager, Charley Casserly, into considering Visi for *his* daughter.

> **Charley Casserly:** "For years Johnny told my wife, Bev, and I about how great Visitation was. When my daughter, Shannon, was ready to choose her high school, Johnny met me over at the school for a tour. The plan was for two students to show us around, but we couldn't go two feet without someone stopping us. Johnny knew everybody in the building.
>
> "The two 'tour' girls met us, took us to a foyer, and started telling us about the history of paintings on the wall. This went on about 15 minutes, and I finally said, 'Girls. Stop. Let's eliminate all the history of paintings. I taught in high school. I was a guidance counselor. It's an all-girls' school, so what do you do about boys? How do you handle that? Let's talk about the class. Let's talk about homework. Let's talk about sports. Let's not worry about paintings.'
>
> "Johnny politely told the girls that he'd handle it from there and gently dismissed them back to class. Johnny took over and gave me the tour. My daughter graduated from Visitation."

Kellie was first to show her budding theatrical talents at Visi when she was cast in the role of Myrtle May in the comedy classic *Harvey*. Mary Clare and I were very nervous parents as we sat in the audience watching Kellie perform. Not to worry. She pulled off a flawless performance.

"I knew she had it. She's a chip off the old block," said her drama teacher, a five-foot fireball named Sr. Marie Louise. I assumed she was referring to me, although she could have meant Mary Clare. This is how I first met Sr. Marie Louise Kirkland, better known around the halls of the school as "Weezie."

Weezie was born in D.C., and we heard she played some mean basketball in high school. She later attended Immaculata College and worked as a courthouse clerk in Rockville, Maryland until she hit her 30s.

"When I joined the convent, I was afraid I wouldn't be able to love sports anymore," she once said. Her family didn't think she'd last in the cloister, but she "lasted" for over 50 years. She remained a sports fan, too. Especially a Redskins fan.

When Moira's turn came around we noticed that she had inherited the Holliday "performance" genes, too. Moira and I would play many of Sister Marie Louise's benefits, as Sister always seemed to request that I emcee her events. Have you ever tried to say no to a little nun who stood only five feet tall? You can't. It's impossible. Besides, I loved the shows, and so did Moira.

I can directly attribute the kind of people my daughters are today to the Visitation experience. Their lessons extended far beyond the classroom. Kellie is a family physician today, largely because of the encouragement she received from Mother Mary Philomena, her biology teacher. The same is true of Tracie, a neonatal nurse at Shady Grove Adventist Hospital. I believe my daughters received the best possible education. We will never forget the Visi faculty: Sister Mary Berchmans Hannan, Sister Anne Marie, Sister Jacqueline, Mother Mary De Sales, Sister Philomena, Sister Suzanne, Sister Clare Joseph, Sister Mary Virginia, headmaster Dan Kearns, and Sister Marie Louise.

If you can send your girls to a Visitation school, take it from Johnny Holliday and his family. Do it! You won't find a better education for your daughters.

And who would have guessed that Weezie would go on to become a national sport celebrity? To explain how this happened requires a profile of another D.C. legend, the late sportscaster Glenn Brenner. But to do that properly also involves getting my old boss at WINS, Joel Chaseman, into the story.

In 1973, Joel came to Washington to run WTOP-TV Channel 9. He had always been involved in college radio, so when the University of Pennsylvania college station got itself into a jam—through no fault of its own—he drove up there to help out. In one of his prior incarnations he had also been head of Philadelphia's KYW-TV Channel 3. On that visit to the university, he tuned in KYW to see what his former station was up to.

Joel Chaseman: "I had helped put the KYW news team together—Jessica Savitch, Mort Crim, Al Melsor—so I watched it for old times' sake. This underplayed sports segment came on, which I really didn't understand, with this big guy sitting there, with what I thought was a congenial, ingratiating manner. It was a really bad set with terrible drapes, and the lighting wasn't good, but the guy interviewing someone was terrific.

"He was this third-string sports guy named Glenn Brenner. We were going through agony at Channel 9. Warner Wolf had left, replaced by Mike Wolf, who was a disaster. So we needed somebody. I knew the manager at KYW, Allan Bell, and called him, made some conversation, and finally got around to the real subject of the call:

'How are you doing at sports? Is Al Melsor holding up well?'

'Yeah, he's all right,' said Allan.

'And your second-string guy's OK, too?'

'Yeah, fine.'

'You know I saw that guy, Glenn Brenner. What's he doing?'

'Oh, I don't know. We put him under contract. We really don't want to keep him around any more, but I don't know what to do with him,' Allan said.

"You know I can probably do a save here. Let me talk to Jim Snyder (the late Channel 9 news director, also a widely respected and well-loved guy). I was also scouting Andrea Mitchell at the time—there was lots of talent in Philadelphia—and Snyder said fine. That's how Glenn came to Washington. I'm not sure if Glenn ever knew this story.

"There was a mischief about Glenn that was fun. A joy for life, and an irrepressible humor that he could translate with intelligence. He was unconventional, but it was clear he wasn't ego-crazy. He was just enjoying sports.

"Sports have always been thought of as toys and games within the news arena. The second part of Glenn's success was his link with the anchor, Gordon Peterson.

"Gordon Peterson is a man who was a marine, and he was a monk. He's honest, intelligent, with a wisdom and experience that is rare in any human being, much less in an on-the-air newscaster. People admire Gordon Peterson, and well they should. People spark to something in Gordon that is an essential honesty, integrity, and unassuming wisdom.

"The link between the two of them helped launch Glenn.

"It's no surprise that Johnny should think so highly of people like Gordon and Glenn. There are no false steps here. I think the dominant difference that set Glenn Brenner and Johnny Holliday apart from others was, and is, their irrepressible good nature. It bubbled up and was effervescent without ever being mean, petty, or small-minded. People like that.

"And, unfortunately, those are rare qualities, and seldom leavened with wit and humor."

Glenn always called me "Holliday." We met when we cohosted a telethon together shortly after he arrived in D.C. in 1977. A former pitcher in both the New York Mets and Philadelphia farm systems, I instantly knew he would take the market by storm. I was right.

Glenn knew what he was talking about. He was funny, likeable, and irreverent. People just loved the guy. His "Weenie of the Week" awards for stupid plays or poor management decisions were audience favorites.

"The Glenn," as his friends called him, kept it entertaining, and not just for sports fans.

He once told *Washington Post* reporter Tom Shales: "I'm talking to a group of people who are not that interested in what I have to say. Statistically, they've proven that. So what I want to do is keep their interest. And the way I can best do that is to relate to them."

Relate he did. No one has come close to owning the Washington sports market like the Glenn.

He once took a one-day suspension from his boss rather than apologize a second time for a comic airing of two Redskins mangling the Star-Spangled Banner on Veterans' Day. Glenn didn't suffer fools, and he made sure to stay honest with his audience.

Glenn had a good line about Charley Casserly. Glenn said, "I'd want Charley to be a POW, because I know he'd never say anything. Every time I've interviewed him I've walked away realizing that he never said anything. He can say more about nothing than anyone I've known."

After Glenn cracked the joke, Charley was asked how he learned to be so evasive at times. Charley said, "By watching the politicians on the news each night."

One of Glenn's best bits was to line up various celebrities to pick the winners of the week's NFL games. It just so happened that Kevin Enright, one of Brenner's staff, suggested he get in touch with a nun who apparently was a huge Washington Redskins fan.

It turned out to be our own Sister Marie Louise.

She guessed more winners than any of Glenn's celebrity prognosticators. The losers included newscasters Dan Rather, Maureen Bunyan and Connie Chung; boxer Sugar Ray Leonard; actors William Shatner and Paul Reubens (Pee Wee Herman); members of the Temptations; and football stars Sonny Jurgensen and Mark Rypien. Weezie beat them all. TV appearances and a *People* magazine profile earned her, and the school, nationwide publicity.

Weezie stopped short of predicting the point spread. Remember, she's a nun. She felt that odds-making for the listeners would be wrong. By predicting the most wins, she earned $1,000 for a Visi scholarship fund.

Glenn Brenner, Gordon Peterson, and I emceed Sister Marie Louise's 90th birthday celebration. It was a black-tie event with proceeds earmarked for another scholarship fund. "A scholarship fund is dearest to my heart," said Weezie during a tearful thank-you to the assembled guests.

For her birthday Glenn Brenner gave her *a set of golf clubs* and soon had the audience cracking up with one-liners.

"Sister, are you going to pick the Saints to win this week?" asked Brenner from the podium. "I think you should. It's a good career move."

"Oh, I don't bother with the Saints. They always let you down," Weezie answered.

He said, "Okay, how 'bout the Cardinals?"

"Oh, I don't know any Cardinals."

Weezie managed to not only keep up with Glenn joke for joke, but actually upstaged him in her own quiet way. This almost never happened when you shared a mic with the Glenn.

For my part, I sang, "Once in Love With Weezie," accompanied by Angela Enright (Kevin's mom) on the grand piano. Weezie hugged me when it was over. The crowd loved it.

We were alarmed to hear that Glenn had collapsed one year later during a Marine Corp marathon. His illness was first attributed to stress from the run. However, the community was shocked when the true diagnosis was disclosed later in the week.

The diagnosis was inoperable brain cancer.

His enormous popularity was instantly overshadowed by sadness as his fans coped with the bad news. Sister Mary Louise got permission to leave the cloister and visit him in the hospital to say her goodbye. Glenn was comatose when she arrived.

By his bedside, she held his hand and spoke to him. Glenn did not open his eyes, but did respond, almost miraculously, by squeezing her hand in reply. He knew she was there with him. Glenn Brenner died later that day on January 14, 1992. He was 44.

All the local TV and radio stations led with news of Glenn's death. Sr. Marie Louise was among those interviewed in Channel 9's coverage. "Well, in the first place, I loved him," she said.

WRC's sports reporter, George Michael, was visibly emotional as he shared his feelings with viewers. I think George best said what we were all feeling.

"Glenn has become more than just a sportscaster for Channel 9. He has become a very large part of our city. At one time or another, he's made every single one of us put a big smile on our face. No matter what the circumstance, Glenn could make us laugh at even the worst of times. Thank you, God, for letting me work with him."

It came as no surprise when President Bush issued the First Family's condolences:

> *"Barbara and I are greatly saddened by the untimely death of Glenn Brenner, a man whose wit and ability has endeared him to so many Washingtonians. The suddenness of his death and the warmth of his personality leave all of us with a painful emptiness. Sometimes we think we know television personalities better than we really do. But Glenn Brenner's life and his many friends demonstrate that the man we saw was real, a man who loved his work, his family, and the community he served. We will remember him for those qualities that made him so special. Barbara and I offer our prayers and sympathy to his family and friends."*

As her own health began to fail in later years, Weezie would remind me that she was planning to throw the grandest birthday party that Washington had ever seen when she hit the big 100.

She passed away July 10, 1999, a little more than three months shy of her centennial. The Hollidays are among the many who will never forget her.

Chapter 19

Pitching the Commercials, Sharing the Stage

"Sport Automotive. That's where you and your family will be sports fans, too."

How many people on the planet can claim to have been the spokesperson for Levi jeans and the United Association of Plumbers, Pipe Fitters, and Sprinkler Fitters? Or how about Harrah's Tahoe Casino and Mug root beer?

Imagine that you've just been hired by President Bush to serve in his cabinet. Before you start work, you'll be required to watch an instructional film on administration transition, hosted and narrated by yours truly. And if you're lucky enough to get jury duty in Montgomery County, Maryland, you'll sit through a film on the process. Guess who narrates it?

I've been spokesperson for some top-notch advertisers and agencies over the years. Voice-over commercials in radio and television can give a performer that extra exposure all of us are looking for. This work can be tremendously positive for your career if the commercial is a good one. If not, it can hurt you, especially if the audience knows it's you.

I'm thankful to my WINS boss, Joel Chaseman, for pointing me in the right direction regarding commercials. Joel already had experience as executive producer for Steve Allen's syndicated show when Steve left New York for Hollywood by the time we met. It was a wild show with bits like their "man on the street," but that's a different story. Joel retired as president of *Post-Newsweek*. What a career.

Joel Chaseman: "At WINS, we had a group of disc jockeys that had become accustomed to New York and the fame and glory. They were kind of hard-shelled, semi-cynical, and very much proud of themselves. Johnny wasn't like that. He was a good human being. So I took more than a normal interest in his work.

"He was enthusiastic about the music and a lot of other things. But he threw the commercials away and kind of droned them. I hated to see that in John, because the rest of his work was so good. It wasn't good for him to become a different person when he read the commercials than who he was on the rest of the show. At some point I told him that.

"It had to do with John's presentation of who he was—a lively, smart, engaging, cheerful person. But he became something other than that when he did commercials. He became dull. I pointed that out to him and he was very quick to understand and adapt to it."

The commercials that gave me the greatest national attention were the ones produced by my friend Gordon Falkner for Nissan automobiles. He ran his own ad agency out of Baltimore and saw me do a TV spot in 1975 for Perpetual Savings and Loan. My daughters Kellie and Tracie were in the spot. Moira would have been with us, too, had she been born.

Gordon thought I'd be perfect for his new client, Bill Shaeffer's Nationwide Datsun. This began my long Datsun/Nissan run. Gordon picked up more than 75 additional Nissan dealerships from coast to coast. I was the on- and off-camera spokesman for all of these. We'd do up to three commercials at a session, and then I'd add each individual city tag.

The spots we filmed ran on almost every channel, every night. You couldn't miss them. I got paid in 13-week cycles. These spots were never repeated, because we were constantly doing new ones.

The Nissan ads were as campy as they were creative. On one, we were pilgrims heading for the Datsun "Sell-a-thon"("This sure beats the Mayflower.") We filmed a Nissan 50th anniversary spot with me in white tux fronting a full orchestra. One showed a man in shorts walking up to his garage and opening the door. Up popped Holliday. Behind me was a showroom with shiny cars and a busy, milling crowd in motion. The crowds, however, would ultimately become a problem for my union, AFTRA.

In 1984, I received a letter instructing me to cease and desist working with Gordon Falkner. Why? AFTRA got wind that Gordon was not paying the union rate to all the extras in the showroom crowds. Gordon's defense? He was paying the actors and actresses a good salary for doing nothing besides standing around the cars. He reasoned that he needed the "showrooms" to be filled with up to 30 actors, and he couldn't afford to pay top union scale to everyone.

AFTRA didn't agree and put him on the unfair list.

I went before the AFTRA board and made my case. "He's fair to me," I told them. "What will you accomplish by putting him on the unfair list? All you'll end up doing is costing me the biggest freelance account that I've ever had, and he will continue with nonunion talent."

AFTRA still didn't budge, and that ended the gig for me. I couldn't go up against my union. Today, AFTRA would have handled something like this more cooperatively, but back then they took a hard-line approach.

Falkner replaced me with a nonunion spokesman—just as I predicted to my union reps—and the ads continued. He made a ton of money. Today, he owns an automobile dealership in Hilton Head, South Carolina. The only person who lost money was me.

Fortunately I was later picked up by Rick Kell's Kell Communications and their client, Sport Automotive Chevrolet Jeep and Honda, which I've done with Rick for ten years. The relationship I have with Sport's owner Robert Fogarty and his general manager Tony Landini turned out to be even better than the one I had with Nissan. Only problem with Robert is that he's a Duke fan. But I'm working on that. Landini is a Maryland grad and seldom misses a game.

Rick Kell: "There are two things I really enjoy about working with Johnny. He's the consummate pro. I produce his Maryland coaches' shows too, and he takes the worry out of the business. I've never found a time when he wasn't prepared.

"He's also the best guy to make fun of because he has a great sense of humor. He's just like the ad says, 'He's fun and hassle-free.' We often think of technology getting better, but Johnny's the one who keeps getting better."

My first nationwide exposure was a ten-second commercial on Phil Rizzutto's national sports show. My freelance work really shifted into high gear in San Francisco. I began to concentrate even harder on style, delivery, and flexibility. I realized that the more versatile I could become with commercials—both broadcast and nonbroadcast—the more successful I would be. My second national spot was for Levi jeans, joined by the Jefferson Airplane. Other Frisco ads that come to mind are Vox guitars, Hastings, Harrah's Tahoe, and Shakey's Pizza.

My freelance work in Washington has kept me busy. I've worked with some great talent. Paul Anthony (whom I first got to know in Rochester), Willard Scott, Ed Walker, John Badilla, Carroll James, Dude Walker, Brian Clark, Walt Teas, Rhea Feiken, Naomi Robin, Bill O'Connor, Martha Manning, Elliott Denniberg, Stan Brandorff, Lew Grenville, Mike Pengra, Colgate Salisbury, Sheldon Smith, Henry Strozier, Michael Willis, Betsy Ames, Nancy Calo, Melissa Collins, Ilona Dulaski, Francis Glick, and Doris McMillon are just a few of the best I've worked with.

Other accounts I've enjoyed include Worldgate Athletic Club, which I did with former Redskins coach Joe Gibbs, the American Red Cross, PBS, the Discovery Channel, Sears, the Kennedy Center, Lee Sports, McDonald's, U.S. Air Arena, London Fog, the State Farm Senior Golf Classic, the U.S. Postal Service, the May Company Stores, AARP, the IRS, and Kroger Foods.

One of our WMAL radio interns, Mike Dawson, once noticed a stack of checks in my briefcase. He asked me what was up with this money. I noticed I hadn't deposited my freelance checks in the bank for a while.

One tool of the radio trade is the ability to do impressions. My first impression was Ed Sullivan, performed nearly 45 years ago at my high school assembly with buddy Don Lewis.

Following our "really big shew" I soon mastered easy impressions like Dracula, W. C. Fields, Cary Grant, and Jimmy "Inka-Dinka-Do" Durante. Eventually my radio career required a serious approach to getting the intonation and words just right as I began building a wider range of character voices. Because I was working in the nation's capital, it made sense to add Reagan, Humphrey, McGovern, Perot, and other politicians to the arsenal. All in all, I think I can do about 50 characters. The only time I blew one was when I interviewed Roger Miller at KYA. Roger already knew I did an impression of him and put me on the spot by requesting to hear it. I found that I couldn't mimic him face to face. I choked.

Once I joined Larry Lewman for a commercial taping. Rene Funk, of Rodel Productions, gave me my instructions.

"You'll be doing 'Richard Nixon' for this spot," Rene said.

"Who told you I could do Nixon?" I asked.

Larry pulled me aside and said, "You can do Nixon. You can do any voices. Besides, they don't have anyone else for this job. At least try." And so we did.

Lewman was arguably the top voice-over talent in the Washington/Baltimore market. His later health problems forced him to retire much too early from the business.

Washington D.C.'s original Wax Museum used my John F. Kennedy impression for their wax figure's "real voice" for years. In the early seventies I lost track of the museum when they relocated across town and added a live dolphin show to the mix. Now long gone, I wonder whatever happened to the wax dummies *and* my Kennedy voice.

An ad campaign for the old *Washington Star* newspaper paired my Jimmy Carter with a young Alma Viator doing an Amy Carter impression. Alma Viator later became the public relations tour de force at the National Theatre and now heads her own PR firm. Readers who know Alma will get a big kick out of learning she once did a radio spot as Amy Carter.

For many years before the Kennedy Center for the Performing Arts opened its doors, Washington D.C. was not regarded as much of a "performing arts" city. Yet *Showboat, West Side Story, Fiddler on the Roof, Hello Dolly, Crazy for You,* and others first played to Washington audiences at the National Theatre and then on to Broadway fame

I saw my first Broadway show in 1964. *How to Succeed in Business Without Really Trying* at the Schubert theatre. The gorgeous Michelle Lee glowed in the role of Rosemary. Darryl Hickman, brother to Dwayne, of "Dobie Gillis" TV fame, played Finch. I had just missed seeing Robert Morse, who originated the role, which was a disappointment. Still, I remember being so impressed with the whole show.

As I sat in the audience, however, I kept thinking, "Hey, I can sing those songs. I can act. I could be doing that. This would be a perfect role *for me.*"

That chance came a few years later when I read a notice for *How to Succeed* ... auditions held at the Contra Costa Musical Theatre in Walnut Creek, California. Walnut Creek was not exactly around the corner from my job at KYA, but the auditions were the same night I was playing a KYA Radio Oneders softball game, and the field was not far from Walnut Creek. I figured, "Let's give it a shot."

I sang "The Brotherhood of Man" and the show's title song, still in my Oneders uniform. I thought it went well since the director thanked me and said he would call.

Sure enough, I was cast as Finch, the lead role. Was I ever thrilled? The cast was very good and included Barbara Nunn (Rosemary), Bill Disbrow (J.B. Bigley), Vince Aiello (Bud Frump), and Sandy Dudley (Howdy). None of us were paid. We did it for the love of theatre. I also knew the cross-promotion would be great for both KYA and Contra Costa.

Later I would repeat the role in Oakland for the Woodminster Summer theatre, a step up from Contra Costa. Having played Finch before, I really felt comfortable in the role the second time around, and it was a much better show. Director, James Schlater, and fellow cast members Maureen Lee, Guy Ezelle, and Georgeane Zavo were wonderful.

When I arrived in Washington, I had four productions under my belt: *Finian's Rainbow* and *Oklahoma,* in Cleveland, and *How to Succeed In Business* in Walnut Creek and Oakland California.

The Longworth Dinner Theatre held auditions for—you guessed it— *How to Succeed.* Only this time it was a paying gig. Not much, mind you, but still a step up the musical ladder. The big question for me was did I want to do this show a third time? Yes, I did.

Keith Donaldson directed. Lew Ressigue produced and also acted in Longworth shows with his talented wife, Barbara. Lew would later tour as Barry Nelson's understudy in the national company of *42nd Street.* Other standouts in the cast were the talented Lonnie Lohfield as Rosemary and Dan Higgs as Bigley.

On a WGMS radio report, critic David Richards said, *"And then is a young man named Johnny Holliday, who has the face of a chipmunk that has spirited away a week's worth of acorns in his cheek and a smile that reminded me of a harvest moon."*

Next would come my Harlequin Dinner Theatre years, simply some of the best times of my life. With an initial investment of $7,500, Dr. Nicholas Howey, along with Kary Walker and Ken Gentry, founded the Harlequin on East Gude Drive in Rockville, Maryland. Two productions, *Stop the World* and *Promises, Promises* had opened the 400-seat facility before I got a chance to audition for their third show, Stephen Sondheim's *Company.*

Since it was Sondheim, the first obstacle I had to overcome was reading the music charts. I kept thinking back to Mr. Dutton's high school chorus class for inspiration.

My rather nerve-wracking audition was held at American University, with Kary at the piano and the good Nicholas Howey (with his Ph.D. in Theatre), sitting in the first row.

Kary asked me what key I wanted for my song.

"Uh…whatever key you normally play it in," was my clever response.

I soon got the feeling that they knew I *might* be able to sing Sondheim, but there would be work ahead.

After I landed the job, Nick asked me what I did for a living. It was at that moment that I thought he was nuts. Here I was the big morning man on WWDC radio making serious inroads on WMAL's Harden and Weaver show. I did commercials. I'd been in the newspaper; I was the famous disc jockey from New York. How could he not know who I was? *Didn't everybody know Johnny Holliday?*

The answer seemed to be no. Neither Howey nor Walker appeared to have a clue.

Driving home that night it dawned on me that I had won the role based on my performance at the audition, and not because of my work on the radio. This gave me a warm satisfaction.

Company turned out to be a big hit for the Harlequin. The cast included Larry Shue, who had so impressed me when I saw him perform in the previous show, *Promises, Promises.* Shue was a wonderfully talented character actor who drew your attention even when the focus should have been on someone else. Larry and his talented wife, Linda, were a great team. Clearly, Larry was destined for Broadway.

And so it was. Larry wrote some well-reviewed plays. One was *The Foreigner* that opened at NYC's Astor Palace theatre in 1985. Another was the *The Nerd* that played Broadway's Helen Hayes Theatre in 1987.

Tragically, Larry's life ended when his commuter plane crashed in Virginia's Blue Ridge Mountains in 1985. Ironically, Larry had written about a rough ride in a commuter plane in the second act of his play, *The Nerd*. He was 39 years old.

With Larry and Linda, Nick Howey put together a resident company that also included Jack Kyrieleison, Michelle Mundell (later Jack's wife), and Buddy Piccolino.

The shows were built around them, and when I say built, that's exactly what they did. They worked on costumes, the sets, and waited on tables. They did it all.

Buddy Piccolino is a funny performer and a good man. I always enjoyed teaming with him.

> **Buddy Piccolino:** "My first show at Harlequin was also with John in *Company*. I was already a fan from his WWDC radio show. Before he came to rehearsal, many of us wondered if he was going to be a prima donna. But he wasn't. He joined right in with the cast, treated us kindly, gave us lots of publicity on his show, and John and I became very close. There were instances in my younger life when I had personal problems, and Johnny was always there to lend a shoulder, an ear, or just a friendly word. Both Johnny and Mary Clare instilled in their family and by example the importance of giving back to those less fortunate. I have always admired that and have tried to do it in my own life because of them.
>
> "He and I once did two shows back to back, *The Odd Couple* and *The Music Man*. John had been complaining during our shows that he wasn't getting much time with Mary Clare. One day after a meal with the cast, he suddenly announced that Mary Clare was pregnant.
>
> "I asked, 'Who's the father?'"

Another Harlequin player and friend, Jack Kyrieleison, coauthored with Ron Holgate a successful play, *Reunion—A Musical Epic in Miniature*, presented at Ford's Theatre. It's about the Civil War and why the North almost lost. Jack received some powerful notices for *Reunion*:

> **Jack Kyrieleison:** "I'd been a huge fan of his morning show at WWDC while going to school at UMD as a theatre student. I'd grown up listening to Ed Walker & Willard Scott's 'Joy Boys' on WRC, staying up till 10 and taping entire shows as a kid to try to learn how to write that kind of material. Harden & Weaver were the morning drive kings then, and while acknowledging their mastery of the medium, it has to be said that they were just unlistenable as far as I was concerned—stale, safe and cliched.

"But Johnny's morning show was different—edgier, hipper, a combination of the Joy Boys and Bob & Ray, but solo, and played at 45RPM instead of 33. It could only have been done by someone who'd come from rock 'n' roll. But without the meanness or cynicism of Imus. (My appreciation of him would come later, after life had kicked me around a little!)

"Loaded with voice characterizations, and quick as a whippet on Benzedrine, Johnny somehow managed to appeal across the board to 9-to-5ers as well as long-haired, would-be hippy theatre students like me. I can still remember a morning sitting in a traffic standstill on the BW Parkway heading for my summer day job, car radio tuned to WWDC. John was in the middle of a bit that had me howling, when I glanced over at the car next to me. The woman in the car was doubled over herself. I glanced to the left and saw the guy driving that car laughing. I kept track for the rest of the bit, and there was no doubt they were listening to the same thing as I.

"In the middle of a July Washington traffic jam there were uncounted numbers laughing out loud at the radio—not chuckling, not smiling blandly, but guffawing. I'd never seen such a powerful demonstration of mass media and what it can accomplish in the hands of a master.

"A few months later, I was on stage with Johnny in *Company* at the Harlequin, replacing an actor who was extremely overweight. My first night in the show, disaster loomed when the word came backstage that Johnny's pants weren't set for his quick change out of the current scene—played sitting under the covers in bed. After the next blackout, the star was about to be caught standing in nothing but his boxers. Eager to prove my indispensability, I raced to the dressing room and called to the dresser to give me Johnny's pants so I could slip them to him in the blackout. She tossed me the pants. I slithered out from the wings in the blackout and handed them to John, as proud as if I'd arrived with a fresh heart for transplant. I sat back to wait for the wave of gratitude sure to come my way.

"The lights came up on stage, and there stood Johnny, bare-chested and standing in what must have been size 68 pants, vast enough to accommodate at least three more of him. In her panic, the dresser had tossed me the departed actor's pants, and I'd passed them along to Johnny in the dark. There followed about two minutes of nonstop audience laughter fueled by Holliday ad-libs, Johnny taking a disaster and mining it into pure gold—a lesson I made use of many times in the next 30 years on stage.

"I don't know how he kept up the schedule then, and I still don't, as he hasn't let up at all. And never showing a bad mood. Actors get bored and tired and moody during a long run. I can still remember the dig I got from him when I didn't bother to say hello one night. I've remembered ever since that a lousy mood is never an acceptable excuse for ignoring the simple courtesies of the workplace.

"His generosity is well-known, but here are a few instances shown toward a penniless young actor. Inviting me to join him courtside at the announcer's table for an NBA game, saying hello to the players at the shoot-around— "Jack, you know Wes Unseld?" Ummmm, actually, no.

"Making sure I got to meet and hang out with his friend Rick Barry when the great ex-Warrior came to see Johnny at the Harlequin. Having me call in to do occasional bits with him on his morning show— you can imagine how that went over with a guy who grew up dreaming of doing 'The Joy Boys.'

"Many years later, I was on radio doing PR for a show I had written that was about to open at Ford's Theatre. It was about 9 p.m. on a Monday night, garbage time in radio, and not the most incisive interview in broadcasting history. Near the end of the hour, the engineer broke in to say they had a caller who wanted to get on the air. For the rest of the hour, anyone listening to WMAL heard Johnny Holliday sell my show and me as if he'd had money in it, as if the station were fortunate enough to have in the studio a cross between John Barrymore and Bill Shakespeare. He'd been driving home from ABC and flipped the radio on, heard me on the air and could tell the interview needed a little goose. Nothing in it for him, except the opportunity to help out a friend."

The Harlequin would be my showcase for the next 20 years. Nick and I once calculated that over 750,000 tickets were sold to the shows I was in. That's a staggering number.

Critics were always kindhearted to me. For some reason, they never slammed me. I don't know how I escaped their wrath. I guess I was always in good shows, surrounded by talented people. In 40 years of doing theatre, the highlight came with my Helen Hayes award nomination for best actor in a musical for Harlequin's *Me and My Gal.* Nominations for best actress and best musical went to my costar Liz Donohue Weber and to the show itself. Stacey Keach and Victor Garber were also nominees that season. Tough competition.

In a *Washington City Paper* article (published the day after the World Trade Center attack, so I doubt many caught it), Dave McKenna wrote:

> *Johnny's clip file shows that he's broken more legs than the Sopranos. Richard Coe, the Washington Post's main theater critic for four decades and the guy credited with bringing D.C. stages into the major leagues, took a shine to Holliday.*
>
> *"In voice and movement he's in humorous control," wrote Coe of Holliday's work in* The Apple Tree *in April 1977.*

Coe, who died in 1995 at 81, had a reputation among actors as an easy touch, but even critics known to wield a far sharper pen have fallen for Holliday's charms.

"He is curiously reminiscent of Donald O'Connor,"wrote former Post *critic David Richards of Holliday after catching him at the Harlequin Dinner Theatre's production of* Bye Bye Birdie *in May 1982.*

"Richards also gave Holliday two big thumbs up for a 1987 "pistol-driven" performance in 42nd Street: *"Holliday will have you marveling at how much is up there on stage.... Holliday's sonorous, seasoned delivery makes Julian formidable and effective."*

Richards, it should be noted, has since become a theater critic for the New York Times... "

A significant void in local theatre, especially in the northern area of Montgomery County, was created when Harlequin closed its doors in 1991. Nick Howey moved on to launch Troika Entertainment and now runs successful touring companies of such hit shows as *Grand Hotel* and *Cats*. I know he's done well.

Nick Howey: "It had been 20 years for Harlequin, which was a pretty good run, but we were just starting a touring company, so we closed the theatre to explore other options. There was a time when dinner theatre was hot and we were getting past that time. Johnny never learned to pronounce the name correctly. I've been correcting him constantly. It was HarleQuin, not HarleKin. It's become a running gag. I think he does it to spite me."

With Harlequin gone, there were only a few options left to me if I wanted to continue performing in musicals. The Burn Brae in Burtonsville was still in business and had the distinction of being the area's first dinner theatre.

It was John Kinnamon, the driving force behind Burn Brae, who called to see if I'd be interested in doing *42nd Street* again. Sure, why not? I'd be reunited with Tricia Pearce who had played Dorothy Brock with me at the Harlequin in 1987. Tricia would later pair with Jerry Lewis in *Damn Yankees* on Broadway.

Burn Brae's production was very good. Many former Harlequin fans were drawn to Burtonsville to check us out. John turned out to be a good director, and he also shot a mean game of golf.

He and I played 18 holes once at Chevy Chase's Columbia Country Club. While backing out of a sand trap, John tripped over a short chain fence, twisting his leg. Shrugging it off as a sprain, we continued to play. He shot 76 that day.

The next day I saw John in a walking cast. It turned out he had broken his leg. *And he still shot a 76.*

The lure of *42nd Street* attracted some wonderful talent to Burn Brae, including Bill Pierson, Tina Desimone, and Mark Minnick.

My next director was Toby Orenstein, who has a strong reputation among Washington-Baltimore theater goers. At her Toby's Dinner Theatre in Columbia, Maryland, she stages shows in the round, with live orchestra and fine cuisine. Toby has won many accolades, from recognition for excellence by the Helen Hayes Awards to Baltimore Magazine's "Best of Baltimore."

I visited Toby shortly before vacationing with Mary Clare in Bermuda. I thought Toby might have wanted to discuss *42nd Street* for the coming season.

Instead, she offered me the role of Buddy Plummer in the area premier of Stephen Sondheim's *Follies*, a show that very few theatres had done. I was unfamiliar with the script and the music, but Toby had both on hand for our chat. I admit I was not that excited about the role or the show, but Toby did one heck of a selling job, promising me it would be one of the most rewarding roles of my life. It turned out she was exactly right. *Follies* was a real challenge for me but also a stage experience I'll never forget.

Toby Orenstein: "Johnny Holliday is one of the most beautiful people I've ever worked with. He has a humility that many people who have been around as long as he has do not possess. His willingness to stretch [for *Follies*] and work as hard as he did was a joy to watch. I had no idea what it would be like to work with him. He had done a lot of shows, and he did University of Maryland and many other things. Sometimes folks like that come with some baggage, but John's baggage was nonexistent.

The cast Toby assembled was a Who's Who of area talent that included Itzy Friedman, Dan McDonald, Jason Fulmer, Penny Friesland, Adrienne Athanas, Mary Jo Brenner, Jean Ann Kain, Tricia Pierce, Patsy Abrams, and Gary Dieter. It was a powerful show that dealt with present and past relationships. I doubt many of the audience knew what to expect when they came to see *Follies*. Indeed, there were nights when a few left at intermission in puzzlement.

As always, Toby directed *Follies* with flair. I came away having learned so much from her. Local critic Richard Gist wrote, "*Mr. Holliday's Buddy Plummer is full of all the superficial charm and swagger the role demands.*" I hoped for another chance to work with Toby when *Follies* closed.

My chance came seven months later when Toby's version of *42nd Street* opened. I'd be Julian Marsh again, and hopefully for the last time. After all, how many times could I sing "Lullaby of Broadway?"

The show was a success. Doug Lawler's music was first rate, Nora Shaw created a stunning wardrobe of out-of-this-world costumes, and Ilona Kessell was nominated for a Helen Hayes award for best choreographer.

Toby and I had some discussions about me playing the devil in *Damn Yankees* for her next show, but I ended up passing when I agreed to do *The Music Man*, which would be the first show to open the University of Maryland's gorgeous new Clarice Smith Performing Arts Center at Maryland.

The Music Man was sensational and featured a surprise encore every night by the University of Maryland Marching Band. It was a stunning effect when the entire band appeared from nowhere at the curtain call, blaring "76 Trombones."

This show would also yield one my worst reviews, penned by a student critic in the University newspaper, *The Diamondback*. The student called my performance creepy and implied I was too old to be playing romantic leads. Maybe he's right, though I still had a wonderful time on stage, and the audiences seemed to love the shows.

Before Dr. Mote, William "Britt" Kiwin was the university president. Mary Clare and I became close friends with Dr. Kirwin and his wife, Patty. Like Dan and Patsy Mote, the Kirwins were very supportive of the Terps athletic program. When Britt accepted the offer to become president of Ohio State University, Maryland lost a terrific president.

Fred Frederick, former president of the Terrapin Club and a longtime Maryland supporter, hosted a going-away dinner party for the Kirwins at Columbia Country Club. As you could imagine, it was a very emotional evening, built around a "This is Your Life" theme. I had the pleasure of holding the Ralph Edwards role as emcee. Britt was moved to tears by the outpouring of love that night.

The old saying is what comes around goes around. Britt had returned to Maryland as Chancellor. I doubt any school has two such dynamic leaders as Drs. Mote and Kirwin.

Dr. Dan Mote, University of Maryland President: "After we were shaken by 9/11 and our first tornado in 75 years, Johnny lifted our spirits with his rousing performance as Harold Hill in the gala opening of the Clarice Smith Performing Arts Center. He is a characteristically generous person, giving his many talents to the University community with enthusiasm."

Opening the Clarice Smith Center was very special. The student cast was great: Danielle Pastin, Sara Hale, Adam Shapiro, Abigale Bortnick, and Laura Lichtenberger. Carmen Balthrop, a faculty member of the school of music, and Drury Bagwell, who recently retired as VP for student affairs also played key roles. Noted Washington director Nick Olcott directed. Musical director was Richard Sparks.

Just one week before the show opened, two Maryland students, Colleen Marlatt, 23, and her sister, Erin Marlatt, 20, of Triadelphia Mill Road in Clarksville, Maryland, were killed when a freak tornado moved through College Park and lifted their car 75 feet into the air, clearing one of the high-rise dormitories. Colleen had been studying environmental policy and looking forward to graduating in January. Erin was a sophomore sociology student. They were visiting the their father, who worked with the Maryland Fire and Rescue Institute on campus. His trailer was adjacent to the theatre.

The tornado did extensive damage to the College Park campus, but other than broken windows, the new theatre was spared. The show went on, as it must.

From Harlequin, Burn Brae and Toby's, the road I traveled has been well worth it.

I've been extremely fortunate to work with those directors, actors and actresses I've mentioned previously and also fine performers like Michelle Kyrieleison, Lonnie Lohfeld, Robin Deck, Matt McCoy, Steve Schmidt, Tony Gilbert, Barbara Walsh, Susan Dawn Carson, Pam Bierly, Mary Ellen Nester, Mike Caruthers, Dick and Susie Bigelow, Megan McFarland, Amy Pierson, Liz Donohoe Weber, Brad Watkins, Gordon Paddison, Gerry McCarthy, Danny Paolucci, Rosemary Pollen, Michelle Summer, Lani Howe, Dottie Mach, Gary Best, and Charley Abel.

I thank all of my dear theatre friends for making me look good on stage.

A chance to meet and interview music stars came when I took a TV job doing "On Stage" segments for WRC Channel 4 news in 1978, when WRC expanded to an hour news format. Jim Vance was anchor then and he continues as strong as ever today. I did segments with Emmylou Harris, Sha Na Na, Perry Como, the Starland Vocal Band, and many others. I even rode on a motorcycle with soul crooner Isaac Hayes.

In 1988, the Maryland chapter of "Right To Life" filmed a documentary called *Eclipse of Reason*. Produced by antiabortionist Dr. Bernard Nathanson, this film became hotly controversial because of its one-minute graphic depiction of a late-term abortion. Heading this effort was Dr. William Colliton, whose daughter, Mary Kay, attended Visitation with my own daughter, Tracie.

The film was scheduled to air on Baltimore's Channel 54 (WNUV), but five days before the airing, WNUV station officials unexpectedly announced that the abortion subject matter was "too controversial." Maryland Congresswoman Helen Delich Bentley intervened and pushed Channel 54 to honor the agreement to show the film.

At that point, Dr. Colliton invited Mary Clare and me over for dinner. Initially, I didn't want to get involved with this, but after our meal, we watched the film. Although I had been previously against abortion, I was *really* against it after actually viewing the procedure. I was shocked. Colliton asked me to lead a panel discussion on abortion, which he planned to film and add to the original content in *Eclipse*. I agreed.

Producer Mark Bowen became involved, and the panel included Sandra Walton, a Maryland woman who felt she had been personally exploited by abortion, Sue Keusal of the Pregnancy Centers of Maryland, and Lynn Page, a spokeswoman for the Right to Life speakers' bureau. Mark added our discussion to the original film, and it aired on Channel 54 on January 10, 1988. The original graphic footage, however, was still omitted. If there was any criticism of my involvement, I didn't hear about it.

Looking back on my public service broadcasting, I can honestly say that nothing has given me more satisfaction than being able to help others through my hosting of nearly every major telethon in Washington. These include Muscular Dystrophy, Cerebral Palsy, March of Dimes, Children's Hospital, Easter Seals, the Arthritis Foundation, and the Leukemia Society's HTS Leukemia Sports-a-Thon.

In May 2002 Nick Olcott cast me in three roles for his LA Theatre Works radio production of Gore Vidal's *The Best Man*. Actress Marsha Mason and Senator Fred Thompson headed the cast of Paul Morella, Terrance Currier, Naomi Jacobson, Timmy Ray James, Michael Kramer, Kevin Murray, Judy Simmons, and Gary Sloan. This star-studded group was assembled by Olcott and executive producer Susan Albert Loewenberg. It was neat to work with "the Goodbye Girl," a U.S. Senator, and a great cast.

The Best Man was broadcast on National Public Radio and the Voice of America. One of my roles was Walter Cronkite. I'd never done him before.

My latest public service work on radio is enormously rewarding. I'm working with the talented Carol Lehan on Catholic Radio Weekly, a production of the Catholic Communication Campaign (www.usccb.org/ccc) that airs nationwide.

Three weeks after the World Trade Center attack I had the honor of reading the following program introduction to Catholic Radio Weekly listeners throughout the United States:

"The second Tuesday of September 2001 began with a glorious, cloudless day in our nation's capital where more than 40 U.S. Catholic bishops had gathered for a meeting. Soon after their meeting began, news of the horrific attacks on New York and Washington began to filter in.

"At noon the meeting adjourned, and the Bishops began walking two blocks from their headquarters to the Basilica of the Shrine of the Immaculate Conception, where they joined Washington's Cardinal Theodore McCarrick in a mass for the nation.

"In his homily at that mass, Cardinal McCarrick recalled the last time he had felt such a sense of despair for our country. It was nearly 40 years ago when President John F. Kennedy was assassinated.

"As he urged prayers for the victims, he also warned against vengeance, asking the nation's leaders to never cease building this nation as it has always been built. With the values of faith and trust in the Living God."

As we come to the last page of my story, I feel a little self-conscious echoing these great words of the cardinal. I've never felt comfortable being thought of as a preachy kind of guy, and I'm not going to try to conclude my life story by becoming something that I'm not.

But Cardinal McCarrick's words ring true for me. The values of faith and trust in God, family, and our country made everything else possible for me. I've been constantly surprised by life. I tried to enjoy the surprises and made the most out of whatever came my way.

I've grown a bit older while writing this book, and you've aged a little, too, by reading it. Let's put it behind us now, and go out and enjoy some new adventures.

AFTERWORD

By Dick Vitale

There are certain guys in the world of broadcasting who become legends along the way. The late Cawood Ledford was such a legend down in Kentucky. Broadcasters like Johnny Holliday and Woody Durham fit that mold.

What makes them so special is that even though they are associated with their given university, they have great credibility and objectivity. With a special spirit, they are so vital and important to their universities and to the whole areas where their voices are heard.

The University of Maryland is very fortunate to have a voice like Johnny Holliday, because Johnny brings such passion and so much enthusiasm to what he does.

If I were describing my man Mr. Holliday, I would simply say he's a prime-time performer. To put it in real Vitalese, Johnny's the three "S" man: super, scintillating, and sensational. Johnny Holliday is a solid gold Rolls Roycer, baby. Awesome with a capital "A."

INDEX

Index

Index

Index

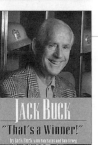
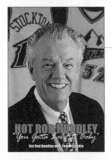
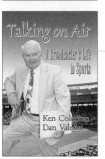
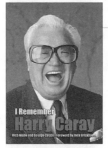

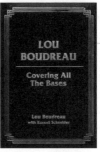

6/13/12